JO MALONE
MY STORY

JO MALONE
MY STORY

**SIMON &
SCHUSTER**

London · New York · Sydney · Toronto · New Delhi

A CBS COMPANY

First published in Great Britain by Simon & Schuster UK Ltd, 2016
A CBS COMPANY

1 3 5 7 9 10 8 6 4 2

Simon & Schuster UK Ltd
1st Floor
222 Gray's Inn Road
London WC1X 8HB

www.simonandschuster.co.uk

Simon & Schuster Australia, Sydney
Simon & Schuster India, New Delhi

The author and publishers have made all reasonable efforts
to contact copyright-holders for permission, and apologise for
any omissions or errors in the form of credits given.
Corrections may be made to future printings.

A CIP catalogue record for this book
is available from the British Library

Hardback ISBN: 978-1-4711-4300-7
Trade Paperback ISBN: 978-1-4711-4301-4
Ebook ISBN: 978-1-4711-4303-8

Typeset in the UK by M Rules
Printed and bound by CPI Group (UK) Ltd, Croydon, CR0 4YY

Simon & Schuster UK Ltd are committed to sourcing paper that is
made from wood grown in sustainable forests and support the Forest Stewardship
Council, the leading international forest certification organisation. Our books
displaying the FSC logo are printed on FSC certified paper.

To the three great loves of my life:
Gary, Josh and Teri.

And to every entrepreneur who each day
takes one more step of courage and
never gives up their dream.

Man cannot discover new oceans unless he
first has the courage to lose sight of the shore.

André Gide

CONTENTS

PROLOGUE

The journalist is curious, as she has to be. 'So, we know you can create amazing fragrances, but tell us something about Jo Malone that we don't know.'

That question always makes me smile because I have long understood that people know more about my fragrances than they do about me. Such is the power of branding.

So I tell her what she and everyone else never expects to hear. 'Well, I'm not the posh bird everyone thinks I am. I was raised on a council estate, dropped out of school at fifteen, and have zero qualifications. I'm also dyslexic. I struggle to tell the time, often get confused between my left and right, and can barely drive. I've actually never been brilliant at anything except for making fragrances. And I didn't even understand that much when I first started out with four plastic jugs, two saucepans, and a wing and a prayer.'

It's almost become my stock response to the question everyone thinks will stump me – many of my speeches start in a similar vein – and it always elicits a look of surprise.

I'm in Dublin, doing a round of interviews ahead of a breakfast event where I'll be 'in conversation with' Melanie Morris, the editor-in-chief of IMAGE magazine. On the five hundred chairs at that event, each *member of the audience will walk in to find a Jo Loves gift bag waiting for them. And that's something else that I find tends to surprise people.*

Strangely, it doesn't seem to be common knowledge that I'm no longer a part of the company I first founded, Jo Malone London – and I haven't been since 2006. Jo Loves is a whole new personal venture, which I launched in 2011 after five years away from the industry.

As sure as night follows day, someone will approach me after the breakfast event and say, 'I had absolutely no idea you'd left Jo Malone!' It happens all the time. I don't blame people for not knowing – there was hardly any PR at the time of my departure, and my name remains on product all over the world. But that name and my identity have had to become two very different things in recent years.

'Why did you choose to do it all over again?' the journalist asks.

I've often asked myself that same question.

'The truth is that the hunger and spirit that was there in the beginning still lives within me.'

'Where does that hunger come from?'

'Where does anyone's drive come from?' I ask. 'I suppose it all started in my childhood . . .'

PART ONE

Roots

ONE

Crackling fire. Burnt sulphur. Wet leaves. Charred wood. Toffee apples. And the kind of grimy, wispy smoke that leaves its invisible trace on clothes. In a life to be governed by the sense of smell, my nose likes to imagine that these were the aromas in the air as I arrived in the world on Bonfire Night 1963.

Named Joanne Malone, I was the first of two daughters to Eileen and Andy. Mum, then aged thirty-one, said she was instantly enamoured with me that first night at St Stephen's Hospital (now Chelsea and Westminster). 'You were like this perfect, little French doll, and I used to sit and stare at you, observing every detail.'

Dad, several years her senior, probably didn't envisage becoming a parent in his late thirties but doubtless took it in his stride. I would eventually learn that he had great adaptability when it came to dealing with the unexpected.

For a short while, we lived in a poky bedsit above a garage in Hayes Hill, outside Bromley. Dad was a draftsman at a local double-glazing firm, and Mum, like her father, had worked for the gas board, but their two meagre wages barely covered the rent. I can't imagine what it must have been like, squeezed into a place not big enough to swing a cat, but my optimistic parents would have likely convinced themselves that their fortunes would soon change. Sure enough, when I was about six months old, we moved to a semi-detached, two-up, two-down in Barnehurst, near Bexleyheath, on the south-east fringes of London's suburbs, then part of the Crayford Urban District of Kent.

A street of uniform, sandy-bricked properties on a council estate would become my home for the next sixteen years. My bedroom was at the front, above the living room, overlooking a small patch of grass and low brick wall. At the rear, above the kitchen, Mum and Dad's room had a view of the oblong back garden, and a neighbouring block of flats. The house must have felt huge compared to a bedsit, but there was only one problem in the week before we moved in – we didn't have a stitch of furniture except for my cot. Dad told Mum not to worry; he'd sort it. And he did, with forty-eight hours to spare.

Mum hadn't a clue what he'd chosen as they drove to Barnehurst, with me asleep in her arms. Ideally, she would have preferred to pick out the furniture as a couple, but Dad had wanted to surprise and impress. Mum figured that if the dapper way he dressed was any measure, then he would choose well.

But she soon discovered that while clothes maketh the man, they don't necessarily maketh the interior designer. 'I walked in with you still asleep,' she told me, 'and my heart sank – he'd kitted out the whole place in *dark brown*. Dark brown sofa, dark brown dining table, dark brown chairs, dark brown armchair. And green and brown cheap velvet curtains!'

As a young woman sensitive to the approval of others, and because she didn't wish to hurt Dad's feelings, she didn't verbalise her displeasure; instead, she forced a smile and learned to live with it. As to where the furniture came from, she preferred not to ask about that either. Dad said he'd bought it on the never-never, to be paid off in weekly instalments. Mum privately doubted him, suspecting that he'd won it by gambling.

My dad was a dab hand at poker, playing at casinos or the homes of people in his social circle. He was a real wheeler-dealer, too. If opponents couldn't pay, he'd claim the equivalent value in whatever else they could stump up. Like a set of furniture, for example. In the end, Mum needn't have worried – the payment arrangements proved legitimate – but she could never be sure when it came to any new purchase or gift. All that mattered on this occasion was that she had somewhere to put down roots, to feel secure, and to be with the man she loved. When you've made do in a bedsit, landing your own house on an estate is going up in the world.

These humble beginnings illustrate the theme of my childhood: the sense of struggle, the just-about-getting-by, and the resourcefulness of two hard-working people who did everything they could to keep the balls in the air. I wouldn't know any other way to live or be. If we could make ends meet week after week, then we were in good shape.

Mum grew up in Harrow with her parents, Len and Edie, and two sisters, Vera and Dorothy, enjoying a close-knit, contented, working-class life. But as much as she was positively influenced by her parents, she yearned for something more, something unknowable, something beyond the pedestrian pace of the suburbs. No wonder, then, that the bright lights of London proved enticing.

Mum's sense of style belonged in the capital, too. She prided herself on being the best-dressed woman in town. Together with her best friend from the gas board, Irene, she would head into the city to sample its nightclubs as a more stable, post-war era heralded better times for everyone. Regardless of how little money she had, Mum always dressed to the nines. She was a real lady, and I mean that in a graceful not a grand sense; in the way she carried herself, the first impression she sought to make, and the proper manners she upheld.

For me, this practised poise is illustrated in a treasured photo showing my infant self sitting between her and Aunty Dot in our back garden. Mum is sat on the steps, hands folded on her lap, knees together, looking the epitome of well-put-together grace, with not a hair out of place. Yet, behind that serene demeanour, there existed a restless spirit. And if it's true that she sought something more exciting and unpredictable, she got what she wished for in Dad.

Tall, broad-shouldered, with a Clark Gable-esque panache, he was also someone whose pristine appearance belied his more humble roots – from his hand-made leather shoes, the silk ties, and classical gold wristwatch, to the sharp Chesterfield suits that finished off his look. I can well imagine that when my parents stepped out together, they looked quite the couple, driving around in whatever second-hand Mercedes or BMW Dad drove at the time.

They met in a nightclub in central London. Dad was out with friends and Mum was working part-time in the cloakroom. Apparently, they fell in love the moment she handed him the ticket for his overcoat. Andy Malone was new to London, having recently moved from north of the border, yet he had only the slightest hint of a Scottish accent. Mum would later learn that he was actually English but had moved after being orphaned at the age of seven.

His father had been killed in the Great War and then his mother died indirectly from breast cancer – she suffered a fatal haemorrhage in the days after undergoing surgery to have a mastectomy. Dad was taken in by his grandparents, Ginger and Agnes – the only names I heard him reference.

Ginger was a gamekeeper on a landed estate in the Scottish Highlands, where he created the most idyllic childhood for his grandson. In later years, Dad would regale me with the odd story, telling us how he'd go poaching and 'sit with my hand in the river, tickling the salmon and, as they shot out of the water, I'd catch one and put it in the pocket down the side of my trousers, ready to sell to the local hotels'. Or there was the time, as a nine-year-old, when he was a 'beater', braying a stick on the ground to flush out wild game for hunting parties. During one lunch break on the moors, he ended up sharing a sandwich on a stump, sitting beside the King of Egypt who, apparently, was a guest of the Duke of Buccleuch. Knowing Dad, these may well have been tall tales with a grain of truth – he was a bit Alice in Wonderland when it came to storytelling – but I didn't care. I wanted to hear his stories again and again because the things he spoke of, and the life he'd led, seemed a world away to a girl on a council estate in Kent.

Dad's carefully selected and often repeated anecdotes never strayed into personal territory, though, almost as if he had erected his own wall on the border, keeping his past from encroaching any further. There was obviously a life before us, but it was never a topic I heard him discuss. I'm not even sure Mum asked too many questions, probably because she was focused on their happy-ever-after.

A dynamic couple with similar values, they were young, care-free, and passionately in love. Dad was certainly extroverted, and I think his more gregarious spirit gradually coaxed out Mum's confidence. He spoiled her, taking her to some of London's fancy restaurants and casinos. That's where she first noticed his penchant for gambling, understanding that poker was how he made some extra money. The fact that he seemed to win more than he lost can only have added to his air of apparent invincibility. Andy Malone worked hard and played hard, and was clearly fun company.

By day, they held down regular, nine-to-five jobs, but that was never more than a means to an end. Life for them was about the evenings, weekends and being together: what they would do, where they would go, what they would wear, and the good times they would enjoy. Then came the Arctic, record-breaking winter of January and February 1963.

From New Year's Day onwards, London, like most of the country, was blanketed in a thick layer of snow sealed to the streets by temperatures of minus two degrees Celsius – cold enough to turn the upper reaches of the River Thames into a skating rink. 'The Big Freeze' lasted two months. Buses and trains didn't run, rubbish didn't get collected, and power cuts – aided and abetted by unions issuing 'work to rule' orders – became frequent, which led to the closure of nightclubs, cinemas, casinos, and theatres. People even resorted to wearing their coats at home and work in order to keep warm.

I don't know how Mum and Dad were personally affected because they never mentioned anything but, one thing's for sure, it certainly would have curtailed their socialising. I dare say they had never spent so many nights indoors. Maybe that explains why, one day in March, Mum found out she was pregnant.

And that's where I would come in, eight months later.

Smells unlock my every memory, like I'm moving through a sensory doorway to the past where all my senses translate into a scent or an aroma, conjuring a vivid recall. Transported to a specific time and place, I'm suddenly seeing, hearing, tasting and touching everything around me. This link between the sense of smell and human emotion would be one of the truths of fragrance I would come to understand, and it's well known that Marcel Proust was the first to write about this phenomenon. But no description better sums it up than the one from Patrick Süskind in his novel

Perfume: '*Odors have a power of persuasion stronger than that of words, appearances, emotions, or will ... it enters into us like breath into our lungs, it fills us up, imbues us totally. There is no remedy for it.*'

We breathe them in to be stored in our subconscious, for remembrance, for nostalgia, for the truth of how we once felt. Smells are our olfactory reminders – emotional threads from the past that tug on us from nowhere. And all I have to do is close my eyes, and my nose will take me back.

Eau Sauvage, a cologne by Christian Dior: unmistakably Dad, with his starched collar and crisp, white shirts ironed to within an inch of their life. He's sitting in his armchair, right ankle resting on left knee, creating a cradle between his legs. He called this his 'dip' the spot where I would sit, listening to his stories, facing his moustached smile, seeing the reflection of myself in his black, thick-rimmed glasses. This was my favourite place in the world.

Joy by Jean Patou: the grace of Mum, and her signature floral fragrance – an invisible vapour trail of jasmine and rose, as much a part of her elegant uniform as the Yves St Laurent-dominated wardrobe, Jaeger velvet skirts and beautiful silk shirts she saved up to buy. And then I'm five again, hugging her legs, not wanting her to go to work, looking up at her as she stands at the mirror in her bedroom, applying her Revlon burnt orange lipstick, setting the pearls in her ears *just so*.

Even as a little girl, I knew from Mum's choice of fragrance what her mood or the occasion was: *Je Reviens* by Worth – headed to work, serious, professional; *Joy* – going to London, feeling confident, out to impress at somewhere fancy; *Ma Griffe* by Carven – summer time, a spring in her step, holidays in Cornwall; and Mary Chess *Tapestry* bath oil – Friday night, unwinding, time to herself, the scent that infused the rest of the house whenever she took a bath. She also used the same talcum powder, and I can still see those snowy footprints leading out of the bathroom, across the landing, into the bedroom.

Whatever she wore, its composition nearly always contained notes of jasmine and rose, and I could often smell her before seeing her, either as a reassurance that she was close – upstairs or in the garden – or the relief that she was coming home, as confirmed by the sound of her high-heeled boots clipping up the garden path. As soon as she stepped inside, I'd run to her before she had time to take off her forest green, hooded cape, and she'd sweep me up in her arms, eager to express how much she'd missed me. Mum didn't return to work until I was four or five, but I understood the urgency for her to earn a wage.

I didn't smell much money in my childhood.

Instead, I can recall the array of scents from the amazing flowers in our back garden: the apricot, white and red roses; the blue lobelia, the greengage tree, the lemon-scented geraniums, and the fresh mint – the ingredients for my first home-made perfume mixed in a jam jar and left to ferment in Dad's garden shed. This was no flashforward of my future – most girls experiment in this way, I think – but it was perhaps me trying to capture the pleasant smells of days spent in the garden, either with Dad tending the rabbit hutch, or with Mum and Aunty Dot, sitting on the steps on blazing August afternoons. Even as a child, family meant everything to me, but that sense of cohesive togetherness was inconsistent and fleeting.

I could fill that same jam jar today with an abundance of fragrant memories from my early years: the damp wood of the garden shed where Dad found his peace; the tomatoes he'd cut into jagged crowns to place on the salads he'd make; the breaking of a digestive biscuit which, for some reason, reminded me of our dog's paws; the apricot madeleines that evoke the nonstop baking of Nanny Edie, my mum's mum; Sunday roast beef with gravy, meaning we got to sit together, gathered around the fire, with plates on our laps; the woody tobacco packed inside Dad's roll-ups; the Ajax and bleach that greeted me after school, which meant 'Aunty' Maureen, our neighbour, had cleaned because Mum hadn't the time; the linseed oil and its turpentine scent from Dad's paintings; the fresh carrot from feeding the rabbits in our hutch; pine needles from a tree on Christmas morning; freshly cut grass from summer; and even the musty laundry, which didn't get tackled as much as I'd have liked. Those are some of my happy smells, there to remind me of all the good times. Lest I forget.

TWO

'Jo Malone, child star' doesn't quite have the same ring to it, but I do wonder if that was Mum's first idea of how my future looked when she signed me up for an audition to appear in a Heinz baked beans TV ad. Sadly, if she did harbour any hopes for me to be an actress, I imagine she walked away disappointed. I proved to be no Shirley Temple.

I must have been four, all innocent-faced and blonde hair. Mum had submitted a photo to the Bonnie Kids Agency, and I ended up filming my audition reel at a studio somewhere on the outskirts of London. I vividly remember sitting on the edge of a sofa, surrounded by blinding lights and feeling painfully shy in my tartan skirt and a furry, white jumper while a man seated about fifteen feet away asked me to speak into the camera above his head.

Behind him stood Mum, a silhouette caught in the haze of lights. I squinted, wanting to make sure she was close. She wasn't hard to pick out in her black, three-quarter-length leather coat – a treat from Dad (or rather, a treat he'd won at a poker game). In fact, he had returned home with an entire rail of leather coats that he went on to sell after Mum kept one for herself. As commanding as she looked in her new garment, I could see she was more nervous about this audition than me. The general idea of the audition, she had explained on the train, was to get across how much I *loved* Heinz. I was a fussy eater as a toddler and the only thing Mum and Dad could get me to eat was Heinz tomato soup or Heinz baked beans on toast.

'It's going to be great,' she said, trying to drum some excitement into me. 'You know how much you love baked beans? Just tell them!'

When the cameras were rolling, it didn't prove as straightforward as that. I totally clammed up, to the extent that the man sitting beneath the camera tossed me cuddly toys, presumably to help me feel relaxed and playful. His ploy had limited success. 'Go on, Jo, go on …' said Mum, urging me from the sidelines. But I sat there, swinging my legs, head down, completely forgetting what I was meant to say.

'Can you say, "Beanz meanz Heinz", Jo?' asked the man. Actually, I was meant to sing that line but the first challenge was getting me to utter the three syllables at all, when what I wanted to do was go and sit with Mum.

He mouthed the words for me. 'Beeeeenz. Meeeeenz. Hyyyyynz.'

Mum stepped into full view, clearly sharing the collective frustration. 'Joanne. Just say, "*Beanz … meanz … Heinz!*"' she said. Whenever she called me 'Joanne', I knew I was in trouble or she wanted me to do something serious. And so, like a horse feeling a whip on its hide, I blurted out the required line, probably a little overeagerly. 'BEANZMEANZHEINZ!'

I blurted it out several more times, too, trying to slow my delivery, but I soon grew bored with saying the same thing over and over again. As we walked away from the studio, I could tell by Mum's silence that she was disappointed. That upset me. I *hated* disappointing her, which was why my bottom lip started to quiver.

Mum saw the tears in my eyes. 'Don't worry, Jo – you did your best,' she said, crouching down so her eyes were level with mine. 'I'll tell you what, why don't we go have a nice cup of tea and a pastry?'

Mum's idea of a treat, whenever we had the time and extra money, was to go to the antiquated J. Lyons tea house on The Strand, opposite Charing Cross railway station, which is where we headed to catch the train back to Kent. For Mum, the tearoom was a throwback to the war years, with its 1940s background music, elaborate decor and famous 'nippies', or waitresses, dressed in black with white pinnies, who treated everyone like royalty. Lyons was a posh and luxurious establishment, which was probably what appealed to Mum. My eyes were only ever interested in the speciality products – the cakes, pastries, and chocolates – but I also liked going there because it was a special place only Mum and I went. For a snatched half an hour or so, I had her all to myself. That time felt precious because, in the coming years, such occasions would prove rare.

I soon forgot about the fluffed TV audition when a giant Danish pastry was placed in front of me. Mum smiled as I shoved too much of it in my mouth, which was a relief because that smile told me I remained in her good books. I'm not sure what happened to that Heinz reel but, suffice it to say, I was never again put forward for an audition by the Bonnie Kids Agency.

As a toddler, I had no idea that even two cups of tea and a pastry were a stretch for my parents but these financial pressures would become harder to hide as I got older, especially when we didn't have enough money for the electricity meter. When that happened, we depended on heat from both the coal fire and the oven, turned on and left open. Dad was obsessed with trapping the heat in the living room. Whenever we nipped upstairs to the bathroom, he'd feel the blast of cold air from the hallway. 'Close the bloody door!' he'd shout, hurrying to put the draught excluder back.

Upstairs was Arctic in the winter. Ice on the inside of the windows was as common as ice on the pavements, meaning that I'd often wear layers and socks in bed. Bedtime could sometimes feel like camping indoors. I couldn't wait to get up the next morning and sit in front of the living-room fire, legs tucked to chest, eating my toast.

Every birthday, I would sit in front of that fire and open my cards and presents. The year I turned five, I opened a card from Aunty Winnie, my granddad's adorable sister, and several shillings fell out. It was the first time I'd been given coins of my own so I tucked them in my pocket, not wanting to let them go.

Later that afternoon while out with Mum, she nipped into the local shop. 'Joanne, can I borrow your money? I'll give you it back later.' But she never did, and it wouldn't be the last birthday cash she'd 'borrow' to top up the kitty.

What didn't help my parents' cause was the fact they were hardly the prudent type; if anything, they lived beyond their means. They were proud, proud people who shared a fierce desire to live in a league higher than the one in which they found themselves. Mum and Dad didn't believe in limitations – they aspired to grow and achieve life-transforming success. They had chased pots of gold at the ends of rainbows for as long as I can remember. Their determination would leave its positive mark, but I never understood why, if our finances were stretched, Mum would still buy expensive new clothes, and order taxis *everywhere*. Or how Dad could afford to stay out late so often.

My parents' ambitious lifestyle could be glimpsed in the smallest ways, from Mum's fashionable wardrobe to Dad's top-of-the-range suits, from her gold bracelets to his fancy cufflinks, and from the bone china tea set to Mum's pride and joy – her three crystal, colourless glass decanters with stoppers, set in a wooden, antique chest that was only ever opened on special occasions for Dad's not-so-cheap brandy and whisky, which he referred to as 'a wee dram'.

That's not to say that they didn't do their damnedest to make ends meet, put food on the table and keep a roof over our heads. Somehow, they scrimped and scraped and balanced it all. Dad adopted the 'you only live once' mindset, not believing in giving in to struggle; he would far rather embrace the self-reward of spending hard-earned cash. Another pay day – from work or poker – was around the next corner. In that regard, he was a true gambler, unafraid of taking risks, focused only on what he could gain, not what he could lose.

In fact, he approached much of life as though it were a poker game: luck and fortunes were capable of changing at a moment's notice. Each pack of cards contains four kings and four aces waiting to be dealt, he said, but luck finds people, we don't make our own. Hence why he was superstitious, to the extent that if he saw one magpie (for sorrow), he'd need to spot a second (for joy), otherwise he wouldn't play poker that night. Another bad omen was if he spotted three nuns in the street – a terrible sign in his book. Conversely, when he spotted three 7s on a car registration, that was a sign that he should definitely be 'dealt in' at cards.

He soon had a little bit more money to play with when he landed a new job at a small architects' firm in London. I don't know what his precise role was, but he started catching the train to Charing Cross, and I heard him tell Mum that he had his own drawing board in an office. Mum hadn't returned to the gas board, choosing to devote herself to being a full-time mum for my first four years, although she did take a part-time job as an usherette at the local cinema, working weekends and the odd midweek evening. On those occasions, my chief babysitter was Jenette, the teenage daughter of the wonderful Aunty Maureen, one of Mum's closest friends who lived down the road. I grew up calling all Mum's friends 'Aunty' – that's what most kids in our neighbourhood did back then. There was Aunty Sheila next door, Aunty May over the road, Aunty Beryl at the top of the street, and Aunty Shani who made the best curries and lived opposite Aunty Maureen. (I don't remember friends of Dad ever coming to the house, hence why you won't find me referring to any 'uncles'.) Out of everyone, Maureen, with her big blonde bun, bright pink lipstick, and salt-of-the-earth personality, was a mainstay in our lives. Whenever there was a crisis, an argument between my parents, or a last-minute panic to find someone to look after me, she was always there.

I liked going to her house because we'd often bake and everywhere was so neat, tidy, and clean – forever-smelling-of-Jif clean. I doubt there was a speck of dust on the carpet, let alone the mantlepiece above the fire.

I particularly remember that carpet because I ended up practically kissing it on one occasion.

'Right, Jo,' she said in a hushed voice, the way adults do when they are about to tell a child something that is morally questionable, 'if anyone knocks on the door, we hit the floor, okay?'

I nodded. It sounded like a grown-up version of *Ring a Ring o' Roses*.

'We don't say a word. We don't let anyone know we're in,' she added, nodding in encouragement of her own advice. 'Don't be frightened now. It's all okay. Understand?'

'I think so,' I said. 'But why, Aunty Maureen?'

'Ssshh ... remember, a knock on the door, a ring of the bell, we go down on the floor.'

She must have been expecting a visitor because, within the

hour, while I was helping her polish the telephone table and bottom of the banister in the hall, the bell sounded and we both dropped to our hands and knees, behind the front door. Maureen was also on all fours, facing me, barely moving. *Ring a Ring o' Roses* had turned into musical statues. Even the curtains in the living room dared not twitch. I sensed something wasn't quite right when the visitor drilled the bell one more time, and then started knocking. I didn't take my eyes off Maureen. Stay still, she mouthed, as if she knew how this would pan out. Seconds later, we heard footsteps walking away. She weighed the silence, wondering if it was safe to get up.

While suspended in that abeyance – me looking at her; her looking at me – we heard the back door open. That was when our heads turned toward the kitchen to find the council rent man standing at the far end of the living room, staring at us on our hands and knees.

Without missing a beat, Maureen looked at me as if we were doing the most natural thing in the world. 'Jo, can you see that shirt button?'

She had clearly been in this situation before.

I shook my head. She shook hers, pretending to be baffled, then jumped up, dusted herself down and walked into the kitchen, closing the door behind her. I didn't hear much of the serious conversation that followed, but that was the day I realised someone from the council came to collect the rent. And not everyone on our estate was ready for him.

My sister Tracey was born on 3 June 1968 and we became a family of four. I remember her imminent arrival by the smell of grass: I was alone in the front garden, darting around with an empty jam jar, collecting caterpillars and butterflies. I could easily kill an hour or two playing catch-and-release with nature, although, on this particular day, I was probably taking my mind off the fact that Mum was poorly. When I woke up that morning, Dad had explained that she'd been admitted to hospital. He said she was 'sick'. I would later find out that she was suffering from hyperemesis gravidarum – a condition that causes severe nausea and vomiting during pregnancy, and one that I would inherit. That day, I was lying on my front, chin on the grass, peering into the jam jar, wondering how on earth caterpillars ever became fly-away butterflies, when the shrill of the telephone disturbed my peace. Dad called my name. 'It's Mummy!'

She was in bed on the ward, calling from one of those portable pay phones. Mum worried when she was away from us, even when she had her head in a bowl and was hours away from going into labour. She grew anxious when away from home, fretting about whether Dad had everything under control and whether I was okay. Mum only really felt calm when we were all home and together. Before Tracey came along, I loved nothing more than snuggling on the sofa with Mum and Dad, mesmerised by the black-and-white television in the corner that flickered almost as much as the open fire to its left. They were both tactile, tender parents and all I wanted to do was sit and cuddle with them. And then our unit of three made room for one more.

Mum gave birth to Tracey the day after calling from hospital, and I came to dote on my little sister, 'playing mum' by holding her whenever Mum had to make dinner, and rocking the pram in front of the fire when it was naptime.

From the beginning, I felt a strong bond of sisterhood, even though we would have diametrically opposed personalities. I was self-sufficient, she leaned on Mum; I was more reserved, she was a gregarious tomboy; I had to work hard at everything I did, she seemed naturally talented at whatever she tried. But the biggest difference to develop over the years would be her joined-at-the-hip affinity with Mum.

Whatever she did, Tracey mirrored; whatever she said, Tracey agreed with. And if my sister ever did something wrong or an accident happened in the house, her finger would instantly point in my direction and Mum would believe her. Like the occasion when she was a little older and daubed paint on the bathroom tiles, or tie-dyed Mum's bed sheets in a bucket – when there are only two sets of bed sheets, that's a big deal, and Mum rightly went berserk. But it was my fault. 'You should have been watching her!' became an echo of childhood.

The big benefit of having a sister was that I had a summer playmate, and our favourite pastime was re-enacting the madcap BBC show *It's a Knockout* in the back garden. We invented our own fun version of the games, and one memorable challenge involved tying water balloons to the low-hanging washing line. Tracey climbed into Dad's wheelbarrow, stood up and then, on the whistle, I'd push and run as she craned her neck to burst as many balloons as possible with her teeth, soaking us in the process. Our giggles and squeals of laughter matched those that we had heard on the television.

I got used to the sound of Tracey's blood-curdling screams, too. That's because she would stuff anything and everything in her mouth, requiring at least two panic-stricken dashes to A&E.

One day, she decided to go ferreting under the kitchen sink. Dad wasn't home, Mum was in her room, and I must have been in the living room – 'looking after my sister' – when Tracey's cry brought Mum thundering down the stairs, only to stop her in her tracks at the kitchen door. The horror in her voice scared me. 'TRACEEEEEE!'

My sister was sitting on the black-and-white tiles, in front of an open cupboard door, with an opened bottle of bleach to one side, and a dribble of liquid coming out the corner of her mouth. Startled by Mum's reaction, Tracey turned hysterical, especially when force-fed a carton of milk to dilute whatever quantities of bleach she had ingested. Before I knew it, this milky-mouthed infant was in Mum's arms and out the door, leaving me to inform Dad, whenever he returned home for dinner. Mercifully, after a stomach flush and one night in hospital, Tracey quickly recovered. But no sooner had she survived that episode than she was being rushed back in after using a cousin's Airfix kit to glue together the left side of her mouth.

It's not hard to see why I felt the need to look out for my young sister, who was also severely asthmatic. Mum seemed always to be calling out, 'Watch her, Jo!' or 'What's Tracey doing? Is she okay?' I became Mum's second pair of eyes, sensing that Tracey's welfare was as much my responsibility as hers.

I'll never forget the time I arrived home from school to discover my sister was missing. Mum was out. Dad was asleep on the sofa, off sick with a bad back that had plagued him since boyhood – a rugby injury led to a steel pin being inserted in his spine. I was upstairs changing out of my school clothes when I realised Tracey wasn't in the house. She wasn't in the garden, either.

'Dad! Dad!' I yelled, waking him. 'Where's Tracey?!'

'Upstairs, isn't she?' he said, groggily.

'Dad, she's not here!'

Bad back or no bad back, I had never seen him bolt up so fast. And then, a frantic minute or so later, there was a knock on the door. 'Excuse me,' said the man from down the street, 'I think this is your daughter.' He had his hands on the shoulders of Tracey, standing in front of him in a cardigan and red Wellington boots that she'd put on the wrong feet. The man had found her in the newsagent's, where she had bought a pile of comics, sweets, and a plastic doll – items she now clutched to her chest as she stood there.

Where did she find the money to buy those?

And that was the thought that sent me racing upstairs.

Ever since Mum had used my birthday money from Aunty Winnie, I had learned to secrete any cash gifts under some clothes in my drawer, and I had saved the handsome sum of £5. But it turned out that Mum wasn't the one I should have been worried about. It never occurred to me that Tracey knew the whereabouts of my money, let alone that she – a four-year-old – would go out and spend it.

Dad wasn't bothered about this minor incident of petty theft. My £5 haul was a small price to pay for having her home safe and sound. But I couldn't stop stewing over the injustice and I needed to exact revenge in the way that kids do. So I made my sister a sandwich. A Pedigree Chum sandwich.

I gave three-quarters of one tin to our golden Labrador Shandy, and then served up the last quarter between two slices of bread, telling Tracey it was pâté. I figured that once you've tasted bleach and Airfix glue, the dog's dinner wouldn't be all that bad. But she took two bites and spat it out. Years later, while I was washing my hair by leaning over the sink, she once stood on the toilet seat and tied my plaits to the taps before running off, so I suppose we were even.

My abiding memory of Tracey as a child is that of an over-exuberant, impish dynamo who would drive me to the edge of frustration before flashing an irresistible, cheeky grin. She was needier of Mum's attention than I, and seemed to act out more than I ever did. I don't know whether she required more attention as the second child but, I'll say this about my parents, they were even-handed with their love, ensuring there was no favouritism or imbalance. They were also hugely protective. Mum especially. Almost overprotective . . .

*

Other children in the street played outside to their heart's content, running free, allowed to wander off down the street to the local green and wherever else, as long as they were back home at a certain hour. Not us. Mum didn't want us out of sight, so the front garden wall, about eight bricks high, was our strictly enforced boundary. Even as the eldest, I wasn't allowed to go beyond that point. All I could do was sit there, or watch from my bedroom window as classmates bombed around on their bikes and rollerskates. The only other option was for those kids to come play with me in the garden.

'Why can't I go play outside?' I'd ask.

'Because I say so!' Mum would say.

Our only concession was when the ice-cream man trundled down the road in his van and Mum allowed me and Tracey to run out and buy a 10p cornet, on the condition that we came straight back. Even then, she never took her eyes off us, watching from the front door or top window. The odd thing about this rule was that, while I couldn't play in the road with friends directly outside our house, I was allowed to walk on my own to infant school, from the age of seven, down the road and around the corner. I can only guess that Mum didn't think much could happen en route to school, whereas larking about with kids in the neighbourhood knew no bounds. Either way, I learned to love the freedom of that ten-minute dawdle, even if I remained watchful of the time.

'Why aren't you ever allowed to come and play?' a girl once asked.

'I'm just not allowed,' I said, matter-of-factly.

Mum's concern about our safety wasn't only restricted to outside the house. Every night – *every single night* – when Tracey and I were about to go to sleep, she would look under our beds and check inside the wardrobes.

'Why you doing that, Mum?' I asked.

'Just in case anyone has come through the window and is hiding.'

She said it as though this was a probability; that this was what every parent did. Mum couldn't rest until her compulsion to check our environment had been calmed. I became so used to it that I would have probably double-checked myself had she ever forgotten the drill. I saw nothing odd in this at the time, but it obviously speaks to a neurosis – a deep anxiety that entertained the irrational notion of strangers climbing in through windows. Even in winter. And so it follows that if we weren't safe in our home, there was no way we were safe when playing out in the street.

I didn't really care what the other children in the street thought, though. I had one best friend, Dawn Cossar, and she'd often be round at ours, or we'd be at hers having tea – her mum was sometimes our child minder in my early years. In my eyes, as long as Tracey and Dawn were around, I saw nothing negative about my restricted boundaries.

Other friends probably thought our street curfew was weird but Mum redeemed herself by hosting the best game-filled parties for my birthday, inviting as many school friends as the house would take, and festooning the living room with balloons and banners. Dad also came into his own, gathering my classmates into a cross-legged circle where he'd wow them with a card trick or a sleight of hand that miraculously produced a penny from behind someone's ear.

He was a brilliant magician and a long-time member of the Magic Circle, inspired by his 'friend' and comedic magician Ali Bongo, who would go on to have his own BBC series, *Ali Bongo's Cartoon Carnival*. Dad would practise on relatives by tucking a cigarette into a clenched fist, then pulling it out from inside someone's ear. (On Mum's instruction, he soon stopped doing that when one cousin started stuffing cigarettes down his own earhole.)

At my parties, I'd note the disbelief on my friends' faces as he produced a missing ace of spades or queen of hearts. I felt proud that Dad was the one everyone went home raving about. He'd be the talk of the class on Monday mornings, too. My parents went all out to make birthdays special. The same can be said about our Christmases.

Dad virtually turned our front room into Santa's grotto. As well as a masterfully decorated, real tree, the entire ceiling would be covered with colourful foil garlands, and each wall festooned with tinsel. Mum cut her tights in half and they became our makeshift stockings hanging over the fireplace. When Dad had finished wrapping the tree in multi-coloured lights, he'd sit with me in the dark, in front of the roaring coal fire, and hold me as we marvelled at how twinkly everything was. To me, our tree dazzled with a hundred jewels and it felt like every ounce of Christmas spirit had been squeezed into our four walls, to bursting point. And then there were the smells: the fresh pine, the box of sticky, sweet dates, and Dad's festive drink – a snowball.

No matter how tight things were financially, my parents constantly delivered a magical, happy Christmas – it's why it remains my favourite time of year. Don't ask me how they afforded it but, without fail, we woke to a generous amount of presents. We never went short in that regard. But one year, as we sat at the bottom of the stairs full of anticipation, raring to burst into the living room and tear open our gifts, Mum prepared us for the fact, that 'This year, we're having a Swedish Christmas!' The hyped tone of her voice suggested this was going to be a real treat, even if we had no idea where Sweden was.

I must have been nine, Tracey four. Mum slowly opened the door and our presents came into view ... unwrapped and fully visible. My pile was to the right of the fire: a wooden cot with a doll, a Waddingtons board game and a bottle of perfume whose name escapes me. Christmas done and dusted in one glimpse. My heart sank. If this was what Swedish kids faced every year, I felt sorry for them, I thought. Without any element of reveal, our bubble was well and truly punctured. For reasons that were not made clear, it turned out that Mum and Dad hadn't had the time to wrap our last-minute gifts. Something was off between them even if we didn't know what. But while Tracey and I concealed our crushing disappointment – we had been taught to be grateful no matter what we received – we were not to be outdone.

As Mum prepared the turkey, we held our own impromptu 'take two' – wrapping and Sellotaping our gifts in newspaper before taking turns to open them, one by one, on the stairs. We did what we had seen our parents do: we improvised. We made do. We handled life's unexpected events without complaint.

One Friday evening, when I was about six, and Tracey eighteen months, Mum and Dad disappeared into the kitchen for a hushed, serious-sounding conversation. Within the hour, they joined us in front of the television and our evening resumed as normal. It wasn't until the next day that I thought something strange was going on.

Dad was upstairs getting ready when Mum dropped us off at Maureen's, with no explanation other than a promise to pick us up at the end of the day. I knew they were headed somewhere fancy because she was wearing *Joy* by Jean Patou.

The next thing I knew, after a day of baking and playing games, Mum and Dad walked in to collect us, faces beaming with happiness. She was wearing a beautiful silk suit with pearls in her ears and high heels on her feet; he looked every inch the refined gentleman in a dark suit, white shirt and royal navy tie. Their mood definitely felt upbeat and, when we arrived home, Dad nipped out for a Chinese takeaway – a sure sign that they were celebrating something. A Chinese meal was a 'treat' reserved for special occasions.

Mum and Dad never mentioned a word about where they had been or what they had done, and it didn't seem to matter – they were cuddled up on the sofa, laughing like love-struck teenagers. I didn't want to go to bed that night. I didn't want the day to end. And I'll forever remember that evening for how happy the entire house felt.

It would be another four decades before I learned the truth about that day, as relayed by Mum's sister, my Aunty Dot, long after my parents had passed. 'That was when they came back from the registry office after getting married,' she said.

And then she unfurled another secret from the past. 'Your dad's name, before he was known as "Andy Malone", was originally Frank,' she said. (She provided his original surname, too, but I don't think it serves anyone to detail it here.)

That was how I found out that Dad had been someone else in a life that preceded us, making sense of the limited stories from his years in Scotland – a period he clearly wished to box away and not revisit. For that reason, I will respect his wishes. Suffice it to say that this revelation, as surprising as it was, didn't make me question him in any way. It felt like a piece of information so distant, and from another time, that it couldn't touch us. Then and now, it really didn't matter to me whether he was Andy or Frank because, whatever his past and whatever his business, he was, quite simply, Dad, and nothing could diminish who he was to me in childhood.

As a family, we couldn't afford too many day trips or activities that required an admission ticket, so Dad often got creative to keep us entertained. One afternoon, I arrived home from school to find that he'd built Tracey and me a den in the living room.

Most kids do that kind of thing, but Dad had constructed it on his own, commandeering airers and chairs for the three walls, before draping them in bed sheets and using a duvet for the roof. One side was left open, facing the fireplace. 'And in there,' he said, 'is where you are going to have your dinner tonight!'

Dad was a brilliant chef, even if he did insist on using every tin, utensil and piece of cutlery, leaving the kitchen in a right state. Mum didn't love cooking, probably because she got easily distracted. I lost count of the times she left the chicken or roast potatoes in the oven, wandered off to see a neighbour, realised the time and rushed back only to find dinner was ruined. Rustling up a meat and two veg dinner was something Dad could do with his eyes closed, but his specialty was 'stovies', a dish he'd inherited from Scotland, using leftovers from a Sunday roast. Together with cheese and onion turnovers and Spam fritters, these were ideal for a family short on money. We had a serving hatch that opened into the living room and, with a dramatic flourish, he'd pull open the doors, poke his head through and yell, 'STOVIES ARE READY!'

His smile – at the hatch, before bed, or first thing in the morning – reassured us that everything was all right with the world. But when that smile slipped, I knew something was up. He smoked like a chimney at the best of times, but he inhaled more deeply when stressed, breathing it into his lungs as if each breath calmed him.

He made his own roll-ups and had that craft down to a fine art: sliding a tiny sheet of Rizla paper along his tongue before packing it with Golden Virginia tobacco, then rolling it between his thumbs and forefingers, in ten seconds flat. If it wasn't a cigarette in his hand, it was a deck of cards, which he constantly shuffled in two different ways – the overhand chop-chop-chop, or the riffling of two halves to merge into one.

One night, he sat in his armchair and lit up, and I knew he was off in his own world, lost in his thoughts. I found out what was wrong a few days later – he had been laid off from the architects' firm near Charing Cross. I can't remember if this was Harold Wilson's Britain or whether Edward Heath had become prime minister, but a skilled and clever man had been turfed on to the unemployment heap at a time when jobs and opportunity were few and far between. Mum and Dad hadn't seen it coming, and I don't think my parents knew how they were going to cope.

THREE

As I arrived home from school, I pushed open the door to be greeted by the flinty whiff of sulphur, as if an indoor firework had gone off. Mum and Tracey were out somewhere, so I knew Dad was home alone. I called out his name from the bottom of the stairs.

'In here!' he shouted.

I found him standing in the middle of the living room, surrounded by cardboard boxes, pieces of paper, and all sorts of tools, including a saw.

'What's that burnt popcorn smell?' I asked, frowning.

Dad took my enquiry as an invitation. 'Wait until you see this!' he said. He bent down, picked up a magic wand, fiddled with its end, and extended it outward. 'Go on, touch the tip!'

As soon as my finger made contact, the white tip crackled and sparked. I yelped and jumped back. Dad's eyes lit up. His latest home-made magic trick was a triumph. This, as far as he was concerned, meant another productive day at 'the office' and, in the circumstances, his buoyant mood was a good thing.

Dad would be unemployed for a good couple of years, so magic became one of the creative ways he attempted to earn a crust, combining his skilled hands with a lifetime's knowledge from inside the Magic Circle. When word spread locally about his hobby, he started to land bookings for birthday parties, which was why he was honing his act and devising new tricks. This proactive response to his unemployment was typical Dad – he always found a way to adapt or bounce back. Rather than becoming a victim to a bad situation, he would try to turn it around. I did admire how he rolled up his sleeves and turned a hobby into an income, however minor his magician's earnings may have been.

The tables had turned in our house. Mum, forced back to work due to Dad's unemployment, was now the main breadwinner after landing a job as a manicurist for Revlon, encouraging women to have 'matching lips and fingertips', as the ad campaigns said. Once home, she'd open her own box of tricks – a red and gold case that contained a collection of lipsticks and nail enamels, from Orange Sherbet and Fatal Apple Red, to Persian Melon and Blase Apricot. In my eyes, Mum worked with magic, too.

According to different relatives, she was 'the best manicurist they had', which surprised no one because Mum had a charisma, a great sense of humour and an ability to get along with almost anyone. With the job came the importance of image, and she never looked anything other than exceptionally well put together – hair pristine, fingernails perfect, shoes shiny. A walking, elegant advertisement for Revlon.

Dad was rarely up when she left for work, struggling to get out of bed to face another unstructured day. When he did rise, he soon got busy and turned the garden shed into a magician's den, creating a little workspace for the tricks he'd make. The ones that stick in my mind are the metal linking rings that mysteriously separated; a wooden box – painted black with big red dots – that had a false bottom in order to conceal a white rabbit; and a wand that drooped when he fed a hidden rope through its centre. And it wasn't only props he stored, he had magic pets, too – one dove and nine rabbits.

The dove, which had clipped wings to prevent her flying away, was kept in a cage in the living room. When home from school, I'd let her out and she'd perch on my shoulder and accompany me throughout the house: to the toilet, into my bedroom as I read a book, and on the sofa while watching TV. We called her Suki and she used to brush her head up and down my neck, quietly cooing in my ear. When she knew I was settling in for a long night in front of the TV, she hopped down to nest on top of the sofa. When I got up, she jumped back on to my shoulder, responding to me like our golden Labrador, Shandy. For the year we had Suki, she was my constant companion and Dad's star act, along with his nine Netherland Dwarf bunnies – the smallest breed of rabbit, which made them the ideal size to be pulled out of a black hat.

We kept them in a long hutch that ran down one side of the garden. One of them, Spanky, became my pet and followed me around almost as much as Suki. Keeping an eye on Spanky was my job; keeping an eye on the other eight was Dad's, which he seemed to forget one day when they escaped and started marauding across a neighbour's garden.

We were woken one Saturday morning by frantic banging on our front door. The woman from three doors down was almost hyperventilating as she yelled, 'YOUR SODDING DOG AND RABBITS ARE IN MY GARDEN!' The next thing I knew, I was in my pyjamas and slippers running around her back garden with Dad, trying to round them up. Shandy had burrowed under our fence and bolted for freedom, followed by what must have looked like the cast of *Watership Down*. What a caper that proved to be, shepherding nine rabbits, using a cardboard box and a sheet of chicken wire as a guiding device. Once they were captured, Dad started making profuse apologies to our neighbour about the trampled flower beds when I noticed Shandy in the woman's house, in the living room, doing a number two on the carpet. I screamed. The woman turned around and screamed even louder. And Dad cursed like a sailor.

His magic seemed to leave a mess everywhere, and it drove Mum, and me, nuts because he didn't restrict his trick-making to the shed; he preferred to bring his DIY skills inside, where he had more room to spread out and rehearse. But that meant that our living room was often filled with his boxes, instructions, and bits and bobs – what Mum called his 'tut'. Sometimes, there would be nails, pieces of plastic, and wood shavings left on the carpet around the dinner table, because he'd been sawing away, making last-minute adjustments. I'd be the one running around with a Hoover, clearing up after him, because mess made me anxious. I also rearranged the airing cupboard in Mum and Dad's room, placing the sheets and towels in neatly folded stacks and rows. I swear that Dad's constant 'tut' made me a little obsessive compulsive! Not only was I a fastidious child naturally, but I wanted everything to be tidy for when Mum walked in the door, otherwise she'd have a go at him. I'd do anything I could to avoid friction. Since Dad had lost his job, their arguments were a little too frequent for my liking – a situation not helped by his continued gambling.

In his mind, he was only ever one big win away from putting everything right again. I knew when he'd won at poker because his mood was upbeat and chirpy, and our house could breathe again. But when he lost, I'd hear the blazing rows as I lay in bed listening to Mum's accusations of recklessness, barely muffled by the paper-thin walls. Some nights, I'd hear her crying into her pillow with frustration.

Two famous arguments have stuck with me: the time she discovered her precious collection of crystal decanters had been staked as collateral and lost; and the evening when Dad was given a lift home ... because he'd gambled away the family car. The longer he was out of work, the more he seemed to speculate to accumulate, and I'm sure this unacknowledged addiction was a source of endless anxiety for Mum. She couldn't know if he was going to come home with big winnings, or turned-out pockets and an empty wallet. As much as I adored my dad, and as much as he tried his best in so many other ways, his actions seemed wilfully blind to the consequences of losing.

If the financial pressure, together with their differing professional fortunes, revealed anything, it was how much tougher Mum had become, no longer afraid to speak her mind and upset the apple cart. She seemed to tolerate his ways less and less as she came to realise that the man she'd married would never change.

All I wanted was the harmony to be restored; for Dad to wave his magic wand and make everything okay again. Even at the age of seven, I felt the discomfort of our circumstances, no longer oblivious to the stresses and strains that clenched our home like an iron fist, refusing to let go.

In between the broad brushstrokes of Dad's magic and gambling, he developed another lifelong pursuit: art. As a skilled draftsman, it was perhaps no surprise that he was a talented painter, creating the most stunning watercolours and oils that nearly always depicted wild seas, angry skies or serene countryside landscapes. Each painting conveyed the theme of a journey: someone walking off into a wintry distance, or down a beautiful path through a copse of trees, or a galleon cutting through the waves.

I'd watch him start with a blank canvas as he sat at his architect's drawing board propped on the dining table, rolling one of his cigarettes, waiting for inspiration to strike. If there was one thing I learned from watching him stare into space, puffing away, it is the truth that you can't force creativity. He could sit there for hours without picking up his brushes, but, as he explained, creativity needs to be respected. It is not a tap that can simply be turned on; it comes when ready, not when forced or unfelt. Waiting, he said, was part of the creative process. Let inspiration come to you. Don't chase it.

As he waited and painted, the table resembled a cluttered art studio with miniature pots of paint, palette knives, jugs, and different brushes – flats and rounds – scattered around the smudged rainbow on his thumbhole palette. When you add his tricks, boxes, sawdust and piles of magazines to the scene, it's not hard to picture the mess that was our living room and kitchen, and it wasn't helped by the piles of laundry that kept growing into overwhelming mounds because Mum didn't have the time and Dad didn't bother.

His art even spilled into the bathroom. He'd fill the bath with jugs of cold tea, to a depth of about one foot, and leave his blank canvasses in there for twenty-four hours, staining them for an aged effect. And if the bath wasn't filled with canvasses, then the living room would be, stacked against the wall to the left of the fireplace, together with long pieces of wood that he'd cut up and use for framing, leading to more sawdust. He'd cut four pieces of wood before joining them together with individual vice-like brackets, and then mounting the painting behind glass. Most of the time, I found it easier to retreat to the neat enclave of the room I shared with Tracey rather than confront that whole scene.

Lying on the top of the bunk bed we shared, I often imagined living at Aunty Maureen's because it was everything I wanted our house to be: a) she was always there, the ever-present parent; b) a cooked meal was always on the table at 6 p.m., which meant 'family'; and c) she kept her home meticulously clean and so it felt like a cosy, well-looked-after home, where there only seemed to be harmony. How I envied that kind of existence.

I soon became the magician's assistant, which was a role I fell into by virtue of wanting to be around Dad all the time. If Tracey was Mum's shadow, I was his. And so, when I started tagging along to different children's parties, I found myself called on to arrange the props, look after the dove and rabbits, and fetch his next trick, placing it on Dad's little table which had a curtain draped around its front.

We didn't have costumes – we couldn't afford such luxuries – but Dad looked swish in a black suit, white shirt, and bow tie. He took his act seriously, so he first swore me to secrecy, emphasising that a magician never breaks the secret code. 'If you ever reveal to anyone how any of these tricks are done, you will never come with me again. Understand?'

I never did tell a soul.

I made my debut at Northwick Park Hospital in Mum's old stomping ground of Harrow, which was where Aunty Vera worked. The London Palladium it was not, but you wouldn't have guessed from the energy Dad put into his act. Wherever we went, he dazzled his child audiences with a deft execution of his tricks. What's more, he wanted to make the kids believe that *they* were the ones capable of magic, too.

I found him in the living room one Saturday morning before a show, messing around with a needle and thread, weaving it through an unpeeled banana. 'You'll see what I'm doing later,' he said, with a wink.

At the next children's party, the banana was his first trick and he picked out a young boy, telling him, 'You be the magician and let your index finger be the wand, okay?'

The boy stood up and my dad told him to tap the banana with his right index finger in three different places along its length. 'Once you do that, we're both going to say, "Abracadabra! Alakazam!" Ready?' The youngster tapped the banana 1-2-3, they both shouted the magic words, the boy peeled back the skin . . . and the fruit was sliced into three segments. The look on that child's face was magic itself. I can well imagine that the dramatic gasps of children were a sound that kept Dad going back, despite the limited money he earned.

After a few weeks as his assistant, I viewed us as an unbeatable, formidable duo, and I particularly cherished our father–daughter time. In the car to and from the events, we'd chat about this and that – inconsequential talk, but talk that made me feel close to him nonetheless; light, upbeat, full of laughter.

One time, when we were mid-conversation, the person in front of us stopped suddenly, forcing Dad to slam on his brakes. With that, nine tins of John West pink salmon rolled out from under my seat, washing up around my feet. Dad looked like the kid who'd been caught with his fingers in the cookie jar. I wasn't daft. I knew he'd acquired these tins 'off the back of a lorry', which made me feel distinctly uncomfortable, but he wanted to serve them as a treat for when Aunty Dot came round for dinner later. I think he wanted to prove that he could still provide by whatever means possible. He kept trying to get back on his feet, which was why I didn't only become his magician's assistant but his right-hand woman at the market, too. Dad had decided to set up a stall, selling his art.

Before he and I walked out the door on a Saturday or Sunday, en route to the markets at Crayford, Dartford, Blackheath, or Tunbridge Wells, we often left with a message ringing in our ears. 'Andy,' said Mum, 'you *have got* to make a sale today – there is nothing in the fridge!'

In the car, which was packed with paintings to its roof and back doors, I'd look at Dad and sense the pressure he was under to deliver. He'd catch me staring and smile back unconvincingly. 'We'll be all right, Jo,' he'd say, patting my knee. 'We'll sell a painting or two today!'

I desperately wanted us to earn that honest money, otherwise I feared more tinned food rolling out from underneath my seat. So I felt the urgency for him to make a sale, too. I'm sure we weren't the only traders who were down to our last coppers, and I think that's what made market life so nerve-wracking and exciting at the same time. Unlike the magic shows, I had no idea what was going to happen next. I had no idea whether Dad was capable of pulling a rabbit out of the hat.

I especially loved the hustle, the bustle and the energy at Crayford market, held at the greyhound track. The traders there felt like one big family of aunts and uncles because they'd see me, this young kid with Dad, and share his sense of protection. I was as safe as houses in that environment, which was why Dad allowed me to wander around the one hundred or so stalls that sold anything and everything: clothes, textiles, fruit and veg, fish, foodstuffs, art, photography, books, records, kitchen utensils. People from all over the boroughs of south-east London and north-west Kent flocked to this market, not only to grab a bargain but also to enjoy the banter and patter of traders selling their wares.

The whole place felt vibrant and alive as I breathed in the working-class air infused with the smells of hot tea, Bovril, bacon sandwiches, crispy chips in a deep-fat fryer, cinnamon, cigarette smoke, and the soot from the track. The soot got everywhere – over my shoes, hands and skirt – and I sometimes returned home looking like a chimney sweep, but it was the one time I didn't mind getting filthy.

'Hello, Jo, luv!' one of the Cockney regulars would shout as I walked around. And someone else would yell, 'Wanna giz an 'and today, Jo?!' Other traders brought their sons but I can't remember any other young girls being around, so I think I was a bit of a novelty. Everyone knew me. Everyone waved. Everyone was on their toes, looking to make a sale.

We would arrive about 7–7.30 a.m., come rain or shine. The market was located on the oval-shaped dirt field in the centre of the track and, before the crowds arrived, Dad had to claim his 10 x 10-foot, metal-framed stall and find his pitch. Together, we would then set up shop, using sheets of hardboard to line the stall's back and sides, which was where we hung and stacked the paintings, creating our own mini-gallery beneath a tarpaulin roof.

Once the paintings were on display – there were about twenty-five at any one time, from foot to eye level – he would stand there, brush off his hands and say: 'All right, Jo, I'll mind the stall, you go get our bacon sandwiches and cups of tea.'

There was always a big queue at the canteen and I'd stand there, a blonde-haired dwarf among giants. The countertop was about two feet higher than me, so the man with the big smile had to lean out and reach down to hand me a small cardboard box containing our bacon butties and two polystyrene cups of steaming hot tea. In the twenty or so minutes that I'd been away from the stall, all I could think about was how Dad was getting on, so my first question to him was always, 'We sold anything yet?'

He laughed. 'Not yet, Jo. Not yet. I nearly had one, though!'

'We've got to sell something soon, Dad!'

'I know, love,' he'd say, 'and we will. They promised me they were coming back.'

I loved being with Dad on the stall because he constantly encouraged me to get involved with a sale or the banter with other traders and customers. Through him, I almost certainly learned the art of the sale, to the extent that, in my own mind, I felt I could do it better. Yes, even at the age of eight.

Within a few weeks, and when I felt confident enough, I started to emerge from his shadow more and more, telling curious customers about the story behind each painting. For example, take the clipper painting: I'd describe its history and the voyage it was embarking on, transporting them from the market and into the painting in the same way Dad had done with me. The hook of a good story often led to a sale – a mental note to be registered for later life. I'd urge Dad to share the stories he'd told me but he could rarely be bothered and my heart would sink when a customer walked away and we lost a sale. The more I grew into the merchant's role, the more seriously I approached it, and I learned to know Dad's rhythms. If he hadn't sold a painting by the end of the day, he'd be attacking the final two hours with gusto and more likely to sell one. But if he'd sold a painting in the morning, he tended to rest on his laurels. With £25 in his pocket, he'd start haggling and be more obstinate, not willing to barter. Dad was more '£25 – that'll do'. I was more '£25 – let's turn it into £100'.

I'd know when he was negotiating and when he had a customer on the hook. In my head, I'd be thinking, 'Now, Dad. Close the sale!' I also sensed when a deal was slipping away. 'They'll give you £30 not £40 – take £30!' But, being the gambler he was, he'd hang out for the extra tenner and invariably lose out. He loathed dropping his price after putting his heart and soul into each painting.

At one point, he completely deviated from his usual genre and started creating these ugly-looking, abstract paintings that weren't his style and, more to the point, never sold. They really were hideous creations – one was blue, one pink, and the other green – and I couldn't believe it when he priced them at £15 each. It didn't surprise me one jot that we were lugging them around for weeks.

I grew so sick of them that when he asked me to mind the stall one day, I decided to do a deal. When he returned from fetching tea, he noticed they had gone. 'You sold them?!'

'I did,' I said proudly. 'I did a deal – twenty pounds for the lot.'

He hit the roof, which was embarrassing because I felt everyone was looking at us. 'Hell's bells, Jo! That could have been a week's money and you sold them for twenty pounds!'

I tried explaining that twenty quid was a fair price but he didn't listen because all he saw was a near-fifty per cent discount. I apologised all the way home, and he eventually forgave me – Dad couldn't stay angry with me for long, although I did receive the lecture about never cutting deals without his permission again. Mum wasn't upset when we handed over that twenty. Beggars couldn't be choosers.

I preferred it when we returned home with something to contribute. I loved it even more when we'd had a good day, when we'd sold four or five paintings priced £25–30. Dad felt flush with that kind of money in his pocket and our reward was a Chinese takeaway collected on the way home. As he and I waited in the restaurant, he'd order a beer and buy me a pineapple juice, and we'd clink our glasses together – a toast to a father and daughter putting in another productive day's shift.

FOUR

Over the space of a year or so, Mum had thrived as a manicurist, growing a loyal customer base and developing an overall passion for skincare. A job taken out of necessity had blossomed into a career, and she was booked solid from morning until evening. It felt as though I only saw her on Saturday evenings and Sundays, but this was our new 'normal'; this, as she continually reminded me, was how we survived.

She would be out of the door to catch the early train before we left for school, and not home until eight o'clock, sometimes ten. She was so preoccupied with keeping us afloat that she didn't even step off the treadmill to celebrate her birthdays. From the age of eight onwards, it became my annual tradition to ensure we marked the occasion. Armed with a recipe, and because her birthday always fell at half term at the end of October, I'd bake a cake, smear on the icing with a knife, buy the candles, and wait at the dining table until she walked in. Sometimes, I'd have to go to bed because she wouldn't be home until late but, whether it was on the actual day or the following day, I made sure that we sang *Happy Birthday* and shared cake. It was never much of a celebration but it was my small way of expressing gratitude for everything she did for us.

In early 1971, there was cause for more celebration when she was offered an opportunity she couldn't refuse, facilitated by a client who also happened to see London's grande dame of skincare, a beauty therapist called Madame Lubatti. A rare opening had arisen to be the receptionist at her Marylebone clinic. The only slight difficulty was that Mum suffered from a form of rosacea-acne – not the greatest advertisement when you are the first impression for arriving clients. Madame Lubatti gave her the job but insisted on treating her skin and, soon enough, the condition cleared up. I think that was the moment Mum truly understood the wonders of skincare.

I would later get to know the warm-hearted, eccentric character that was Madame Lubatti. Aged in her eighties, she was a countess who had once been married to an Italian count. She had lived in Hong Kong, where she mastered homeopathy, before moving to London and starting her own business in the 1930s, creating face creams and doing facials that attracted clients from the middle classes to the aristocracy. Hollywood stars Ava Gardner and Vivien Leigh supposedly swore by her treatments. No wonder Mum jumped at the chance, keen to develop her knowledge in all matters skincare.

It didn't take her new employer long to realise that Mum was a willing, trustworthy, eager-to-learn employee. Within weeks, Mum was not only receiving on-the-job training but coming home from work to revise for beautician exams and diplomas, studied at the Arnould-Taylor Therapy College. On many Sundays, she would sit out on the sun lounger in the back garden, wearing her green cotton summer dress and straw wedge sandals, sipping a Dubonnet and lemonade, and study for hours on end. We weren't allowed to interrupt her concentration but I'd watch her through the kitchen window and observe her intense focus. I could see how much this new job meant to her by the way she threw herself into these studies. Within no time, she had qualified with distinction as an aestheticienne (a beauty therapist) in the subjects of anatomy, physiology, and massage. I felt so proud of her – she had found that one thing in life that made her happy.

From what I would later gather, Madame Lubatti saw a lot of herself in Mum: a woman who wanted to make something of herself, who dreamed of going up in the world, and was unafraid of hard work. I dare say she also recognised a fellow keeping-up-appearances type, because Mum's glamour belied our council estate existence. A polished veneer mattered in the beauty industry and if anyone understood the importance of projecting the correct image, it was Madame Lubatti. Following her divorce, she had retained her title of countess, which she felt gave her an edge in a class-obsessed city like London. She knew the importance of conveying prestige; indeed, for a lady with a clientele comprising aristocratic ladies and movie stars, it was the hallmark of her brand. She had also adopted 'Madame' because it conveniently cloaked her first and middle names. She kept them to herself, preferring simply to use her initials, and so she became known as 'Madame D.H. Lubatti'. 'Doris Hilda Lubatti' didn't quite have the same ring to it.

From now, my weekends were either spent with Dad as he sold his wares or performed magic, or with Mum at the skincare salon. I never stopped enjoying being Dad's able assistant, but shadowing Mum in her glamorous new world, and the prospect of meeting a countess, pulled on me the strongest.

I was transfixed the first time I met Madame Lubatti: initially, by her scent – an amazing mix of sandalwood and rose oil; then, by her appearance – a six-foot-tall, white-haired lady who appeared so grand and polished, even as she mixed lotions and potions, darting between her lab and two treatment rooms.

She wore the same 'uniform' almost every day: a long, white lab coat over white fishnet tights with the dramatic accent of black, high-heeled, peep-toe shoes. Then there was the striking use of make-up: the blood-red lipstick, the stark, black eyeliner, and the generously powdered complexion, beneath her fringe and short, elfin hairstyle. She looked so regal to me. And yet, behind the formidable exterior was a soul with the kindest eyes and the silkiest hands that defied their aged and brittle appearance.

Her skincare salon was housed at No.14 Montagu Mansions, within a Victorian, four-storey, red-brick mansion block, a stone's throw from Baker Street. At one end of the road was York Street, with its regiment of Georgian terraced houses; at the other was Crawford Street, with its expensive apartments and a small parade of shops. To my young eyes, the neighbourhood was the poshest place I had ever been. Residents had flower boxes on the sills of canted bay windows, and the cars in the street looked like the kind that Dad drove in his dreams. No wonder Mum had me dress up all nice in my green Billie Kilt skirt with straps, white jumper and navy blue Clarks sandals with white socks pulled to the knee. I doubt that other kids at my school dressed as well for church.

We walked up a set of marble steps into a lobby where a uniformed porter was on hand, and then we turned left into a ground-floor apartment that opened into a reception hall. Mum told me that BBC Radio disc jockey Pete Murray lived in the same building, but that meant nothing to me. The only 'star' who excited me was Madame Lubatti, and she always took my hand and led me inside her lab, leaving Mum to carry out treatments on clients.

Beyond two treatment rooms and the lab, the apartment comprised a large kitchen, a bathroom and a drawing room, which were the private quarters where Madame Lubatti and her 'companion' Mr West lived. But it was the lab, 'where all the

magic happened', that left me endlessly fascinated. It was as heavenly white as a John Lennon *Imagine* video: white paint, white
shelves, white cupboards, white cups, white plates, white racks.
Underfoot, the black-and-white tiles ran throughout; on the walls
were bevelled mirrors; on the ceilings, twinkling chandeliers. The
whiteness of everything made the place feel so serene and safe.

At the far end of the lab, beneath the window that let in the
daylight, there was a countertop covered with glass sweetie jars
containing ingredients such as slippery elm, sandalwood, rosehip,
camphor crystal, dried marigold flowers, and amber crystals; you
name it, she stocked it. On other shelves, there were different-
sized tubs of cream and corked, antique poison bottles containing
oils and tonics, each one clearly labelled with a handwritten tag
tied around its neck. Imagine a pharmacist's room at the back of a
chemist's – with clear, green and brown glass bottles neatly stacked
on different shelves – and you get the picture.

If there was one overriding smell that kicks open that memory,
it would be the combination of rosemary, lavender and camphor,
and I can see Madame Lubatti mixing a lotion in a glass cylinder
as she walked around, forever on the go, exuding an undiluted
passion for her craft, almost bouncing around the room with her
creative spirit.

The laboratory was where she took me under her wing, and I
had my own exclusive spectator's spot, sitting in the gap between
a bookcase and desk on a set of portable wooden steps that were
used whenever Mum or Madame Lubatti needed to grab an ingredient from out-of-reach shelving. I observed *everything* from this
vantage point, taking in every detail and imbibing every scent. I
also watched Mum come alive in between appointments, grab-
bing this or that ingredient before crushing it all together with a
pestle and mortar, adding a touch of goat's milk to everything she
did – that was one of Mum's touches. Dad was a genius with his

hands but I now saw that she was equally talented, able to make the perfect face mask.

This was a completely different world to the rough and ready environment of the markets, and I definitely felt more at home in the lab — it felt like the most natural place for me to be. Indeed, all I wanted to do was spend my Saturdays with Mum and Madame Lubatti.

One afternoon, while Mum was locked away in one of the treatment rooms, the countess waltzed in holding a bottle of Shloer grape juice, but I didn't know it was grape juice because I'd never had it before.

'Jo, let's celebrate!' she said as she carried two crystal, engraved champagne coupes over to the table near her desk. 'Would you like some champagne?'

'I-I-I would, but I don't think Mummy would let me!'

'Ohhhhh, you can have *this* champagne!' she said, pouring it into my glass.

She patted the other seat, inviting me to join her, and we clinked our glasses as she made a toast I now forget. The toast isn't what mattered; what mattered was that I was being a real lady, sipping pretend champagne with my new favourite person, drinking from a glass that felt like a fish bowl in my hands. Then Mum walked in. I can see her face now as she saw me with a champagne coupe to my lips, which I slowly lowered as a frown formed on her brow.

'M-Mad-Madame! What is she drinking?!'

I looked at Mum, looked at my drinking partner, and wondered how much trouble I was in. 'It's grape juice, Mum! Look, taste it!'

Madame Lubatti laughed as Mum approached the table and spotted the bottle; suddenly her frown dissolved into a smile. She put one hand on my shoulder, picked up my glass with the other, and clinked Madame Lubatti's glass. 'Cheers!' she said.

She, like me, started to see the countess as my surrogate grandma.

Sometimes, Mr West – or Vernon, as the countess referred to him – invited me to go outside and grab some fresh air, but I never did warm to him; he smelled of beer all the time and seemed distant and aloof. Besides, he wasn't as inspiring or as entertaining as the countess. She used to do yoga, even though she was in her eighties, and we once found her doing a handstand against the wall.

'Madame, how long have you been in this position?' Mum asked.

'Oh, about an hour!' she said. 'Almost done.'

She used to say that if you stood on your head for an hour a day, the blood rush to the brain would make you more intelligent. She was a student of yoga long before it became fashionable, which was evident in how nimble she remained; indeed, it was her flexibility that likely saved her from serious injury one Saturday morning.

In the bathroom, she had one of those extendable washing lines that stretched from wall to wall – that was how she dried her fishnet stockings. Mum and I showed up at 9 a.m. and Madame Lubatti must have heard the door go.

'EILEEEEEEN! EILEEEEEEN!' she screamed, sounding in distress.

We hurried through – me trailing behind Mum – and there she was, hanging upside down, head and shoulders on the floor, with one leg awkwardly slung over the drooping washing line. She had apparently been doing another headstand when one of her fishnets got caught. Once Mum had freed her, she sat on a chair to catch her breath, looking a little confused and disoriented. Mum had a treatment to carry out so she asked me to keep an eye on Madame Lubatti.

In the kitchen, I could see her shaking slightly as I made her some lapsang souchong tea, served with a drop of honey in china teacups. A drop of honey was her medicine for everything, to soothe a stye in the eye, to treat a sore on the face, and, in this instance, to calm her nerves. The tea was awful – it smelled like burning rubber – but it seemed to do for Madame Lubatti. As I watched her hold the cup in both hands, I knew what would take her mind off the embarrassment: a story. She always liked going back to her glorious past to retrieve a fantastical episode, and I couldn't think of a better distraction, for her and for me. 'Madame, tell me about the time when ...'

Like Dad, Madame Lubatti was flamboyant with her storytelling. When the words fell from her lips, with drama conveyed by widening eyes and do-you-know-what-happened-next cliffhangers, I hung on every theatrical anecdote. Two worldly tales lodged in my mind. The first involved her mother, who owned an evening dress that had the most divine bejewelled lilies, and in the centre of each lily was 'a diamond *the size of a quail egg!*' I had no idea what a quail was and so, in my mind's eye, this egg was the size of the boiled egg I'd eaten that morning. Her mother's show-stopping outfit was worn to one high-society party where everyone dressed in their finest and quaffed champagne. 'Do you know what happened next, Jo?'

'No, Madame ... Tell me!'

'My mother went to grab her cape from a chair and just as she was about to pick it up, a waiter screamed, "Stop, Madam! Stop!" And she looked down to find *a python* coiled on top of the cape!'

'A real snake? A big one?' I asked.

'*Eee-normous*,' she said. 'About this big ...' and her hands measured thin air, about five feet apart.

One of my favourite stories was about her time in Hong Kong

when she was working as a homeopath, learning about fruit, plant and flower extracts. 'Everyone thought that was all I did,' she said, 'but do you know what I *really* did, Jo?'

I shook my head.

'Can you keep a secret?'

I nodded.

'Well, I worked . . .' and she approached me, bent down and whispered, '*as a spy!*'

I gasped. 'Madame Lubatti!'

'And do you know how we passed secret messages back and forth?' She took one of the face creams and removed the lid. 'In here, in one of these tubs, under the wadding. No one was going to look inside a woman's face cream for a tiny piece of folded paper!'

There were so many other exotic stories from Hong Kong, China, London and Italy, and each one almost made me forget that Mum was in another room, doing a facial. Half the time, it felt as though it was only the countess and me in the salon. But it was more than simply her stories that impacted me; she was the one who opened the door into fragrance.

Over the next two years, I would unwittingly soak up the knowledge she imparted, along with my own observations that I unconsciously collected. She showed me the beauty of creativity, the fantasy world of product, the magic of mixing lotions, and what it was to be an artist. She turned on a light in the deepest parts of me, and that light would only glow brighter with time. It was almost as if she saw my future as much as she did Mum's, which was probably why she decided to train my senses by regularly testing my nose.

She would bring over three unlabelled bottles of different rose oils, remove the stoppers, place each one under my nose and ask: 'What do you think that smells of?'

I'd close my eyes and sniff. 'Tea rose?'

It impressed her that I could tell the difference between the woody muskiness of a garden rose, the clean, apple-green notes of a tea rose, and the rich, regal scent of a Bulgarian rose. 'Very well done,' she said, producing another bottle. 'And what about this one?'

'French lavender!'

The next day brought a new test. 'What's this?'

'Camphor. It's camphor, isn't it?!'

'Now try this. Not as easy . . .'

I screwed up my eyes, inhaling deeply and thinking hard about this sticky, waxy, gloopy smell. And then it came to me. 'Jojoba oil!' It is the ingredient that brings thickness and texture to a face cream. It is one of those characters that is a slight chameleon because it turns as hard as wax in cold temperatures yet as loose as yoghurt on a hot day. The fact I nailed it in one earned me extra brownie points. In fact, I didn't get many wrong, as Madame Lubatti coaxed out my love of fragrance and essentially trained my instincts. She said that I had a nose for the business – a comment that never ceases to make me chuckle today.

She also divulged a little-known tip that made me understand the reasoning behind whiteness in a room: one interior colour, plus very little sound, allows the eyes and ears to relax so that the scents in the air are the only stimulant for the senses. But that wasn't the only inside tip I learned, because, on her desk, she kept the biggest secret to her unrivalled success – a precious, well-thumbed, black leather ledger, filled with more than four decades' worth of recipes for her skincare products: the pink moisturiser that smelled of marshmallow; the orange skin food that reminded me of geraniums; the white nourishing cream derived from Bulgarian rose oil; the rosemary and lavender body oil; the sandalwood exfoliating mask . . . the lot. She allowed me to flick through its pages one day and that's when I noticed her intricate, spidery handwriting, in black or blue ink, that recorded her precise formulations. I stood there scanning, if not reading, an invaluable archive that most of London's beauty industry would have died to get their hands on, even if I didn't realise it at the time. That precious artefact contained the secrets to eternal youth. What I could not have known was that it would one day end up in my mum's possession, and help change the course of my life.

Madame Lubatti decided out of the blue that I needed to apply my new-found knowledge. 'Jo, come here. I want you to make a slippery elm mask. Do you think you can do it?'

'I do. You use—'

'No, don't tell me. Show me.'

My heart pounded because I was worried whether any attempt I made could be good enough. *What if I disappoint her? What if I disappoint Mum?*

My head was barely above counter height, so she dragged over a stool for me to stand on, and then I opened one of her big glass sweetie jars and scooped out some of the oatmeal-coloured slippery elm powder, added a tablespoon of plain yoghurt, a few drops of avocado oil, jojoba oil and some vitamin E, with a dash of freshly squeezed lemon juice and a spoonful of honey. I mixed everything in a bowl with a spatula and, once I'd finished my feverish stirring, I poured this mousse-thick mixture into a white plastic jar with a black lid and handed it to her. Madame Lubatti placed her nose to the rim and then dabbed a finger into the cream, like a chef testing the texture of a sauce.

'Wonderful ... wonderful!' she said, and gave me a big, tight hug.

At that moment, Mum walked into the room. 'Eileen,' said Madame Lubatti, 'look what Jo has made!'

Mum was impressed, too. 'Oh darling, well done – that's wonderful.' I don't think she realised until that moment how much attention I had been paying to the whole operation.

I learned so much under Madame Lubatti's tutelage, including two skincare tips that have remained with me to this day: mashing up avocado to treat dry, dehydrated skin, and using cotton-wool pads soaked in ice-cold milk to bathe tired, swollen eyes. I knew this because it was my job to slice the avocado and mash it in a bowl, and I would also cut the lint into little squares to fit snugly on clients' eyes.

My education at the school of Madame Lubatti wasn't only limited to the lab; she also took me along to Goulds homeopathic chemist in Crowndale Road, where she bought her pills, powders and oils by the kilo and half-kilo, as well as Baldwin's in Walworth Road, one of the great herbalists, where she sourced different herbs, waxes and dried flowers.

The days I looked forward to the most were those when she took me to Marylebone High Street to a Viennese coffee shop that became our regular haunt. She'd have a chicken vol-au-vent and I'd devour a chocolate marzipan in the shape of a seal. Sometimes, we'd go there for brunch, sitting at a small round table near the window, and she'd tell me more outlandish stories or talk about different teas, herbs, and face creams. I soon saw for myself why her incredibly high standards had played a huge part in her success: if a pastry or cup of tea wasn't perfect, she'd send it back, in the same way she would reject a face cream if it wasn't *absolutely perfect*. 'If you can't do something perfectly,' she told me once, 'then don't do it all. You must do everything brilliantly!'

She hardly drew breath when talking and I could have listened to her all day long. Maybe it was because she spoke to me like one adult does to another. 'Do you know,' she said to me one day as we sat there, 'I think you are my best friend . . .'

Apart from Mr West, I don't think she had anyone else in her life except for me, Mum and her clients. And I doubt she had anyone who was quite as enraptured as I was.

She seemed so sprightly and alert that it was easy to forget her age. But one day, a glaring moment of forgetfulness caught me unawares. Bless her heart, we were about to walk into the café when she stopped dead in her tracks and gripped my hand. 'We have to go back, Jo!' she said, sounding alarmed.

'Why, Madame. Why?'

She put a hand to her mouth. 'I've forgotten to put my under-wear on!'

When we returned to the salon, she seemed quieter than usual, as if she was too busy thinking. I didn't realise at the time that she was probably mortified. I also failed to see the significance in why she was spending more time with me, leaving Mum to do more and more treatments.

Another incident happened two or three weeks later: we were walking along streets that had been her backyard for years when she stopped and stood rooted to the spot, looking utterly lost. 'Do you know where we are, Jo?'

'Yes, I do. Marylebone High Street, Madame.'

She looked relieved but the way her grip tightened around my hand suggested she was scared, almost holding on to me. 'Oh, good girl . . . You show us the way home, then.'

When I told Mum what had happened, she didn't seem sur-prised. From that day on, she made sure that Madame Lubatti had her address written down on a tag we used to pin inside her coat. I saw nothing odd in that; to me, it was no different than having my name stitched into the one I wore to school.

I had no idea that the woman I adored was beginning to unravel and lose her mind, slowly and imperceptibly becoming a stranger to all that she was familiar with.

FIVE

One Sunday evening, a bunch of tall men in suits turned up at our house and seemed to catch Dad off guard. Tracey and I were ushered upstairs the moment Mum answered the door, so I have no idea what they wanted or what was said. But after they left, the intense argument that ensued between my parents was enough to suggest that our unexpected visitors had something to do with a gambling debt.

Dad had been staying out until three or four in the morning, which, I came to learn, meant he had been chasing his losses. Consequently, my parents started to squabble *a lot*. The reasons behind their numerous blow-ups were mostly shielded from us but, more than once, I heard the exasperated refrain from Mum that she was 'sick of cleaning up your mess!'

Another one of those messes was revealed when a letter from the council arrived in the post, detailing numerous unpaid parking fines dating back months. Mum had no idea about this mounting debt so she grabbed Dad's car keys, marched outside to his car, flipped the boot and there they were – a stash of unpaid, crumpled tickets still in the envelopes that traffic wardens had left on the windscreen. Dad didn't return home for two days following that discovery.

There was no shielding the tension in a house as small as ours. Mum's simmering frustrations seemed to keep her on edge, and Dad's stubbornness left him brooding and monosyllabic. The uneasy silences at mealtimes were only interrupted by the sound of cutlery on ceramic, and Tracey and I learned to keep our heads down in that deeply uncomfortable atmosphere.

When their marriage was good, they were in harmony, but when things got bad, it was awful – the way they yelled at one another left my stomach in knots. From this point on, when I was aged eight and Tracey three, there would be many a time when I'd sit on the stairs, hands over ears, trying to shut out the noise. Sometimes their arguments could drag on for days. But I knew things were *really* serious when I smelled roast lamb, because I knew exactly what that meant. It was Mum's idea of payback.

Dad hadn't been able to bear the smell since he was a young man in the navy when the only edible thing left in the freezer was mutton that had turned bad. Days from land, hardy sailors didn't grumble about things such as out-of-date food, so he had to eat what was placed in front of him, which explained why the faintest whiff of lamb would make him retch. And it was a button that Mum didn't hesitate to press.

I'd smell her preparing the lamb and I'd dread Dad coming home because he'd walk in the door . . . and gag. Cue another blazing row. For that reason, the rich aroma of roast lamb is not a smell that unlocks any happy memories for me now. I prefer to dwell on the image of Dad, all smiles, sitting in his armchair as Mum hands him a mug of tea, as if no row had ever happened. That's how swiftly their conflicts could end; the switch between night and day. If lamb signalled trouble, a good old British cuppa meant there was a truce, however short-lived those truces tended to be.

*

I can't say that my school years were a bed of roses, either. I have few fond memories of my time at comprehensive school. For me, this period was a rite of passage – the quagmire between childhood and adulthood that I had to wade through.

I struggled academically, seemingly unable to retain any information; nothing would go in. Take French, for example – I couldn't fathom the language or the text. The words on the page looked more like scrambled Morse code and it didn't help that the teacher came from north of the border and had a thick Scottish accent. The harder I tried to concentrate, the more jumbled the text became.

Outside of the classroom, there was one sport I loved: netball. I played centre and made it into the school team. I loved being centre, in the thick of the action. But, ultimately, playing netball didn't help my grades.

Some afternoons, I'd come home and want to cry with frustration because I felt stupid; in fact, I worried endlessly that *I was stupid*. The teachers were of little help, and I didn't feel able to speak with Mum and Dad because they seemed to have enough on their plates; moreover, I didn't want to let them down with my poor performance. Not that they took much interest anyway. I can't remember one parents' evening or sports day that they attended. I used to run around the 200m track looking for their faces in the crowd, but they never showed and I never made a big deal about it.

Besides, my academic struggle seemed incidental compared to my parents' financial struggle. Mum often appeared harried or overwhelmed, and we hardly ever had mother-daughter time any more. The tactile days of being snuggled up on the sofa watching TV were long gone. But I understood the reason – she was single-handedly running Madame Lubatti's salon. When she did manage to take a breath, it was Tracey, as the youngest child, who needed her attention first. I understood that, too. And when Mum found real downtime, she would 'sugar off' down the road, seeking refuge and a good chat with a friend. I was the one who had to go and find her to say dinner was ready, guessing which house she was in: Maureen's, Sheila's or May's.

One of the times I remember receiving a concentrated period of TLC was when I suffered a bout of chicken pox, and Mum managed to drop everything to be with me for five days. I lay on the sofa, she nursed me, stroked my hair, and rubbed calamine lotion into my spots. Sickness brought rare one-on-one time with Mum and she was wonderfully attentive. After recovering, I returned to school but something wasn't quite right with my eyes afterwards – I couldn't see the blackboard clearly and my left vision was blurred. A routine eye test led to a referral to hospital where I was initially diagnosed with a lazy eye. The solution? A hideous pair of ice-blue, thick-framed NHS glasses.

I wanted to cry when I looked in the mirror – they were so ugly-looking. But the specialist wasn't done: underneath the glasses, he placed a big, white, sticky plaster over my 'good' right eye, which was designed to make the lazy one work harder. And he wanted me to walk around for the next two weeks looking like that! Bearing in mind that I was, by now, also wearing a set of metal clamps on my teeth, it's not hard to imagine why my self-consciousness increased tenfold.

I hated those specs so much that I flushed them down the toilet at home, telling Mum that I'd lost them during PE. She ordered me another pair. I 'mislaid' them again. So we returned to the optician to seek another option and, during my next examination, it became clear that my bout of chicken pox had actually damaged the nerves in my left eye. No amount of glasses or patches would have solved it, he said.

At the age of eight, the news that I no longer had to wear NHS glasses seemed to eclipse the somewhat grimmer news that my left eye was permanently damaged. But I never felt handicapped by this impairment because my good right eye compensated and I learned to muddle through without glasses. That's not to say I'd seen the last of my NHS specs.

One morning, Dad came downstairs grumbling that the toilet was blocked, so he called Spot, our window cleaner/plumber who lived up the road. Within ten minutes, Spot walked into the kitchen holding two pairs of dripping spectacles. Mum's face! She was furious that I had lied, and probably a little shocked because I was the responsible daughter; the goody two-shoes who never got into trouble. Discarding my NHS glasses rated as the most trouble I'd get into as a child, even if Tracey and I were constantly at loggerheads.

As she got older, her tantrums became more regular and she started acting out, presumably in response to the unsettled atmosphere in the house. We went through a sibling bickering stage — the annoying little sister versus the ten-year-old with pretensions of independence.

When she started voicing the fact that she 'hated' sharing a bunk bed and room with me, Dad came up with a solution: he installed a plywood partition that acted as a dividing wall across the centre of our already average-sized room, leaving each of us with a window. One edge of the partition ran flush to the front wall, the other fell short of the interior wall, leaving a narrow gap that allowed me access to the door. Tracey took this set-up seriously, literally laying down a border in white sticky tape. 'You're not allowed in my side!' she said. 'Only walk on that line!'

She received a single bed while I ended up with a flat, sunshine-yellow, faux-leather sofa that was so shiny it looked plastic. I never understood why I couldn't have a normal bed like Tracey but Mum must have traded these items for some face creams or something, so I begrudgingly accepted its arrival, even though it provided the most uncomfortable sleep. It was cold in the winter and sticky in the summer, even with sheets on. In fact, putting down a sheet made things worse because, when restless, I'd find myself slipping and sliding on to the floor. The only benefit was the two drawers underneath which gave me extra space to put away all my 'tut'.

I spent more time in my section than Tracey ever did in hers. As long as I had my books, *Jackie* and *My Guy* magazines and vinyl records, I was content. I'd lock myself away and listen to the Motown tunes of the Jackson 5 and the Supremes. *Baby Love*, released the year after I was born, was the first record I bought but I would have other favourites over the years, like *Kung Fu Fighting* by Carl Douglas, and *Rock the Boat* from The Hues Corporation. On Sunday nights, I religiously tuned in to the Top 20 on BBC Radio 1. I wouldn't say I was the biggest music fan but I did go through a stage of tying a tartan scarf to my wrist in homage to the Bay City Rollers, whose posters fought for wall space along-side David Cassidy and Donny Osmond. But beyond music at home and netball at school, I had no real hobbies to speak of, mainly because my weekend pursuits had largely revolved around magic shows, the markets and the skincare salon.

Elsewhere in the house, the discord between Mum and Dad meant they rarely slept together any more, so my sister often shared Mum's bed, making our partition feel even more redundant. I essentially got my bedroom back when the lights were out. Dad used the sofa downstairs – on the nights he came home, at least. He stayed out more now; sometimes, even for entire weekends. But when he was around, the living room suited him – and Mum – because he could stumble in at whatever hour and not wake anyone.

On the surface, everyday life appeared unchanged. I accepted my parents' arguments as part of that routine, the same way we Brits accept lousy weather as part of our summers. The weather between Mum and Dad was forever changeable. Dramatic comings and goings were part of their ebb and flow. Arguing is what they did. Not too many weeks passed by without a shouting match. In the end, it reached the point where it became noise, and you learned to live with it.

SIX

I t felt like I became an adult around the age of ten.

From that time onwards, ordinary childhood memories are scant, replaced, or maybe eclipsed, by the responsibility of effectively running our household and taking care of my little sister. I became the person my parents relied on, leaned on. 'It's okay, Jo's here – she's got it!' Dad would say. 'Jo, can you do this? Have you done that?' asked Mum. Or I constantly heard, 'Where's Jo?' from one of them.

Even though Maureen would occasionally pop round to help with the housework, and Beryl would sometimes babysit, I felt the onus was on me to keep on top of everything. And I took on that responsibility, wanting to help.

Mum was spending longer at the salon, due to Madame Lubatti taking more of a back seat, and Dad, like every other man of his generation, didn't really do the chores, so those duties, by default, fell to me. I would clean the house from top to bottom: hoover, polish, make the beds, wash and dry the dishes, empty the bins, build the fire, babysit for Tracey, cook for Tracey, put Tracey to bed, and get Tracey ready for school. I also tackled the laundry that piled up beside the washing machine without ever being placed inside – we had a twin tub, and I'd do everyone's clothes first before having to wash and tumble dry the sheets before going to bed. The funny thing is that none of this work felt like a chore because I found it calming to put everything in order, to make the house as clean as Aunty Maureen's. On some deeper level, I believed that if I kept everything neat and tidy, perhaps everything else in our house would fall into place and feel calmer, too.

I also felt the need to keep our fridge and cupboards stocked, especially when our provisions were running low. I would rummage down the back of the sofa or go through the pockets of Dad's coats and suits to find loose change. Invariably, that hunt would yield enough coppers for me to nip out and buy a loaf of Mother's Pride, tinned soup and Heinz baked beans. I didn't always have to walk to the nearby shop because a white grocery van visited our estate twice a week, courtesy of a nice man called John. It was a galley-sized corner shop on wheels and he'd stop in the same spot down the road from our house, allowing me to top up basic supplies. I knew what we needed more than Mum did, which is why I was the one who wrote out our weekly shopping list before joining her on a hurried dash around Sainsbury's.

My new-found appreciation of how much food cost and how long it lasted meant that I was ever watchful when Mum picked up fillet steak from the butcher's, not braising steak. I'd tentatively question her choice. 'Mum, do we really need that when—' but she'd cut me off and soon put me in my place, so I learned to say nothing. I certainly came to understand the relief that Family Allowance Day brought each Thursday when she, and everyone else on our estate, marched down to the post office to collect the £1-per-child benefit. Mum also depended on Dad's housekeeping money, which he still had to stump up while scraping together an income via his art and magic.

Many working-class men paid housekeeping on Fridays but

Dad consistently struggled to accept, or meet, that responsibility. Mum often had to remind him, and I'd feel the relief as much as she did when he handed over the cash. I was relieved for two reasons: one, it meant we'd be okay for another week; second, it reduced the likelihood of them arguing. It was hard to forget the times when he *didn't* pay.

More than once, Mum was left livid after he snuck out the back door without paying, presumably needing the housekeeping money for cards. My dad had the biggest heart but his perspective and priorities were so cock-eyed. If you'd told him you hadn't eaten for days, he'd have given you his last meal. But, at the same time, he wouldn't stop to think about our needs as a family if a poker game was lined up. The more I did around the house and the more I had to 'make do' for dinner, the more I shared Mum's frustrations and understood her anger.

She had a lot to cope with, on both the home and work fronts. To Tracey and me, she appeared to be the forever-graceful swan, breezing through our days while being all things to all people: mother, wife, career woman, effectively a joint-business owner, and friend to the dear 'aunties' she now struggled to make time for. What we couldn't see was how furiously this swan was paddling, trying not to let the exertion show.

With so much on her plate – keeping us afloat, keeping Madame Lubatti's salon on track, keeping up appearances, and keeping her own equilibrium – she didn't have the room to be the parent she wanted to be, and she certainly didn't have the happy marriage she deserved. I honestly don't know how she kept it together. But, like most ten-year-olds, I thought that was what mums did – they coped, come what may.

As if circumstances weren't challenging enough, the Government cut everyone's electricity supply. The moment Big Ben heralded the arrival of 1974, the prime minister enforced the 'Three-Day Work Order', which restricted households to three consecutive days of power per week in order to conserve coal stocks. Candles and torches were how everyone got by. I remember walking to the local shop to buy a stash of candles in preparation for the austere measures that Mum said wouldn't last long, but we found ourselves switching between the light and the dark from 1 January to 7 March. We were never short on coal, so heating the house – or, rather, the downstairs – was never an issue. One freezing morning, however, my mood managed to match the bleakness of this time.

I woke up feeling profoundly miserable with our lot: the constant friction between Mum and Dad, the constant mess, the constant housework, and the constant cold upstairs that left another sheet of ice on the inside of my bedroom window. I got out of bed, wrapped the duvet around me, pulled back the curtains and stood at the window, after hearing kids' voices outside. I scraped a peephole in the solidified condensation, and watched some children kicking a ball about, making the most of the daylight. Even if I had wanted to join them, I couldn't – the rule about not crossing the boundary of our front wall remained in force.

I then heard Mum and Dad arguing again. It wasn't even breakfast. I remember every detail of this moment. On the window in front of me, a piece of ice dislodged and slid down the pane until it settled and started to melt slowly inside the mouldy crook between the frame and the sill. And I thought to myself, I don't want to live like this when I'm older. I won't. I can't.

When people ask where my drive comes from, I think elements of it can be found in that promise I made myself, however directionless it may have been at the time. I didn't have a clue how I was ever going to break the mould – such minor details rarely concern ten-year-olds – but I had a clarity that told me enough: I didn't want mess; I didn't want a marriage filled with bickering and upset; I didn't want limitations; and I didn't want to wake up in the morning and feel cold. All I knew, and all I silently vowed, was that I'd never grow up to feel this kind of struggle again.

Mum decided to keep me away from the skincare salon because Madame Lubatti's condition had worsened. There had been a couple more incidents in which the countess had wandered down the street and didn't know where she was, and Mum was concerned that this worsening absent-mindedness could lead to an accident, outside or inside.

I didn't realise until a few months after it happened that Madame Lubatti had moved to a nursing home not far from us, nine miles away in Blackheath. She had been placed there by Mum, because there didn't appear to be any other relatives or friends around. She also ensured Mr West was admitted to the same residence, as he suffered his own decline due to an unremitting fondness for alcohol.

When I asked where Madame was, Mum just said, 'She needed to go away to be looked after by doctors.' But I couldn't accept that she had disappeared, so I kept pressing to see her, thinking she was in hospital – and that was when Mum explained about dementia and the nursing home. 'I'll take you to visit, but you might find it upsetting, Jo. She's not well.'

I wish I had listened.

Dad drove us there and, as we pulled up, the whole property looked bleak. Inside, all I could smell was liquid porridge and a mustiness that reminded me of the pages of an old book. But I was beyond excited to be seeing my best friend again, despite Mum's warning.

Madame Lubatti, dressed in a skirt and cardigan, was sitting upright in an armchair in her own room, looking out of a window on to a sun-soaked patio. She didn't even turn her head as I walked in, hand in hand with Mum, and called out her name. As I got nearer, an old, frail lady devoid of lustre had replaced the formidable, fun spirit I knew, and that confused me. Nevertheless, I placed my hand on hers, flat against the armrest. Madame Lubatti's head moved, falteringly, and she looked right at me, or rather, through me. The eyes that once sparkled now looked as empty as a dried-up well. To see someone who has given so much to your life in such a state was the most shocking thing. I know Mum found it distressing, too – her tears told me that.

The room was sparsely decorated with a generic painting on the wall. There wasn't an oil bottle, face cream or herb in sight – nothing that plugged her into her heart and soul. Even as a youngster, I could see how such an ordinary environment hardly helped her cause. In my mind, we needed to rescue and revive her. 'Look at how unhappy she is!' I said. 'We have to take her back!'

I felt so sad for my mum at that moment because I could tell she wanted to, but she explained that the countess wasn't well enough to go anywhere. 'We have to keep her safe, Jo, and she'll be safe here.'

I ran out of the room, down the corridor and burst through the main doors, rushing to Dad's estate car where he and Tracey were waiting. I lay down in the large boot space behind the back seats and sobbed. I sobbed all the way back to Barnehurst, with Tracey leaning over the headrest, eating a pork pie, staring at me, looking puzzled by my tears.

Madame Lubatti passed away within a year or so. I didn't attend the funeral for the same reasons I never again visited the home – my parents didn't want me to face the upset. Ultimately, Mum would become the main beneficiary of the estate. Not that this inheritance meant any great wealth.

Madame Lubatti had been made bankrupt – a fact I had long suspected but didn't have confirmed until researching this book. I know nothing beyond the facts reported in the *London Gazette*: a creditor filed a petition to the High Court of Justice in February 1973, but it wasn't until May 1978, after her death, that the official receiver discharged that bankruptcy. This detail certainly casts fresh light on the pressure Mum was under, trying to keep the business going.

It also explains why everything, including the Montagu Mansions apartment, every piece of furniture, and her entire wardrobe, was sold off. Nothing was left, but Mum was bequeathed a few items of sentimental value: a little black evening clutch that the countess carried to every high-society party; the engraved champagne coupes from which we had drunk bubbly grape juice; and some jewellery that included a pair of diamond earrings that Mum had designed into separate rings – a little rose made of diamonds, set on a gold band that she wore on each third finger. She would give me one of those rings for my twenty-first birthday – a keepsake of the countess who had inspired me to be who I am.

But the biggest legacy – and one that Madame Lubatti entrusted to my mum before her dementia took hold – would be the black leather ledger filled with forty years' worth of skincare formulations. When I saw this treasure on the dining table, I flicked through its recipes and could smell the rosemary and lavender captured in its pages. I then noticed that the last entries had been made in Mum's hand, maintaining the life's work of Madame Lubatti until the end. I think this gift was the countess's way of officially passing the torch, allowing Mum to forge ahead with everything she had been taught.

She started trading under her own name to be free and clear of any bankruptcy. Within no time, she would become the new go-to beauty therapist in London, carrying with her the goodwill of a loyal, affluent customer base, most of whom were clients she had been treating for years. For the first time in her life, Mum didn't work for anyone else. She was her own boss, building her own reputation, and she was determined to make it a success.

At home, Mum and Dad's arguments seemed to intensify. I wasn't sure whether it had anything to do with the pressure Mum felt, or whether Dad was up to no good. But I took my usual position at the top of the stairs, waiting for Mum to storm out of the living room in tears, rush past me and slam the bedroom door, which Tracey would then push ajar to creep inside and be with her. I didn't move, knowing full well the usual pattern that would play itself out.

After calming down, Mum would call me into her room. 'Jo, I need you to tell your dad . . .' and I'd be despatched downstairs to deliver a pointed message. Dad, sitting in his armchair, never blamed the messenger but always returned serve.

'Well, you can tell your mum from me . . .' And that's how it went, with me going back and forth, rushing up and down the stairs – a pinball bouncing around, scoring points for both sides. This futile exercise left me with such a heavy heart, and I could have cried but crying would only have made matters worse.

Sometimes, I'd walk into the living room to find Dad hunched over in a chair, head in his hands; that told me that he was hurting, too. But the worst episodes were when Mum was having a go at him about something or other, and he'd snap, saying he couldn't take it any more. Instead of Mum running to her room, it was Dad who flew up the stairs, venting aloud while dragging his suitcase out of the wardrobe. 'That's it! I'M LEAVING!' he boomed.

The knot in my stomach turned into a tangled ball of yarn that could only be undone if Dad agreed to surrender and stay, but he never did. I'd chase him upstairs and stand in the doorway, feeling distraught as he threw clothes into a case.

'Please don't, Daddy, please don't. Please stay. Please stay!' I'd beg.

But the red mist was too dense for him to hear me. The need to get away from Mum was apparently stronger than his need to remain for my sake. He'd be upstairs, case packed, out of the door, and speeding away in his car within ten minutes, telling me to behave for Mum. His absence made the house feel empty. But the thing about voids is that they start to feel commonplace the more they happen – a missing piece of the jigsaw that you stop noticing after a while. I learned to live with Dad's comings and goings, even when those absences became longer and longer. One time it was a weekend; another time it would be a week. I simply learned to comfort myself with the sure knowledge that he'd return, which he always did. Dad was the magician who made himself vanish, only to reappear when the timing felt right.

Where he went, I have no idea. All I knew was that when he dared to ring, Mum yelled down the telephone, accusing him of being 'at some floozy's'. She'd slam down the receiver and start calling him every name under the sun, providing little filter for my and Tracey's ears.

The trouble with my parents was that they were two tormented souls who adored one another, even though it sometimes didn't sound or feel like it. They were the can't-live-with-can't-live-without type of couple. I know a deep love existed beneath all their ego and resentment. I know it because I witnessed it one Christmas morning.

As ever, they made an extra special effort for the festive season – the one week when *nothing* could interfere with family time. I remember that year for the Mary Quant patterned tights that Mum bought me, a gift that made me feel so fashionable.

After Tracey and I had finished opening our presents in front of the fire, one little, unwrapped red box remained under the tree. 'One more!' I squealed. 'What's this?! What's this?!'

'That's for your mum,' said Dad, taking it from me to present to Mum, who was all aflutter when she realised she had a surprise. Sitting in her dressing gown, she undid the bow, lifted the lid . . . and that was when her face lit up as she picked out the most gorgeous silver necklace with an amethyst cross. She held the cross in the palm of her hand, then held it close to her chest. Dad started to fill up at the sight of her joy.

'Why can't it always be like this?' I thought as I watched them stand and simply hug one another, staying there, in that moment, in that embrace. Two people no doubt remembering how good they used to make each other feel. Before life got in the way.

To launch her new business, Mum rented a room in Chelsea, in a street within spitting distance of The Boltons, one of London's most exclusive residential enclaves. The all-white room had enough space for one treatment table, her seat, and shelving for the product. Essentially, it was an average-sized bedroom turned into a makeshift salon, and that's where the majority of clients would go, though she would also do house-to-house calls for a select few ladies. But however she worked, there was certainly no space for a Madame Lubatti-style laboratory, so the kitchen of our house now became a face-cream factory.

My obsession with cleanliness not only had to contend with Dad's mess but also the clutter of an at-home skincare manufacturer. Imagine Dad with his brushes, paints and canvasses spread out across the table, and then Mum with her ingredients, pots and creams littering the countertop, and you get the general picture. On top of all that, the laundry quadrupled because each night Mum brought home fourteen white sheets that clients had lain down on. It became my job to turn them around for the next day, as well as scrubbing clean the empty glass jars that needed to be refilled with product.

Mum had to make dozens of cleansing and face creams every week, priced at £4.50 each. If she sold out, that was a healthy amount of money for our family, especially because Dad remained unemployed, still plying an occasional trade at the weekend markets. The financial pressure remained very much on Mum's shoulders, which was why she needed the operation to tick along like clockwork, and why I became the eager volunteer.

She had white enamel buckets on the stove to melt various oils and waxes; or she'd be making a skin tonic that had to be strained, so I'd fetch a big funnel, complete with concertinaed paper inside its neck, a bit like a coffee filter, and help her strain it. Eventually, she pulled Dad into the manufacturing process and, when he realised the money that could be made, he was only too happy to muck in.

Mum convinced him that, as he was a good cook who easily followed recipes, he would also make an able assistant. She left him with a copy of *Harry's Cosmeticology* – the must-read book in cosmetic chemistry – and showed him what to do, step by step, over and over again, until satisfied that he knew what he was doing. Dad was a smart man and a fast learner and, equally as important, this new role gave him a sense of renewed purpose. Soon enough, he was running that kitchen-lab like he'd been doing it for years, allowing Mum to focus on her clients.

When I arrived home from school and smelled oils and waxes, it was actually a comforting aroma, since it meant something was being made, something productive was happening and Dad was occupied, which meant Mum would be happy. With all pistons firing and all hands on deck, a busy house pulling in the same direction often meant a harmonious house and that was fine by me. And the biggest irony of this new set-up was that it was Dad, not Mum, who truly taught me the art of making a face cream.

'Dad? How does all this work, then? I don't understand.'

We were in the kitchen. Mum was still at work and I was holding her copy of *Harry's Cosmeticology.* I had seen Dad dip into this cosmetic bible but, for me, its convoluted paragraphs and chemical equations made the pages look as bamboozling as my French textbooks.

Dad, now churning out face creams with the ease of a baker making loaves of bread, was standing at the sink, sterilising one of the enamel buckets when he looked at me, saw my confusion, noticed the book in my hand and said, 'Come with me.'

He sat down at his drawing board on the table, as if to start a new painting, and pulled me in close so that I was standing next to his chair, our heads at the same height. He picked up his wooden palette and placed it in front of him. 'Mixing a cream is no different to paint, Jo,' he said as he took a small tube and squeezed out a wriggly worm from a tube of red oil paint. On the table, there was a tumbler of water, into which he dipped a brush before holding it over the swatch of paint, dripping in droplets of water. On the other side of the palette, he swished another brush around a patch of watercolour then added oil paint. 'It's oil into water or water into oil but it's how you mix and emulsify them that creates the different results and textures,' he added.

'So it's like art?' I asked.

'Exactly,' he said.

To be sure it sank in, he took me back to the stove for a practical demonstration – my own *Blue Peter* experiment courtesy of Dad. I had, of course, copied Madame Lubatti's technique before, but this felt more precise, by the book. I stood at the cooker watching him heat the oil in an enamel bucket, and follow the formulations in Madame Lubatti's book. On the countertop, he had lined up rows of jars with their black lids to one side, waiting for the mixture to be poured in. Once that was done, he placed them into the fridge, one by one.

'We've got to keep an eye on how they set, waiting until a skin forms,' he said. It was a bit like waiting for custard to set, and it took about an hour of constant checking. 'We have to put the lids on *just before it sets* so that no dust or bacteria gets in there.'

That afternoon, under his patient guidance, and with a little trial and error, I started making face creams. And so it was both Mum and Dad who put me on the path I now walk. She involved me in our little kitchen operation and he provided the one-on-one training.

Over many weekends and evenings, my kitchen-lab apprenticeship continued to progress, and Mum seemed impressed that I had a natural knack for sensing when a cream was ready, as informed by my nose.

'Mum!' I'd say. 'The cleansing cream is ready to pour.'

'No, give it a few more minutes,' she'd reply.

'No, Mum, it's ready now. I can smell it. It's ready to pour!'

Another time, I saw that she was adding a touch too much camphor oil to the hot almond in the pot. 'Stop! That's enough!' I said. 'The almond oil is going to burn.'

'Don't be so silly, Jo,' she said. But she checked it anyway, and I was right.

At the time, I didn't realise that my acute sense of smell was guiding me, but there it was, making itself known, registering a quality that I wouldn't fully appreciate until much older. My sense of touch wasn't that bad either: I would check the gel as it came out of the bucket, take a dab on my index finger to see how quickly it solidified. But focus was still required because if you poured it too quickly, it would melt the pot; pour it too slowly and it would congeal. I was obsessed with getting everything *just right*, remembering what Madame Lubatti had taught me, 'If you can't do something perfectly, don't do it at all. Remember that, Jo.'

Mum also ensured that the gold standard was drilled home, impressing her high expectations upon Dad and me. We were left in no doubt that there was zero room for error.

As soon as she arrived home, she headed straight for the kitchen and was immediately on Dad's case. 'Did you sterilise the bucket?' 'Did you put the lids on correctly?' 'How much oil did you use? Not too much I hope!'

I felt for Dad. 'He's spent all day making face creams. The least you could do is thank him,' I thought. I felt that Mum was being too hard, looking to find fault. Increasingly, and probably as a result, Dad started to peel away from our operation and leave things in my hands, especially on weekday evenings when we saw less and less of him.

Mum's scrutiny of my work was no less demanding but I felt confident in my abilities, aware that I had found something that I was good at and passionate about. Although there was the time when Tracey meddled and messed up an entire batch.

It was a summer holiday and I was spending my days in the kitchen-lab while other children my age played games outside or hung around together. But I had a job to do: make sixty or so pots of lemon cleansing cream, using pre-measured ingredients. While I was doing all this, Tracey was in and out of the kitchen, being the bored, annoying little sister. 'Go away, Tracey! You know what Mum said about you not being in here while we're busy!'

She grumpily retreated into the living room, leaving me be. After a few final checks and a clean-up that left the kitchen spotless, I went upstairs to my room, feeling pretty good about the beautiful batch of creams that I felt sure would impress Mum.

I was in my room reading a book when she arrived home, so I shot downstairs, anticipating some hard-earned praise. Instead, I found her standing in front of the open fridge, looking displeased. Each one of my lemon cleansing creams had a finger mark in its skin, a deep impression that had solidified like a handprint in setting concrete. 'Tracey – you little bugger!' I thought. Unsurprisingly, my sister was nowhere to be seen.

Mum angrily unloaded the fridge and tossed the contents into the bin. 'What a complete waste!' she kept saying. 'How could you let this happen!'

'Money down the drain' is what she really meant to say.

I felt gutted, and was angry with myself for being sloppy and letting my guard down but I learned three things that day: always find Tracey something to do, never take your eyes off the ball, and be willing to toss it out and start again if it's not *absolutely perfect*.

Soon enough I had the whole operation down pat, to the point where Dad trusted me to make product alone. I preferred making creams to doing homework, and I couldn't wait for class to end so that I could return to my 'job' in the kitchen. To other kids my age it would probably have been the most tedious thing in the world, but I loved every second. If it's true what Confucius was quoted as saying, 'Choose a job you love and you will never have to work a day in your life', then this was when my soul latched on to my future. This was when all the scattered pieces knitted together – the enterprise of the magic shows and the markets, the days observing Madame Lubatti, and the at-home product-making, combined with the lessons I'd learned from Mum's work ethic and Dad's think-on-his-feet creativity. I like to think this was when the entrepreneur in me was born. At the age of eleven.

SEVEN

O ne Friday evening, Dad piled us all into the car, saying he had a surprise in store. He swivelled around in the driver's seat to face Tracey and me. 'Who wants to go to the seaside?' Our squeals of delight put a smile on Mum's face.

'Okay! Let's go to Brighton for the weekend!' he announced.

We booked into The Old Ship Hotel on the seafront, which seemed like an expensive treat but Mum, like me, probably assumed that Dad had come up trumps playing cards. After fetching the luggage, he gathered us together in the room we all shared. 'Eileen, Tracey, you sit there,' he said, gesturing to one of the single beds, 'and Jo, I'd like you to go reach inside my trouser pocket.'

He spoke to me like he did when guiding a member of the audience through a magic trick, and so I placed my right hand inside his left pocket and fished out a thick, brown envelope stuffed with what felt like paper. 'Go on, open it,' he said.

I ripped open the back and took out a fistful of £20 notes, more money than I had ever seen him have. Mum appeared even more surprised than me. There must have been about £200 in there (the equivalent to £800 today).

'It's for you, Eileen,' he said.

Mum was speechless.

'My first wage packet … from my new job,' said Dad, as I spread out the notes on the bed, counting them.

Dad had landed a job as a conservation architect with English Heritage. He would work on major projects, too: if any feature of an historic monument or building needed repairing or renovating, he and his team had to ensure that all alterations respected and conserved its original character. Years down the line, in 1986, he would be involved with the restoration of Hampton Court when a fire devastated one entire wing.

But the restoration that mattered most was his marriage, which he knew had been brittle for quite a while due to his own neglect. As I continued to count the money, I could see in his face the intent to prove himself to Mum, as if he was saying, 'I will look after you. I *can* look after you.'

I don't know what he got up to when he was away, but the trip to Brighton seemed to signal a sea change; his grand gesture to tell us as a family that things would be different now. Granted, a new job guaranteed nothing but he had clearly smartened himself up and found gainful employment, and that was a start. Dad's soul needed the stimulus of creativity and the respect of being valued by others. This new job, which would sustain him throughout the remainder of my childhood, was the shot in the arm he needed to pick him out of the doldrums.

He took Mum shopping to The Lanes where, in a boutique on one of those famous narrow streets, she picked out the most beautiful black velvet Jaeger coat. Dad's eyes lit up when she tried it on, happy to spoil her for the first time in years.

So much had gone wrong between them, and there had been so much sadness, so many accusations, so much name-calling, that I doubt either of them could truly reclaim the past, but I think

Dad's hope was that they could draw a line and move on. It clearly meant something to Mum, because I saw a flicker of happiness return to her eyes that weekend. As we drove back to Kent, singing along to songs on the radio, I honestly felt that things were going to be different from now on.

A few months passed and my parents managed to maintain a rare equilibrium. I couldn't remember a time when they hadn't argued for so long, and the harmony felt glorious. Mum continued to build her business, working from her rented room in Chelsea. Dad thrived in his new job and continued to find favour on the home front, cooking dinners and generally stepping up to the plate as an attentive husband. Meanwhile, I kept the house ticking along while doubling up as Mum's assistant on that ever-busy production line. No great transformations took place. Life simply slotted back into our version of normal.

By now Dad had a racing green Jaguar XJ6 saloon, which, although second-hand, was an important status symbol as far he was concerned. Complete with the silver, leaping jaguar adornment on the bonnet, that car said, 'I'm back – life is looking up again.'

The addition of his salary also opened up new possibilities for us as a family, which was why Mum decided we could spend the summer at a rental property in Constantine Bay, Cornwall. A real get-away-from-it-all family break, the kind we'd never previously been able to afford.

The all-white property, surrounded by a stone wall, was called 'Crow's Nest', reflecting its commanding cliff-top location, overlooking a windswept expanse of golden beach and grassy dunes. As soon as we pulled up, I sprinted inside to be the first to claim a beach-view room, and I couldn't believe the size of the place. It seemed big enough to get lost in, providing Tracey and me with endless hours of hide-and-seek fun. 'Fun' sums up the holiday – a memorable time that seemed far removed from our usual reality. Mum and Dad weren't running off to work, there were no face creams to make and, for the first time, I had a taste of what blissful, uninterrupted family togetherness meant.

Dad made the most amazing picnics and we'd take the windbreaks down to the beach and find our usual spot in the sand. I had my first schoolgirl crush on a surfer who hardly said two words to me, was ten years my senior, and turned out to be married. Tracey and I flew kites, built sandcastles and paddled in the sea – we paddled because we couldn't swim, having never been taught – and we enjoyed nights playing games in the drawing room in front of the log fire. Mum and Dad truly unwound for the longest time that I could remember. And yet, behind the giggles and lightness of being, something niggled me about Mum. On a couple of mornings, she seemed strangely lethargic; at other times, there were flashes of melancholy. But then she'd be as right as rain, thoroughly in the moment and enjoying herself. Something wasn't quite right about the way she behaved, and something was going on between her and Dad, but I couldn't quite put my finger on it.

We left our happiness behind at Crow's Nest – that house proved to be our Cornish snowglobe, and that holiday marked the end of my parents' second honeymoon period. Within weeks of returning home, and about six months after Brighton, Dad's mask slipped. He stayed out late and sometimes didn't come home; he was back to being the chancer, acting on impulse, triggering the same old arguments. I half-wondered if Mum had seen this coming in Cornwall, and that's what I had observed about her – the private realisation that she had been kidding herself that things could be different. Dad couldn't suppress his old ways any more than she could suppress old resentments.

I was in my third year at comprehensive school when he disappeared again. It was only for a few days but it sideswiped Mum. It was a devastating betrayal, a betrayal of the belief that he had made her hold again. I came to understand its force over the next few weeks as she gradually retreated from us and herself, going inward and growing quieter, even when Dad returned. I think she tried to keep going and stay strong, but that characteristic strength started to drain away and she looked defeated.

I was tackling a load of laundry in the kitchen one Saturday morning when I went to take some towels upstairs to the airing cupboard in my parents' room. I thought Mum was allowing herself a rare sleep-in past 9 a.m., but I found her lying on her side, eyes open, with a glazed look on her face.

'You all right, Mum?' I asked, but she didn't respond. Even when I approached the bed and leaned down, she didn't talk or move; she only breathed and stared ahead.

Terrified that something was seriously wrong, I went to fetch Maureen who, after taking one look at Mum, used our phone to call Dad, who must have been working on this particular Saturday. When he arrived home, Tracey and I were kept from going upstairs while they attended to Mum behind the closed bedroom door. Then the doctor turned up and I sat on the sofa, worried witless, wondering what on earth was happening.

As soon as he left, I bolted upstairs to find Mum wearing her nightie, sitting in a chair, shoulders slumped, with hands crossed over her chest, gently rocking in her seat. One look at Dad's ashen face told me this was serious. In the end, he couldn't take it and went downstairs to the kitchen. Tracey went to hug Mum but Mum only looked through her, and my sister stepped back, looking as confused as I was frightened. Maureen tried to placate our concern. 'Don't you worry, girls. Your mum's having a funny turn, that's all this is. We just need to let her rest. She'll be back to her old self very soon.'

But I knew that wasn't true. I knew it from her unconvincing smile and Dad's shellshocked face.

That night, he put Mum to bed and slept on the sofa downstairs. But I couldn't rest, petrified that she was either going to die or be taken into a home like Madame Lubatti. I checked on her repeatedly and, at some point during the early hours, I prayed for the first time. As a family we were Church of England but we weren't religious and never attended church, so I don't know where the need to pray came from, but it felt the right thing to do. With my eyes tightly shut, lying on my stomach, and hands clasped together, I recited the 'Our Father', as remembered from school assembly. I recited it several times because if there was a God, and He really did listen, then I wanted His attention. I wanted Him to help Mum get better. And I wanted Him to stop me feeling so scared and alone.

When I woke, the smell of a fry-up was drifting through the house. Dad was downstairs making breakfast. I went to check on Mum and she was unchanged, lying on her side, knees half-bent, with the duvet pulled up beneath her chin, eyes open. The most upsetting thing was her silence – she had locked herself away on the inside, retreating to somewhere deep where she presumably felt safe and couldn't hurt any more. Later that day, when the doctor came round again, I overheard the words 'nervous breakdown', and that's when I first understood what had happened.

Many years later, I would discover from a family member that Mum had suffered a breakdown in earlier life, before she married Dad, when living at home with her parents. Clearly, there was a fragility of mind she had shielded from me up until that point. Personally, I was scared enough by the sight of one breakdown, especially when I heard the doctor mention the possibility that she might have to be admitted to hospital if her condition didn't improve.

That prospect generated a multiplicity of invented scenarios as my panicked thoughts went into overdrive, imagining our whole world imploding: *If Mum's taken away and Dad does his usual thing and disappears, there'll be no one to look after us, and if there's no one to look after us, we'll be taken into care and . . .*

And that was how I worked myself into a real tizzy, convinced that Mum was going to be carted away, while Tracey and I were seized by Social Services. In my eyes, the medication left behind by the doctor only seemed to make Mum even more listless and I didn't foresee a speedy recovery. The only option I could see to keep everything together – to protect her and us – was to take charge and fend off all those outside forces that threatened our family.

'Is Mum going to be okay?' I asked Dad in the kitchen.

'I don't know, Jo. I don't know,' he said, shaking his head. He looked like a little boy lost, and I watched him roll cigarette after cigarette, trying to smoke away the stress, taking hurried drags every three or so seconds.

'Dad, I'm going to look after her – you go to work. We need the money,' I said, telling him that I'd skip school for the next two or three weeks. He raised no objections.

I think this was when I well and truly became the adult in the house, because I was worried no one else would. Or perhaps it was that I didn't trust anyone else to be. Of course, neighbours rallied round, bringing food and checking in, but Mum had mumbled something about not wanting anyone to see her, not even her own sisters, Vera and Dot. They stopped by maybe once or twice but I don't think anyone fully realised how much I covered for Dad.

I didn't give school a second thought. I had more important things to worry about, such as, 'How are we going to eat?!' I looked in the kitchen cupboards and we had soup, bread and beans to last us one more day, not that Mum was eating yet. Then

I remembered Family Allowance Day, meaning I'd have £2 to spend, and £2 felt like a football pools win. Based on my experience with John, the van man, I could make a small amount go a long way. I grabbed the allowance book, got Mum to scribble her signature, and raced to the post office to cash that slip. With money in my pocket, I nipped to the butcher's, bought half a pound of mincemeat and then went to the corner shop for the essentials. Sometimes, Dad would bring home a Chinese takeaway, or Maureen would drop round a casserole, but it was mainly me doing the cooking – making a salad, beans on toast, soup, spaghetti bolognese or shepherd's pie. Home economics classes had taught me well.

In the coming days, I quickly realised that my limited supplies wouldn't last much beyond Tuesday, and we still needed to depend on Mum's income. I noticed her enamel buckets stacked on the countertop, and that's when I had a brainwave: if I can be 'mum' in Mum's absence at home, then I can be 'mum' on the work front, too. I didn't know what the clients had thought when she stopped turning up for work – to the best of my knowledge, they hadn't been informed – but I would now earn the money we needed. She had enough ingredients in the house to make up a first batch of product, and I had made countless face creams on my own. I mean, how hard could it be?

I sat at our telephone table in the hallway with a pen and paper, pressed 'play' on the answering machine and wrote down the backlog of messages from clients who had rung in their orders. I called each one of them back and said their orders would be ready for pick-up on the following Wednesday at Mum's clinic in Chelsea.

I knew that her supplier was Fields, so I found the number in the telephone directory and explained that Mum wasn't well, and asked them to make up a repeat order of whatever she had last purchased. They were wonderful, arranging delivery to our door and allowing me to pay later, which provided some valuable breathing space. After ensuring more ingredients were in the pipeline, I set to work, placing the enamel bucket on the stove, preparing the jugs to pour the oil, and setting out the tubs to fill with face cream and the glass jars for juniper tonic.

I struggled at first to read all the labels on the different oils and waxes, but I muddled through, largely relying on my sense of smell to tell me which ingredient was which. By the end of the day, I had filled three dozen bottles and tubs. I told Mum what I was doing, even though I wasn't sure it registered. I told her because I needed her to know that the business was going to be okay. I was fixing it. All she needed to do was rest and get better.

On the following Wednesday, I caught the train into London, carrying the product in a wheelie shopping trolley. Dad gave me money for a taxi to get from Charing Cross to Chelsea. The day before, I had bought a duplicate invoice book and written out all the orders and totals as receipts, running them by Dad to check the figures. I placed each woman's product into a Chinese take-away bag stuffed with white tissue paper and laid them out against the wall. And then I waited for the buzzer at the main entrance to sound.

After half an hour, the silence was broken by the first client – a woman whose face I recognised from the TV. She asked how Mum was doing. 'Still under the weather,' I said. 'Nothing serious, she'll be back soon.' The famous lady left with four jars of face cream worth about £4.50 each. A second customer bought two and didn't leave before ensuring that more product would be available the following week.

Each customer did the same, placing the same order for the following week or fortnight. At the end of some brisk trade, I had made enough money to pay Fields and enough to feed us as a family. I had found a way to keep the money coming in, without depending on family allowance or Dad's inconsistency in meeting his housekeeping responsibilities. No longer was I simply doing the chores – I was earning money on my own. Reliant on no one.

Depending on when the last client walked through the door, I'd be careful about timing my arrival back into Barnehurst station because I was scared that classmates or teachers would spot me and realise I was bunking off. I'd either catch a train long before school finished, or I'd leave it until 5 p.m.

Back home, after that first day, I took my handsome profit to buy food that would last a full week; the second thing I did was treat Tracey to a sorely needed pair of new school shoes and black plimsolls. And then I returned to the kitchen and made more product. The second week, I made an even bigger profit – and this was how I kept our lives rolling along for the next few weeks.

Dad came and went, sometimes going away 'for work' for three days, and I was fine with that because I had everything under control. The business was in good order, the house had never looked so spotless, and there was even a slight improvement in Mum's condition – she had started eating again and getting dressed in the morning, even coming downstairs to make a cup of tea. She didn't say much and remained a shadow of her former self, but it was a flicker of some self-motivation returning.

Everything was going to plan – and then Dad received a phone call from school that forced me back into class. I suppose I had been lucky to get away with being an absentee for so long. Maureen said she'd check up on Mum in the mornings. That didn't stop me worrying, though. I couldn't concentrate in lessons. All I could do was wait until the bell sounded for the one-hour lunch break. School was a fifteen-minute run from door to door so I'd pelt it home, spend half an hour with Mum, and then sprint back to class, clock-watching again until 3.45 p.m. when lessons ended.

I hadn't enjoyed school before and I certainly didn't enjoy it now. The fact that I can't remember any of my teachers' names tells its own story, even if the smells still linger: the leather of my school shoes; the polish we used to cover up scuff marks; the baking of cupcakes and chocolate cornflake cakes; and the burnt dust of the oil heaters in the chilly classrooms.

Only one experience at the hands of a female teacher would stay with me.

I was sitting at a desk, taking a test that must have meant something because everyone had their heads down. The only audible sound was the ticking of the wall clock and the odd chair leg scraping across the floor whenever a pupil shifted position. As so often happened, I looked at the paper and saw jumbled words, and I felt that familiar clammy sweat at the top of my back.

I looked over to my left and noticed the girl ticking boxes on a series of multiple-choice questions, seemingly breezing through the answers. So, I leaned over and matched her ticks in the boxes – and that was when the teacher caught me.

'JO MALONE!' she boomed. 'Stand on your chair this minute!'

She loomed over me, interrupting the test. She had wicked-looking eyes and pinched features, and spoke in a haughty, clipped tone. I climbed on to the chair, looking down on the rows of faces that turned and looked up at me, sniggering at my humiliation. I felt one of my white knee-high socks slip halfway down my shin and, as the teacher was admonishing me, I kept trying to bend down and pull it up with one hand.

'Stand up!' she bellowed. I snapped to attention, ram-rod straight. 'Jo Malone,' she continued, with real anger, 'if you cheat, you'll *never* make anything of your life! Do you hear me?!'

I nodded, feeling my cheeks glow crimson.

'I said, *"Do you hear me?!"'*

'Yes, Mrs [Whateveryournamewas].'

A boy behind me kept whispering, 'I can see up your skirt! I can see up your skirt!', so I kept patting it down at the back, fearing his words were a gust of wind. The teacher left me standing there until the end of the hour, when she took my paper and put a red line right through it, confirming my fail. I couldn't wait for the sound of the bell to get out of there, eager for the next class and the more comfortable waters of English. I didn't drown when it came to that subject.

I walked home convinced that I was stupid and that everyone knew it. But I kept that thought to myself. I tended to keep a lot of thoughts and emotions to myself, never really allowing what I call 'the luxury of feeling'. If a sad thought popped into my head – and many did – then I'd go downstairs and find something to do: read a book; find a chore; bake a cake. I didn't like how sadness took me down – it untangled me and brought on anxiety – so I learned to detach myself and place sad thoughts into mental boxes that I'd push away and refuse to open. Dad had always said that thinking about a headache can bring on a headache; it therefore made sense that thinking about sadness would bring on sadness. So I didn't think about it.

Mum's gloom eventually lifted. She appeared downstairs one morning looking refreshed, as if her missing spirit had found its way back and turned all the lights back on. I can't explain it now, and she couldn't explain it then, but she felt like her normal self again. She gingerly stepped back into her old routine, taking a good week or two before returning to work full time. I told her how busy I had been and showed her the duplicate invoices, explaining who had ordered what and how impressed her clients had seemed.

She smiled. 'That's good,' she said. 'Thank you, Jo.'

I didn't expect anything more than that. No gushing thanks. No huge recognition. I don't think Mum wished to focus on how well I'd been doing because it underlined what she had been unable to do. Mum wouldn't want to be reminded of this time. It became one of those periods we never talked about again. That's how black and white things tended to be in our home. There was no inclination to go back and figure out the whys and wherefores. Don't look back. Keep moving forward. When there's a business to run, run it – that tends to be the best approach.

EIGHT

1979 brought the Winter of Discontent, when everyone but Mum and Dad seemed to go on strike in Britain. As mountains of uncollected rubbish bags built up in streets and parks, and as schools closed and hospitals were reduced to emergency operations only, Margaret Thatcher was voted in as Britain's first lady prime minister, vowing to restore order. But she could do nothing about me downing tools on my education. I didn't sit any exams, not a single mock CSE or O-level. At the age of fifteen, I gave up on school, eager to live my life.

I honestly didn't see the point any more. It's like I told Dad, kids get an education to learn how to earn money and cope on their own in 'the big wide world'. Well, I had already been doing that, making face creams, tonics and a profit. In maths, all I could think about was calculating the precise quantities of product needed. In science, all I could think about was what ingredients I'd mix together. And in home economics, when we made dishes such as chicken casserole, I thought, 'Great, we have dinner tonight.' My head was everywhere but school and I didn't see how staying on would accomplish anything. I didn't sit a single exam because failure was guaranteed, so it made more sense for me to focus on the family business, which made me feel like I was worth something. My parents didn't seem overly concerned by my grades and, as far as I can recall, even the truant officers had stopped noticing my erratic attendance, probably because the public sector had more important things to worry about. As a result, I was allowed to drift away without anyone blowing the whistle. Ironically, in the months after leaving school, I discovered there had been a good reason for my academic limitations.

Mum had noticed my struggle with telling the time, figuring out left from right, and reading books where sentences bled into one another. I ended up seeing our GP and, after a few routine tests, he said, 'I'm afraid that this is looking like dyslexia.'

He said it so gravely, and the word sounded so serious, that I panicked. 'What does that mean? Am I going to die?!'

'It means your brain thinks differently to other people, and, no, you're not going to die, Jo,' he said, smiling. His explanation to Mum was fuller than that, but I can't remember anything except the feeling of relief. Not because it wasn't life-threatening but because the diagnosis meant I *wasn't* stupid and *wasn't* lazy. It made sense of why every class was challenging and every page of text appeared jumbled. In later years, I would come to understand that my brain actually had its own unique structure and organisation but, back in the 1970s, dyslexia wasn't afforded much general awareness. Teachers and parents often mistook this cognitive impairment as a sign of a lapse in education. There were no neuroscientists referring to the hidden potential of dyslexics; no Alan Sugars or Norman Fosters to trump the stigmas; no books like *The Dyslexic Advantage* to explain how 'individuals with dyslexia aren't defective; they're simply different'. None of that.

Our doctor seemed encouraged that my form of dyslexia could process letters and read large amounts of text uninterrupted;

words only started to look confusing when the text was technical or dense, or when I was tired or stressed. Mum told me not to worry. Plenty of other teenagers have the same thing, she said. But that wasn't my experience, not at my school. And if it was such a common occurrence then why, in her telephone call with a neighbour that night, did her voice fall quieter at the mention of my name and 'dyslexia'? I was embarrassed. Had it been up to me, no one would have known because it felt like a handicap of sorts. In the weeks and months afterwards, I'd scour the agony aunt pages of magazines and newspapers to see if there was any mention of the condition, but I found nothing.

My dyslexia isn't severe but it can be erratic. To this day, I have to think through certain situations ahead of time. In business meetings, if someone unexpectedly places a complex-looking graph in front of me, I can momentarily panic, unsure if I'll be able to process it. The inner schoolchild rears her head and worries that she'll be laughed at or mocked. Usually, someone on my team will have requested that any graphs or charts are presented in bright colours or illustrated with an easy-to-follow pattern.

My dyslexia affects me in numerous ways but it is easily managed. Sometimes, it can take me a minute to distinguish left from right, or tell the right time. In public, when giving speeches, I cannot read from a prepared text so I'll use index cards with 'reminder words'. When reading documents, I'll print out a large-font version and use colourful highlighter pens to pick out key phrases. At the bank, when they ask me to fill out a form, I ask if someone can help me. I do the same at airports when I need to use a self-check-in machine. I have learned to remap almost everything, and I'm unafraid to explain the reasons why. I stopped hiding my dyslexia when my business started to take off. It has not hindered me. It is no longer a cause of embarrassment. It is part of who I am and, I like to think, an ingredient in the success that I, and the teacher who made me stand on that chair in class, never thought possible.

For my sixteenth birthday, in November 1979, I had already received the most amazing Ravel clutch bag from Mum, plus a Star of David silver necklace (due to a fleeting wish to convert to Judaism). I thought I'd done well with those gifts until Dad arrived home from work and, as I sat in front of the fire, he leaned down and handed me £100 in ten £10 notes – the equivalent to about £300 today. 'You're an amazing daughter, you know that?' he said, kissing me on the top of my head. 'Happy birthday.'

Mum, standing in the kitchen doorway, literally gawped as she watched me count the money, laying out Monopoly-crisp notes on the carpet. I don't know who was more surprised: her or me. Yet Dad, as nonchalant as ever when it came to cash earned or won, was already in the kitchen, making himself a cup of tea.

That evening, I went to sleep wondering how I was going to spend it. Then an idea came to me after reading a copy of *Drapers' Record*, a directory for the rag trade. 'What if I went out, bought some t-shirts, penned some designs, and sold them?' A warehouse-type place in London, opposite Olympia, sold blank t-shirts of different colours and sizes, and you could choose from a collection of transfer designs, so I took the train the next morning, pulling my wheelie shopping trolley for my bulk purchase.

For some reason, I also decided to smoke for the first and only time in my life. Maybe it had something to do with wanting to act like a grown-up before entering a grown-up's world, but I bought myself a box of matches and a pack of ten More cigarettes at the station, took my seat on the train, popped one in my mouth, crossed my legs like a lady, and puffed away, without inhaling, thinking I was some glamour-puss. That notion soon faded when a wave of nausea swept through me after my second cig. If I didn't turn green then I felt green, and I tossed away the rest of the packet. I also loathed the cloak of tobacco it left on me. Two cigarettes would be the sum total of my childhood experimentation with any substance, including alcohol. I never did drugs and never got drunk, because I hated the prospect of not being in control.

Within thirty minutes of arriving at the warehouse, I had spent most of my birthday money on £1-a-piece, white, black and red t-shirts. I chose four or five different transfers but the only one I can remember is a vivid Union Jack. Once home, I spread out my haul, covering every inch of floor space, and signed my name on each one – 'Jo Malone'.

I spread the word and, over different evenings, most of the kids in my street came round to buy a t-shirt, priced at £2.50 each. I also went house to house in the surrounding neighbourhoods, and even sold a few in Bournemouth when Mum took Tracey and me to see her old friend Irene. I think my initial outlay was about £80 and I made a handsome profit of £120. I bought two fancy grey skirts with pleats down the side and saved the rest. I didn't reinvest in new stock because that didn't interest me. I think I had been testing myself to see if I could make money on my own, without Dad at my side, without Mum's product. I was proving a point to no one but myself, and I lost interest as soon as that motivation had been satisfied. Mum asked what I was going to do for the rest of the summer, but I hadn't really thought about it, so she suggested I find a junior's job somewhere.

'I'd love to, but where?' I asked.

'I know just the place,' she said.

I could smell the giant warehouse of Fields & Co., in Ruislip, west London, before it even came into view. This was the headquarters of Fields, where they formulated and compounded fragrances.

As I approached the building on foot, I could smell the exquisite fusion of extreme jasmine, rose, and lavender from one hundred metres away.

Mum had lined up one month's work for me, and I would love every minute of the experience, understanding more about the methods and science behind handcrafted fragrances. I was basically the runner, carrying out errands, cleaning up, and helping to fill anywhere between 250 and 500 miniature bottles. I viewed it as an extension of the methodical work I'd carried out at home, and that's probably why my ready knowledge impressed Rose, a red-haired, pencil-thin perfumer whose wrinkly hands and kind manner first demonstrated how they made the compounds.

When I string together all my experiences – from Madame Lubatti in the salon and Mum and Dad in the kitchen, to my brief stint at Fields & Co. – I see that I must have breathed in so much know-how as well as all the wonderful scents, an unconscious bank of information that would come to the fore in later life.

At the end of my month's work, I was keen to move on and land proper, paid employment – and that was when another lovely gentleman who knew Mum extended a helping hand, inviting me to work in one of his shops in Belgravia.

Justin de Blank, an architect turned entrepreneur, ran an eponymous, high-end grocery store at No.42 Elizabeth Street, a shop regarded as a mini-Harrods of its time, drawing in gourmet food lovers from all over London. He stocked some of Mum's face creams and I had previously been despatched on the train as an occasional delivery girl, so we had met in passing before.

He was the most unassuming, humble of men, even though 'JUSTIN DE BLANK PROVISIONS LTD', as written on the shop's yellow awning, was constantly featured in different periodicals, from *Country Life* to *New York* magazine. Food critic Fay

Maschler described his operation as 'a gleaming good deed in a then-very-naughty gastronomic world', and yet no one seemed more grounded than the shopkeeper himself. His name was synonymous with quality, which was why he attracted the custom of royalty, aristocracy, and film stars, such as James Stewart and Ingrid Bergman.

The first job he gave me wasn't actually at the delicatessen; instead, I became a junior at his equally busy flower shop, a few doors further down on the corner of Ebury Street and Elizabeth Street. For £19 a week, I swept the floors, cleaned the toilets and generally assisted the staff, and it felt so liberating to be out of school, working in the capital, earning my own wage.

In the same way that I had found the markets mesmerising with Dad, I loved the buzz of being on the shop floor, and I can still conjure the subtle scent of the tuberose, lilies, freesia, roses, together with crushed green stems on the floor and the smell of twine and brown paper. It's hard not to feel happy in such an environment when, in the main, customers are buying bouquets for birthdays, anniversaries, marriage proposals, weddings, celebrations, retirements, and Valentine's Day. Florist's shops are feel-good factories, filled with wonderful aromas and contagious smiles.

Sometimes, I'd join a member of staff at the flower market in Covent Garden. What a treat that was, entering that damp-as-a-cave atmosphere to be met with a fragrant air of summer, the electrifying colours of every conceivable fresh flower, emitting different layers of scents, from the soft to the potent. Even as a teenager who often felt sleepy and not too talkative in a morning, that assault on the senses was a more effective wake-up call than a splash of cold water or a cup of coffee.

Back at the shop, I'd fill different-sized buckets with the assortment of flowers for the window display. On the pavement outside,

I'd put out the trays of geraniums and begonias, and then line up the jasmine plants either side of the doorway. I liked to create a mini-walkway of jasmine so that each time I brushed past, it would leave its scent on my skirt. I loved that smell – jasmine – reminders of Mum and Elizabeth Street.

I also experienced a mad crush on an unbelievably good-looking, twenty-something French man who was recruited for two weeks to help me sort and pack different sachets of seeds for a mail-order deal with the National Trust. He smoked the French brand of Gitanes and there was something dreamy about the way he trapped each cigarette under his top lip. When he caught me distractedly gawping at him, he winked – a sure sign, I thought, that my feelings were reciprocated. As we sat in the basement eating lunch one day and he started telling me how much he enjoyed working with me, I performed an awkward lunge and planted a kiss on his lips, trying to wrap my arms around his neck. He pulled away, looked horrified, and ran upstairs. I suppose that was the price for being a hopeless romantic who was desperate to fall in love, and be loved. Oh, the humiliation. His brief stint ended soon afterwards, but rejection isn't easy as a teenager, so I was a little sore in the days and weeks that followed.

One morning, I felt particularly tired and tetchy. I had watered the geraniums in the trays but, according to the manageress, I hadn't placed that day's fresh flowers in the buckets as neatly as I could have done. She told me to do it again. I refused, so she ripped into me. All my frustrations came to a head. I felt something snap within me and, in response, I picked up a bucket of cold, murky, stinky water and threw it at her.

'Do it yourself!' I yelled, as she stood drenched before me, her white cotton dress covered in old leaves and mushy stems. Not my proudest moment.

She was rightly furious. 'That's it! You're fired!'

'Too late!' I yelled, tearing off my apron and throwing it to the ground. 'I quit!' Sixteen years old. Who on earth did I think I was?! But that's what happened, and I stormed down the street to No.42 Elizabeth Street where Justin de Blank saw my frustrated anger turn into tears. I think he felt sorry for me, because he tossed me a blue-striped smock and put me to work in the deli. In the time it took me to walk up the road, I had landed myself a new job.

My time at the grocery store was an education in gourmet food as I watched customers buy items way beyond my parents' budget. After one week in the shop, I started to understand why it attracted the rich and famous, because it was the type of place that could supply a king's banquet. Due to my somewhat cloistered upbringing, my eyes were only used to a salad that comprised limp iceberg lettuce leaves, cucumber, beetroot, a dollop of Heinz salad cream, and, when Dad was in a creative mood, tomatoes cut into crown shapes. Justin's shop was in a whole other league – not even tins of John West pink salmon made it on to his shelves.

My job was on the shop floor where I helped make up sandwiches and prepare salads, and Tom the greengrocer was always on hand to answer my curiosity. 'What's that?' I said, pointing to one of his displays in the window.

'An asparagus.'

'What about that frilly, purple one?'

'A type of lettuce grown in France.'

'And that plant-looking thing?'

'That's an artichoke,' he said, and proceeded to show me how to eat one.

I didn't turn out to be a fan of artichokes but I got to taste many other delicious foods, from coronation chicken to chocolate brownie cake, from the tastiest curries to hot chicken legs in honey with a dash of rosemary. 'Foodie' wasn't a term in usage back then but my days were spent in a foodie's heaven.

I didn't get to know Justin too well – he was often upstairs in his office – but I noted his accommodating manner with customers, and his perfect presentation of food, even the salads. He made it fun, too, assisted by the banter of Roy the butcher, very East End, very masculine and the comic in the pack. But Tom was the reason I loved working at the grocery store because he took me under his wing. I'd help him unload the van, and he'd talk about apples, and explain some were sweet and some were sour, with the same passion Madame Lubatti talked about face creams. On one occasion, he looked at me, nudged his big, tortoiseshell glasses up the ridge of his nose, and whispered, 'Look here, under my t-shirt!' He pulled down his v-neck to reveal a magnificent string of pearls. Let me tell you, some of the dowagers in Belgravia didn't own pearls half as classy! I'd never met a cross-dresser before but Tom was my first example of how to be unashamedly true to yourself and to never judge someone. Unconventional yet discreet, he knew he was lucky to be working in Belgravia for a brand as prestigious as Justin's, but he never forgot who he really was.

I would always regard myself as fortunate to be working somewhere that brought me experiences and introduced me to people that I wouldn't ordinarily have known. And no experience proved more surreal than the time a regular customer asked me to be her dog-sitter for two weeks, but there was a condition attached – she needed me to stay in her five-storey house, down the road in Chester Square.

The dog, called Powtan, was one of those big white poodles with a topiary-style cut, and his lady owner was an American socialite who lived alone and was involved with politics. Each time they came to the shop, she'd tie up her bundle of fluff outside and I'd race out to see him. In seeing how much I adored Powtan, the owner clearly thought I'd make the ideal sitter, so she offered me £20 for the fortnight. I had no idea where she lived until she wrote down the address and I arrived outside one of those imposing, white, stuccoed mansions in the quietest of Belgravia's three historic garden squares, a minute's walk away.

Mum couldn't believe that a relative stranger had offered me the run of her house, and she couldn't believe I'd accepted. She fretted about it all. How did this come about? What does this lady want? How will I know you're safe? I explained that the house was in Belgravia, the woman was a known customer of Justin's, and I'd have a giant dog for protection. I'm not sure it got any safer than that.

When the woman first showed me round the house, she took me to the basement room to show me where the dog food was – a chest fridge-freezer filled with chicken breasts and thighs. Powtan was one spoiled dog. But he was expressly not allowed anywhere except in his room on the ground floor. When it came to staying in a large house by myself, I soon discovered that I got scared, so Powtan and I broke the rules and he shared my bed. In fact, he followed me everywhere, to the bathroom, to the kitchen, and to 'the TV room', which was big enough to fit our entire downstairs floor. I couldn't believe that people had a dedicated room for watching television, and this one had floor-to-ceiling bookcases occupying three of the four walls. The entire interior was grandly decorated with antique-looking furniture, fine art and crystal chandeliers in the sitting, drawing and dining rooms. I would walk around, with my canine friend on my heels, trying to imagine what it must be like to live such a lifestyle.

This fortnight in Belgravia, plus my time with Justin de Blank, made me truly see into a privileged world that I wanted to know more about. I wanted to be a part of it without ever forgetting my place. In my mind, I'd always be the delivery girl, the flower girl, the shop girl, or the dog-sitter, but I felt inspired to be more, so I'd do what I did with Madame Lubatti: I watched and learned, observing what these upper-crust people bought, how they talked, dressed and conducted themselves. I couldn't tell why I felt the need to pay such close attention – the contrasts simply intrigued me, probably because I was switching between Barnehurst and Belgravia on a daily basis.

Back at the shop, with my dog-sitting stint over, Tom remained on hand with his mini-character sketches for each loyal customer, and his insight on food. He and I would often grab lunch together, sitting on the step of the side door that faced into the alleyway, tucking into our salads in plastic containers. As we ate, I'd notice the odd tramp loitering around the side of the building. Tom told me not to engage them but their evident hunger would pull on me.

One day, during a quiet period, I was left in the back to cut some smoked salmon. It had to be sliced thinly but my inexperience showed: the slices were too thick and I ended up hacking off one big chunk – guaranteed to be rejected for not meeting the presentational standard befitting Justin de Blank. When you've come from a home like mine, the waste-not-want-not mentality kicks in. I popped my head outside into the alleyway and, sure enough, one regular tramp was sitting on the floor with his back to the wall, looking fatigued. 'Are you hungry?' I asked.

He didn't answer, but I returned inside to make him a thick doorstep of a sandwich, filled with my chunks of salmon. He seemed so grateful, and I felt proud of myself for that one good deed. Unfortunately, a girl member of staff who didn't particularly like me had watched the whole thing, and she reported me to Justin for giving free food away, which was a big no-no. Justin came down to see me and we agreed that I'd given both jobs a fair crack of the whip. 'But I don't think you're cut out for this job, Jo,' he said. I agreed, and that was the end of that.

I was grateful. I had learned a lot, about presentation, standards, style, and patience ... something I'm still trying to master! The biggest thing I learned was that I was a disruptor, who perhaps didn't appreciate frameworks, rules and being told what to do. I had been given a free rein at home and was trusted to take charge, so I found it challenging to have a boss laying down the law. Perhaps this was an early indication of the entrepreneur within me, pushing against convention and wanting to go in my own direction. Who knows? But I walked away from Elizabeth Street knowing my time there had been invaluable and had provided me with an apprenticeship in life on the shop floor.

As I looked for a new job, Mum kept me occupied by asking me to deliver face creams to clients in London, knowing I'd jump at the chance to spend a day in the capital. It could only have been two or three weeks since I'd left Justin de Blank's but I already missed the city's buzz. I even missed arriving into Charing Cross each day.

Once I'd done my deliveries around Knightsbridge and Kensington, pulling my wheelie shopping trolley, I was in no rush to return home, so I wandered to Hyde Park and South Kensington on an aimless amble that led me to the Holy Trinity Brompton, a church tucked away off a side street beside the Victoria and Albert Museum. On the noticeboard outside, I spotted a poster advertising an event taking place inside the church that day – Jackie Pullinger, a Protestant missionary, was giving a talk. I'd never heard of her before but the blurb made it sound interesting so I walked inside, took my seat and waited for the place to fill up.

When she was twenty-two, Jackie Pullinger had set up a ministry in Hong Kong to serve 'the poorest of the poor'. Some called her an English Mother Teresa because she worked with drug addicts, prostitutes and Triad gang members in Kowloon Walled City. One by one, she had encouraged these individuals to have faith in God and break free from their patterns of destitution and despair, instilling in them a greater purpose to live.

When this slight, blonde, forty-five-year-old walked on stage, she radiated light; she had a glow that made her presence fill the room. I can't recall the specifics of her talk but its main message was that we each have God within us, calling on us to believe. As she spoke, there was nothing evangelical about her tone; she came across as grounded and real and, as I listened to her story about how she had rebuilt broken lives, I had never felt so inspired and uplifted. Through her eyes, I came to understand that nothing is wasted in life; that no matter who you are, where you come from, or what difficult circumstances you face, there is nothing you cannot achieve. I took away with me the theme of hope that afternoon. Yes, I came from a council estate, had zero qualifications and was dyslexic, but the message of Jackie Pullinger was that none of those factors were obstacles. And if down-and-out addicts in Hong Kong can turn their lives around, I thought, then anyone can.

Something meaningful happened to me that day. I felt strangely exhilarated and couldn't wait to tell Mum. I remembered from her diary that she was working on someone's face at an address in Eaton Terrace, Belgravia, so I bowled over there and knocked on the door – something that regular clients were well used to. The longer Mum had known a client, the more relaxed the client was about me dropping by mid-treatment. She was working on a massage table set up between twin beds, and I think she could tell I was a bit awestruck by something.

'What's the matter with you?'

'I've just been to see this amazing woman called Jackie Pullinger, and I've got to tell you what she said because—'

Mum looked at the client, looked at me, and rolled her eyes. 'Ohhhh, don't you start with any of that!'

But her quick dismissal didn't deter me – I was starting to form my own opinions and beliefs, and the conviction I felt was too strong to be knocked.

As I lay in bed that night, I was convinced by the truth of Jackie Pullinger's message – that in God I'd found someone who wouldn't let me down. I would pray on my own more and more now, trusting an unseen force because it felt more constant and reliable than anything visible. I wanted to believe that there was something out there stronger than me; that when the chips were down, there was a safety net beneath me. This faith felt true because I had found it on my own and, over the years, it would keep growing stronger. As would my belief that I could make something of my life, even if I had no idea what that looked like or in what direction I should head. I instinctively knew one thing, though – my future was in London.

I soon landed another job in the capital, this time at an upmarket florist's called Pulbrook & Gould in Sloane Street, which would be another retail experience where impeccable standards would be impressed upon me, in both customer service and flower arranging. Lady Pulbrook didn't sell everyday flowers like daffodils, gladioli and chrysanthemums because her clientele ordered hyacinths, sweet peas, hellebore, delphiniums and zinnias, as sourced from country estates and private gardens. I couldn't wait for a second opportunity to work in a florist's, and this time I was determined to prove myself.

With that in mind, and aware of the early starts, I told Mum that I didn't want to commute any more. Those two weeks dog-sitting in Belgravia made me thirsty for London and eager to experience more of what it had to offer. Mum might not have understood my spiritual leanings but she understood my need to escape the suburbs, because she had hungered for the same thing at my age. First, she wanted to ensure that I'd be responsible and safe, rather than ricocheting around on the capricious whims of a young girl, and she knew just the person to call on.

Mum had recently turned away from her original C. of E. faith to dive deep into Catholicism and she had found great personal solace in its teachings. Through the church, she had also found a great friend in a mother of three called Vivian Sewell, who had become a sound influence in many ways, sharing woman-to-woman chats with her about life and faith. When she mentioned my wish to move to London, Vivian offered the ideal solution: 'Jo could stay with us for a bit.' And that was how I moved to the capital, becoming a £10-a-week lodger with the Sewell family, and embarking on a path that I felt would lead me somewhere positive.

NINE

What I didn't realise until I moved out was how much I yearned for, and needed, the togetherness of *being a family*. Living with the Sewells demonstrated for the first time what this meant, while simultaneously affording me a degree of autonomy that I had never really known before. In many ways, I became a normal teenager, unconcerned with domesticity, not worrying about money, or being a second mother to Tracey – and it felt wonderfully freeing.

'Home' became an elegant, mid-Victorian, three-storey house down a short, tree-lined street called Edith Terrace, off Fulham Road, a mere stroll from Stamford Bridge, Chelsea FC's ground. My next two years here would be one of the happiest times of my life, largely due to my wonderful landlords Richard and Vivian. They had three grown-up children: Phillip, who had moved away; Emma, who was at boarding school; and James, who still lived at home.

I claimed Emma's room at the top of the stairs on the first floor at the rear of the house. Decorated with pink floral wallpaper, this girly room felt like the height of luxury. Not only did I finally have a proper bed, but there was a sink in the corner and a radiator on the wall. I had *heat*!

Their converted basement was the heart and soul of the house with a long, narrow kitchen, a sitting room/den, and a dining room, which had French doors that opened on to the garden patio. Every mealtime was spent at the big, round table covered with an olive-green tablecloth; this was where we ate, shared news and listened to what each other had to say in a convivial atmosphere, no more so than on Sundays when Vivian cooked a roast and invited friends and relatives over. There was always a new face at the table, and Emma often came home for weekends. Whatever the occasion, and whoever was present, this home bulged with high spirits and laughter.

They were an inclusive family, who made me feel loved and accepted, but I was probably a little timid about being the newly arrived lodger. Removed from the comfort zone of my family's dysfunction, I didn't at first feel confident about interacting socially with strangers, especially in their house. It would take me a little time to become accustomed to being part of a unit that talked, dined and played together, so I initially chose to sit back and be the observer, watching how everyone held a conversation and took interest in each other. As I sat there, I couldn't help but think how privileged I was to feel part of such a happy family.

The Sewells had a beautiful sailing boat, *Thalassa*, docked in Gosport and they invited me to join them on the coast, sailing the Solent. As a non-swimmer, I was apprehensive about being on the water but Richard looked out for me, and I found reassurance in a life vest and safety harness clipped to the railings. Over different weeks, he showed me the ropes and taught me how to tack, and it felt like I had dropped into the life I wanted – the life where a family played, loved and laughed as one. The kind of family that every child deserves. The more I appreciated what they had, the harder it became to push away the niggling thought that made me compare: 'Why couldn't we have been more like this?'

Initially, I'd go home every other weekend but it didn't feel the same. How could it? I felt uncomfortable being back in Kent. Truth be told, I hated it. I hated stepping out of order and into chaos. I hated leaving behind peace and sensing palpable friction again. Being back there felt like wearing an itchy, ill-fitting jumper that I had outgrown.

Eventually I started making excuses as to why I couldn't get to Barnehurst at weekends: a new friend was having a party, work needed an extra pair of hands, or I wasn't feeling well. I still visited but the spaces between visits got longer and longer, and even then I'd limit my time, arriving Saturday morning and leaving around 2 p.m. on Sunday. In contrast, I looked forward to spending my weekday evenings with the Sewells, arriving back to a home-cooked dinner.

When I say 'dinner', I should say 'feast', as it was served from one of those Belling food- and plate-warming cabinets, which, to me, seemed utterly spoiling. They also had puddings – we never had puddings at home. I think the funniest memory is the time when I watched their youngest son James prepare a salad . . . and I was horrified.

He took an avocado, peeled it, removed the stone and started slicing it.

'Wh-what are you doing?!' I said.

James looked confused, probably because the answer was obvious.

'Why are you putting that out to eat?!'

'It's an avocado, Jo.'

'I know what it is – it's for your face, not to eat!'

James couldn't stop laughing. When I think about it, I must have seen avocado used in salads at the deli but, in that moment, all I saw was an ingredient for a face mask, to be mixed with sandalwood not lettuce leaves and tomato.

Within six months, Mum and Tracey followed me to London. Mum had decided finally to leave Dad. 'I can't do it any more,' she told me over the phone. 'I can't live this way – he'll never change.' Emotionally spent, she had already rented a flat from a client in Holland Park.

Of course, my first thought was Dad. I couldn't bear the idea of him being alone. 'I'll be fine, love,' he said when I called, but that was typical him, telling me what I wanted to hear, what he *should* say. Ironically, I would now spend more weekends going home, because *someone* had to check in on him. But his days would largely tick along as before: still working for English Heritage, still painting, still playing poker. He bumbled along just fine in his own erratic kind of way.

The truth that he'd never admit, and never show, was that Mum was his base camp and he was lost without her. Indeed, in the following weeks, she couldn't totally be without him, either – Dad would visit her regularly at her new address in Airlie Gardens. She rented a basement flat just big enough for her and Tracey in a five-storey house. Its quirky layout – you had to walk through a bedroom to reach the drawing room – meant that they could live at the rear, and keep the front free as a treatment room for the business. Tracey enrolled at a Catholic school, and Mum took full advantage of her city location by cramming more appointments into her day.

Her proximity meant that we saw more of each other. There were no memories or tensions to avoid in Airlie Gardens, and Mum seemed buoyant, enjoying a new lease of life. One weekend, I noticed a sporty-type car parked outside – a blue, two-door Honda Prelude coupé. I assumed it belonged to a new client, until I walked in and overheard Mum telling my sister about 'Emmy', the name she had given her new set of wheels. Her extravagant taste was no surprise, but this seemed to be a stretch even for her – that brand-new car must have cost around £9,000. It baffled me. I knew she was doing well, but *not that well*. Over the following weeks, she'd also buy expensive new clothes and shoes, spending money like there was no tomorrow, and at Harrods of all places. I'd spot those green and gold bags lying around and dread to imagine the price tags. I can't say that it didn't bother me but I figured that she deserved to enjoy her new-found freedom, assuming that she had some savings squirrelled away. Besides, it wasn't my business any more, so I told myself to push the worry away.

I attended more services at the Holy Trinity Brompton, eager to learn more about God, the Bible, and the Christian faith. One Sunday, the vicar David Watson spoke about the importance of Bible schools, referring to their close-knit communities and volunteer programmes, not to mention the diplomas in religious studies that each student walked away with. I hadn't made any friends in London and certainly wasn't part of the capital's vibrant youth culture – I didn't go to pubs, clubs or concerts – so the thought of entering a ready-made community of like-minded people sounded appealing.

I joined the Bible school at the beautiful Kennington Church, close to Oval tube station, where around sixty people of different ages met three evenings a week, between 6 and 9 p.m. It was a huge commitment but, at the end of a two-year course, I'd graduate with that diploma – the only qualification I would ever accomplish.

On my first evening, I knew it was a place that would inspire me as we read the Scriptures, discussed how the Bible applies to everyday life, and reflected on how certain meanings helped us in our own lives. In the coming weeks, I would also get involved with the community a lot more, whether it was volunteering to do washing up at restaurants, litter collections, or working the 'Crisis for Christmas' drive to help feed and clothe the homeless – this time, I couldn't get into trouble for giving a tramp a sandwich!

Between work, Bible school and the volunteer programmes, I didn't have time for much else, and I very much kept to the straight and narrow, a lot of which was due to my new-found faith.

When it came to my beliefs, I didn't have any kind of lightning bolt epiphany; it was something that developed gradually. The more you stand close to something, the more you sense its familiarity and that's what finding God felt like: a faint voice in the distance that grew louder until it became sure and clear. To this day, my faith remains an important part of who I am, though it is part of me, not all of me. But I didn't only find God at Bible school. I found my future husband.

Gary Willcox, a bank clerk's son from Beckenham (ten miles from where I grew up), was the charismatic, handsome guy who often sat near me in class, and seemed to be permanently happy, wearing a smile that accentuated a strong jawline and a set of pearly white teeth.

Whenever I heard someone laugh aloud, I'd turn around and trace its source to Gary, either as the person doing the cartoon-like guffawing, or as the joke-teller holding court. Imagine the looks of Robert Redford and the humour of Bill Nighy – that's how I saw him. He was a constant ray of sunshine, and it soon became evident, from his gentle manner and the way he spoke, that he was a decent, kind bloke who held solid-as-a-rock Christian values. Listening to him, I often felt that he had the wisdom of a vicar. As it turned out, I wasn't too far off the mark: he was attending Bible school with a view to going into full-time ministry, somewhat of a diversion from his day job as a building surveyor.

Up until then, I'd had maybe two boyfriends, although calling them 'boyfriends' is a stretch; it would be more accurate to say short-lived dates, going to the movies, parties or restaurants. Beyond that, no one had really shown interest in me, so my experience of relationships was limited. But I knew this much: I was looking for the real thing from a young age.

I remember being aboard *Thalassa* one weekend when Vivian's niece and her boyfriend, both in their twenties, came along. I watched them sit on the deck, with the wind in their faces, as they snuggled into one another while holding mugs of tea. I felt the pang of wanting what they had – closeness and the warm glow of love – even if I was only interpreting what they shared from the outside.

My first date with Gary was on 15 June 1984. I was twenty; he was twenty-four. He invited me to watch him compete in a swimming competition where he won his race doing the butterfly stroke. We celebrated with pizza, a stroll on Wimbledon Common and our first kiss on a park bench. That night, I knew I had met the man I was going to marry even if, like most men, it would take him a while to catch up with my dream.

There was only one small snag in my mind. If he really wanted to go into the ministry, I was pretty sure I wasn't cut out to be a vicar's wife – the prospect of a life of jumble sales, church bazaars and parish business gave me nightmares. As things turned out, I needn't have worried. He ultimately realised that this was not his calling, which was a relief because that had been the only potential obstacle standing in our way.

Mum heard all about my excitement over Gary, and she would meet him soon enough. She had not been used to boys being in my life, so I think she was initially wary of our relationship, not because she had anything personal against him but because, in my opinion, she didn't want anyone else coming between us. She never said as much; it was more a feeling I had.

Our attachment was strong based on our closeness in my early years. Ever since then, she had almost grown used to depending on me, whether that meant keeping Madame Lubatti occupied, looking after the house, babysitting Tracey or running the clinic when she was ill. At this time, I started to sense that she still wanted me to be around – an intuition that would prove to be correct.

One evening, I had gone to Airlie Gardens for dinner and she gingerly broached the subject of us working together; she said how nice it would be and explained how she'd train me up to be a beauty therapist. But as she spoke, there was a vulnerability behind the happy picture she painted.

Just by looking around the flat, I could see that life was beginning to get on top of her. The kitchen was a mess, with unwashed cups and dishes on the side; there was a pile of unopened bills on the table where we were seated, and, in herself, she seemed stressed.

'Is everything okay, Mum?'

She sighed. 'If I'm honest, the business is starting to feel a little too much,' she said. 'So would you consider coming back?'

I almost felt the plea in her voice and, having lived through one breakdown, I worried about what could happen if she felt she wasn't coping. I didn't want to see her struggle and, yes, I felt the tug of an old obligation to step in and help out. But it wasn't only that. I did miss making face creams. In the same way that some girls develop a passion for music classes, netball or ballet, I had loved my time in our old kitchen, aware that I was contributing to the business.

Gary rightly pointed out that I had said I felt freer when away from home. That may have been true, but circumstances were different now: Mum and Dad were separated so there would be no constant friction, and I would be at Vivian's, affording me the space that I needed.

It actually didn't take much thinking about, so I handed in my notice at Pulbrook & Gould and started working for Mum. As things turned out, I wouldn't only be an employee – she would also invite me to be her official partner in business.

Her lawyer had turned up one afternoon after our last appointment and, while we sat together in the living room, a conversation began about my future, and Mum seemed keen on the idea of making me her partner. 'We can now build a great business together and, think about it, Jo – one day, this will be yours.'

I didn't really know what being a partner meant but the fact that she was offering me a future in the business excited me, too.

The following week, and after talking it through with Gary, I signed the legal paperwork that Mum and her lawyer placed in front of me, making me an official partner in her skincare business.

She trained me up as promised, meaning that I could share the workload and start doing treatments, in the same way that she had been schooled by Madame Lubatti. I'd earn no official credentials or certificates but none of that would matter if I mastered the technique, and Mum was the best teacher.

As she carried out a facial, she directed me to sit at the other end of the bed and massage the client's feet, imagining that I was working on someone's face. I sat in a chair, kneading the sole and toes with my thumbs and fingers, and mimicked the movements she did with her hands. The acid test came at the end of the day when she lay on the bed and asked me to give her a facial, guiding me as I went, telling me what oils to use, when to apply the towel, and when to exfoliate. But she wasn't my only teacher.

I have a distinct memory of a short, bald-headed man wearing a white lab coat and dark glasses that shielded his eyes, and all I can smell is camphor. Try as I might, I cannot place this memory and yet I can vividly recall the knowledge and technique he imparted. And what made him particularly special was the fact that he was a blind masseur, which explains why, when I practised a face massage on him, the first thing he told me to do was close my eyes. 'Do not trust what you see,' he said. 'Trust what you feel.'

Guided only by touch, and assisted by his prompts, I mimicked the movements I'd seen Mum do, only the technique felt more intense when practised in the dark. I moved my hands, palms down, as the thumbs worked in synchronicity, over the arches of the eyes and cheekbones, covering the pressure points. 'See how much more you feel with your eyes closed?' he said.

I would keep on refining my technique year on year, performing a facial that only my clients will truly remember. But what they perhaps may not realise is that when it came to giving a face massage, I would often sit there with my eyes closed, led by my senses, as taught by the blind man.

It didn't take me long to realise that I was really good at treatments. Mum would come in, like the grand inspector, and provide her seal of approval with a nod and a compliment. I also perfected my own style, not necessarily following her instructions every time. She may have half-suspected but never complained because as long as the clients were satisfied and the business was coming in, she was happy. And so was I, because increased turnover meant increased take-home pay.

Mum also trusted me to handle the administration. She was an exceptional beauty therapist but no businesswoman so, every Friday, I'd go to the NatWest to cash our salaries, draw the house-keeping and pay the rent. In handling the finances, I knew exactly how much money was coming in and going out. I wasn't surprised to see that she regularly dipped into her account for personal items, but I was disconcerted to see the imbalance between how much we owed suppliers, and how many of her oldest customers had a 'slate' that was never cleared. Many housewives on our council estate had a 'slate' at the local shop or with John, the man who ran the mobile grocery business, but Mum's clients were well off and I couldn't understand why she afforded them the luxury when we had outstanding bills. From then on, each client I treated had to pay – there was nothing 'on account', trusted friend or not. Business was business.

I also started trying to manage the stock more efficiently – Mum tended to order, say, four kilos of avocado oil when we only needed one. The more I saw, the more incredulous I became. Had she and I actually sat down and properly discussed our philosophies and vision, I think we would have seen how ill-suited we were as partners. 'Mum,' I would say, 'you have to pay your suppliers on time because if they stop supplying, we'll all be up shit creek!'

But instead of seeing the common sense in my point, she'd see it as interference, reminding me that it was *her* business, not mine. I wasn't a partner whose voice held much sway. So I said nothing and kept clocking in and clocking off, trying to ignore the nagging doubt that none of this would end well.

Gary and I were by now inseparable. When it came to dating, we had little money between us so we'd only ever go somewhere that was as cheap as chips, sharing a starter, a main course, and a pudding. One evening, while in a little pancake restaurant called Ambrosiana on the Fulham Road, we decided it would be a good idea to spend a few days in Cornwall. I hadn't been back there since my last family getaway and I wanted to show him all the places I loved as a child, from Port Isaac to Padstow. But our first night would be spent in Constantine Bay.

The fact we couldn't afford any of the hotels there wasn't going

Dad and me on the back step of our house in Barnehurst.

Bonnie kid – the photo Mum submitted, earning me the audition for a Heinz commercial.

Aged four, on Mum's lap, alongside Nanny Edie.

The netball team. Here I am (centre, holding ball) with the rest of the girls.

My mum.

My impish sister, Tracey.

Around the dinner table with the Sewells.

Marrying my soulmate, Gary.

Our wedding day. With my bridesmaids, Sarah, Tracey and Emma, and Mum (far right) and Dad (far left).

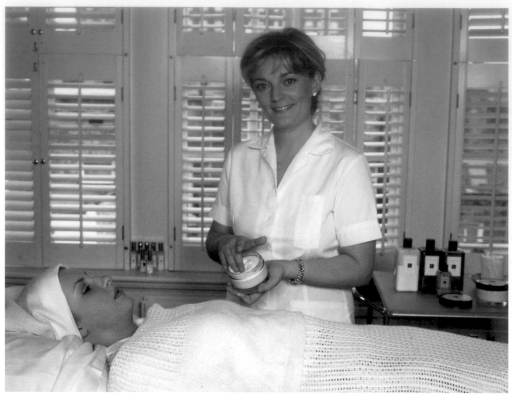

'The face girl' – working on a client in the treatment room at the flat in Chelsea where it all began.

My work desk after branching out into the world of fragrance.

A *People* magazine shoot on the opening of Walton Street.

Two of my greatest loves – fragrance and flowers – at Covent Garden Flower Market.

Steven Horn and me in New York, celebrating the opening of Bergdorf Goodman.

Deborah Bennett and me enjoying the beauty of Petra, Jordan.

Gary and me at
a polo match.

Opening day at our first
shop, 154 Walton Street.

Our precious son Josh – one of the greatest gifts of our lives.

Father's Day.

Celebrating Josh's birthday in Serafina, our favourite pizza restaurant in New York. I'm on my last round of chemo . . . still wearing my *Sex & The City* cap.

to stop us. We grabbed our pillows and duvet, drove to the seafront and slept in the car. Gary had budgeted for us to stay in a B&B further up the coast for the following three nights and we had a great time, taking walks on the beach, enjoying seafood snacks, and talking about our dreams for the future. Those dreams pretty much centred around being together and one day affording our own house. Neither of us entertained any world-conquering goals. With his ministry pretensions consigned to childhood, Gary was keen to make his mark in the construction industry and I was content working for Mum. I didn't look too far into the future in those days.

On the final day of our mini-break, he and I had arranged to spend the night at his grandmother's in Somerset. We had only been there for three or four hours when the phone rang. It was Vivian, calling to tell me that Mum had fallen, hit her head and been taken into hospital.

'How serious is it?' I asked.

'I think you should come back,' she said, choosing her words carefully. I could tell by her voice that I wasn't being given all the details, so Gary and I hightailed it east along the M4.

It would turn out to be an awful but pivotal moment.

Mum had been admitted to St Stephen's Hospital – the same place I was born – and as we drove down Fulham Road and approached the A&E, I saw my sister up ahead, spotting her white cotton skirt patterned with strawberries. She was walking Jodie, our new golden Labrador. As soon as we pulled up, Tracey ran into my arms, utterly distraught. 'Mum's going to die! She's going to die!'

On the inside, I panicked, wondering how bad Mum's injury was, but, for Tracey's sake, I kept my composure. 'It's okay, it's okay,' I said, stroking her hair as Mum used to stroke mine, and offering reassurance without knowing the details. Gary decided to take Tracey home while I went to see Mum on the ward.

I found her in a comatose state, under sedation, with curtains pulled around her bed. Dot was by her side and explained what had happened: Mum had been taking medication to control high blood pressure while simultaneously starting a bizarre diet that involved eating only goat's yoghurt and greens. Apparently, these combined factors had adversely affected the potassium and sodium ratio in her body, and she had fallen or fainted, knocking herself out. I don't remember the complexities of the fuller diagnosis that a doctor went on to explain, but she had suffered a bleed on her brain and had effectively had a stroke.

Her face was swollen and she had stitches from between her eyebrows to the bridge of her nose. Paralysed down her right side, she lay there motionless, in some unreachable place, with hands that were twisted, resting on her chest, as if chronic arthritis had set in.

I pulled up a chair and sat on the opposite side of the bed to Dot, and held one of Mum's contorted hands in between mine. I felt heartbroken for her. First the breakdown, now this. She couldn't seem to get a break. All she'd ever wanted was peace and yet she'd been running around spinning plates ever since I was a kid. She had given everything as a mother and wife, and this was where she had ended up. Life seemed bloody cruel.

Doctors described her condition as 'critical but stable', and I was scared that she wasn't going to make it. I said a silent prayer by her bedside, talking to my new-found God.

Dad turned up that evening and looked as shocked as anyone. He never said much that gave away his feelings, but the lack of his usual talkativeness said enough. I'm sure he felt a degree of guilt that he hadn't been there for her – when she fell and across previous years – even though every one of us knew how much he loved Mum, regardless of his flaws.

He and I, together with Dot and her husband Gordon, took it in turns keeping vigil. Tracey, then fifteen, visited a couple

more times but found the lack of responsiveness too distressing so
tended to stay away. I stayed with her at Airlie Gardens, making
sure she was looked after and went to school.

I don't think Tracey took kindly to me moving back in, insisting
that she was old enough to look after herself. But she didn't understand the predicament – no one knew how long Mum would be ill
and, with no insurance to cover a long-term absence, it was down
to me to keep the clinic going. Frankly, Tracey was a rebellious
nightmare and we clashed a number of times. Looking back, I can
understand her resistance. How confusing it must have been to see
me being sister one minute and playing 'Mum' the next. She had
mostly received parental instructions and discipline from me, which
made it hard for a true sisterly bond to deepen. I cannot know how
she felt, but I can guess that she now wanted to be her own person.

Another thing she didn't appreciate was the state of Mum's
finances. I hadn't realised how dire things were until Dot and
Gordon sat me down to work out the way ahead. We didn't
uncover the entire picture but there was an onerous VAT bill
and a maxed-out Harrods account, which explained some of the
recent shopping sprees. Gordon said we'd have to sell the car to
free up the cash flow.

'But Mum loves that car,' I said. 'She'll kill us if we sell Emmy.'

'Jo, your mum won't be driving again, love,' said Dot.

We sold the car, paid off some of the debt and bought some
new stock. Having gone through the finances – details that
Mum had kept hidden from me – I knew that I had to keep the
clinic busy, otherwise we'd go under in no time. The monthly
amount she owed on the Harrods account alone was as good as
a second rent. So, my new routine was treatments until 6 p.m.,
visiting Mum in the evening, going home to cook dinner for
Tracey, popping back to see Mum and then returning home to
make some product for the next day.

Someone outside the family clearly felt for us because every few weeks we'd open the front door to find a box filled with basic food provisions and home-made meals in Tupperware containers. No note. No label. I asked Vivian. I asked Dot. No one had a clue who it could be, so we assumed that it was one of Mum's clients who wished to remain anonymous. Whoever the food fairy was, they were a godsend at a difficult time.

There was no change in Mum's condition for two or three weeks, but I kept sitting with her, talking to her, believing she could hear me, telling her about the food fairy and how the orders were coming – anything to keep it positive. One evening Gary turned up after 9 p.m., urging me to go home and rest.

When we walked outside, the rain was tipping down so he gave me his jacket, which I held above my head while he got drenched. As soon as we got into the car, I burst into tears. I hadn't cried properly since Mum had first been admitted, and I couldn't keep up the strong act any longer. I can still hear the sound of the rain and hailstones beating down on the roof.

Gary allowed me to have a good cry, waiting until I had composed myself. As I dried my eyes, and sat there snivelling, he decided now would be a good moment to propose to me.

'I really love you, Jo. Will you marry me?'

I burst into tears again. 'Yes, please,' I said.

It wasn't Mills & Boon, it wasn't Paris, it wasn't planned, and there was no ring, but that was the most romantic thing he could have done in my eyes. Marriage is about 'for better or worse' and, at my worst, with no make-up, reddened eyes, and feeling desperately low, he was essentially telling me that he wanted me to be his forever, and that he'd be there by my side. For me, romance is about the intensity and meaning of a moment, and his strength and love had never meant more. I adored every aspect about this man – his heart, kindness, and compassion – and still do. From that day forward, his love would be the most constant thing I would ever know – unwavering and unconditional. Without it, without him, I wouldn't go on to achieve anything.

After three weeks of little improvement in Mum's condition, she was transferred from St Stephen's to the psychiatric ward at the Maudsley Hospital in Camberwell, south London. For me, that place was scarier than any A&E ward, because it was a closed unit where we had to be buzzed in each time. There was a 'lockdown' feel to the place and I hated the fact Mum was there but the hospital had a brain injury unit, which specialised in treating patients who had been involved in road accidents or suffered strokes. When we arrived, we had no idea whether she'd be in there for days, weeks or months because she still hadn't regained consciousness.

As things turned out, we only had to wait another three weeks. Mum, ever the fighter, recovered consciousness one day when Dot was sitting with her. Slowly, over the following week or so, her faculties and memory returned and she was allowed to go home. We were obviously thrilled but the sad reality was that she would never be the same. The Mum I remembered would actually never return home, even if it would take a while for that realisation to dawn. I'm not referring to her slurred speech or restricted mobility – her gait and co-ordination had been badly affected – because we had been braced for that. I'm referring to the altered state in behaviour, which wasn't immediately obvious. As will become apparent, though, the change would be stark and test me to the hilt.

In the initial weeks of Mum convalescing at home, I remained blissfully unaware of what lay ahead, and both Tracey and I wanted to do everything we could possibly do to assist her recovery. One thing was clear from day one: she wouldn't be doing treatments for a while, and would struggle to make face creams again. I think that devastated her, not only because she was prevented from doing what she loved but also because Airlie Gardens was meant to represent a new beginning. Within a year, that fresh start had been snatched away. I suppose it's no wonder that her light dimmed, and I saw how easily upset she would become, first with herself and, later, with me. The times she got most frustrated – probably out of embarrassment more than anything – was when I had to help her in and out of the bath. Mum was a proud woman, and that pride mattered even in front of me.

It was a challenging adjustment for everyone, and I can't say that I found it easy either. I often felt inadequate as a teenager trying to run the business and be a carer at the same time, but there was no other way. It's not as if we had the luxury of choice. I had to get on with it, for all of our sakes.

TEN

Gary and I became husband and wife on Saturday 15 June 1985, one year to the day after we started dating. We got married at his local church, Beckenham Baptist, in front of about forty relatives and friends.

The fact the day went without a hitch was down to no one else but Aunty Dot, who essentially became chief wedding planner, ensuring that I was given the best sendoff. 'I want your day to be so special, Jo,' she said, stepping into the role of mother because Mum was still a little slow and none of us wanted to add extra stress. For the same reason, I didn't leave for church from our home but from Dot and Gordon's in Kingston.

Due to limited funds, it was very much a wedding on a shoe-string. Alcohol wasn't allowed in the church hall for the reception, so there was no booze to pay for; the disc jockey was one of Gary's swimming friends, Angelo; a friend of Dot made my dress; and the morning suits for Gary, his dad, and his brother Cliff, his best man, were hired from Moss Bros.

Dad, wearing tails and a cravat, was unusually quiet in the car during the forty-five-minute journey to Beckenham. Normally, he was a right old chatterbox, but he preferred to gaze out of the window, uncharacteristically lost for words. For a moment or two, I thought he was thinking of something profound to say, but it turned out that he was more twitchy about the ceremony than me. 'I'm so bloody nervous!' he said, blowing his cheeks as we neared the church. 'All I've got to do is walk in, wait for the cue, and walk you down the aisle, correct?'

'Dad, relax! You can't go wrong – everything is going to be fine!' I said.

I thought it was hilarious that even on my wedding day, *I* was the one having to hold his hand and put him at ease. The vicar was waiting on the pavement as the car pulled up. Dad got out, spun round to my side and opened the door. As I stood and smoothed out the creases in my dress, he took me by both hands, took one good look at me, and his eyes brimmed with tears. He didn't say anything – I think he was too choked – but I knew that he felt the moment, and it was probably the closest I was going to get to him expressing his emotions.

He wasn't the only man to get emotional that day. At the altar, Gary's voice cracked as we exchanged vows. We would relive that moment on VHS tape as the cameraman zoomed in on the solitary tear rolling down his cheek – a moment that no amount of builder's bravado could deny. It was only a simple ceremony but its meaning left me walking on air.

At our reception, everyone danced the night away to the hits of the era, including *Walking on Sunshine* by Rockers Revenge; *Feel So Real* by Steve Arrington; and *Rhythm of the Night* by Debarge; though our first dance was to *Make Us One* by Philip Bailey. Cheek to cheek, Gary and I couldn't stop grinning. We were so happy, and, together, we truly felt that anything was possible.

Once we returned from a week-long honeymoon in Greece, we settled into a furnished flat in Kingston – a temporary place because, over the next eight months, we would save like mad for a deposit to buy our first marital home. Gary worked overtime and I filled up the appointments book at Airlie Gardens. Although I hadn't officially acquired any beauty therapy qualifications, I had mastered the art of the facial and even started pulling in my own clients to add to the roster.

Eventually, Gary and I bought a one-bedroom flat in Crystal Palace. This investment drained our building society account, meaning we could only afford the bare essentials when it came to furniture. We purchased a thick piece of pale blue foam to make do as a bed, which, with the addition of sheets, pillows and a duvet, proved comfy enough. Now we had found more space, it felt important to me that my mum and sister could, too. Mum had started to feel cooped up in that basement flat and, with me there Monday to Saturday mornings, everything started to feel cramped.

After searching all over for the right kind of place that could double up as a home and skincare clinic, I found a lovely white-fronted, three-bedroom Victorian terrace in Balfern Street, Battersea, off the busy Battersea Park Road. With Mum's agreement, the business put down a five per cent deposit on a mortgage, and Dad, Dot and Gordon helped us move in. Mum, happier in a more spacious home, would have the master bedroom, with its own ornate fireplace, and Tracey had a good-sized room of her own. The third double bedroom, overlooking a compact, paved garden, was where I'd do the treatments. I felt that domestic and business life would gel well here: the bay-windowed living room at the front would be the private family area where Tracey could hole herself away, watching television; the large kitchen at the rear, with its wooden floor and white cabinets, was big enough to be a dining area as well as lab.

Sometimes, while working there, I would catch myself and think about how I was the sole breadwinner for Mum and Tracey. It seemed almost ironic. But instead of inducing pressure, I realised how much I was thoroughly enjoying the work, interacting with clients under Mum's ever-watchful gaze. Even her mood lifted, as if the move had proved just the tonic she needed. Business was good, we were breaking even, and life generally felt like it was on the up.

One of my favourite clients, who had been coming to Mum for a few years, was a spirited redhead who bounded into our clinic full of the joys of spring. Sarah Ferguson lived in Clapham when we first met, but that was before she became Prince Andrew's fiancée and moved into his quarters at Buckingham Palace.

Sarah and I had struck up a rapport from her first appointment, and she had a wicked sense of humour that often left me in stitches in the treatment room. The transition from regular London girl to soon-to-be HRH Duchess of York didn't change her personality one bit. She remained who she'd always been: kind, down-to-earth, and good fun. But, as much as we got along, the last thing I expected was an invitation to her wedding in July 1986.

If ever there was a moment when it felt like life had picked me up from one world and dropped me into another, it was now, especially when I read the official invitation – a single piece of white card embossed with the gold 'EⅡR' initials sitting beneath a crown.

The Lord Chamberlain is commanded by the Queen and the Duke of Edinburgh to invite: Mr. & Mrs. Gary Willcox to the marriage of His Royal Highness the Prince Andrew and Miss Sarah Ferguson . . .

Sarah really didn't have to invite us. After all, I was only the girl who did her face, but the fact she included us in her big day tells you a lot about who she is. Mum, Dad and Dot shared my excitement – it's not every day you are asked to be a guest at a ceremony where the bride arrives in a Glass Coach pulled by two bay horses, cheered on by one million people in The Mall.

Gary and I, dressed in our finest outfits, couldn't believe that we were there, at Westminster Abbey, among a congregation of two thousand guests about to witness a royal wedding officiated by the Archbishop of Canterbury, Dr Robert Runcie. I'm like the next person, I love a good wedding, but this was something else.

My overriding memory of the day is walking out of the abbey at the end of the ceremony and seeing the hordes of people across the street. We were blown away by the noise of the cheers and the sight of hundreds of handheld Union Jacks being waved in the air. At any other time, we would have been among those crowds, on the outside looking in, and yet, thanks to Sarah, we had been among the privileged few, witnessing one of my founding clients make royal history.

Mum had faced difficult moments during her slow rehabilitation but her mobility improved markedly, so much so that she was able to resume some of her treatments. That said, she got easily upset or snapped over the smallest thing. Doctors had forewarned us about the possibility of her temperament changing, as a consequence of the stroke or the brain injury – I never was clear on the cause. But what I wasn't prepared for was the more hostile change in character, which seemed to unfurl overnight. And, as it unfurled, I detected a subtle cooling between us, as if we had transitioned from mother–daughter to boss–employee, rather than partners.

It was bizarre. The more skilled I became and the more clients

I brought in, the more she found fault with my work and with tasks I performed around the home. I put the sheets in the washing machine 'on the wrong cycle'. I ran her bath 'too hot'. I mixed face masks that 'weren't to standard'. Worst of all, when I didn't react to such criticism, she started putting me down in front of clients. 'I'm so sorry, madam,' she'd say, interrupting a treatment. 'Jo didn't do the facial quite as I would have expected, but I do hope you'll return.' Sometimes, she'd do nothing but stand in the doorway and glare, as if to say, 'I've got my eye on you', which I found the most unsettling because the client would be lying there and I'd be trying to concentrate.

And then, the next day, like dark clouds dissipating to make way for sunshine, everything would be fine again, as if nothing had happened. I could never get an accurate read on her mood, and I arrived at work each morning never knowing what kind of day lay in store. I didn't talk to Mum about it. I didn't feel able to in that kind of atmosphere. Instead, I focused on not putting a foot wrong, but that's not so easy when placed under a microscope. I wish I could say these incidents were occasional but they happened regularly, to the point where I started to dread going in.

My attitude has always been that if you don't like something, there are three choices: change your mindset, change your situation, or accept it. I couldn't accept it because it made me so unhappy. I couldn't change anything because Mum was pulling the strings. So I tried to alter my thinking, because I'm sure my face conveyed how much this whole thing was getting me down. I told myself that if I adopted a positive attitude and approached each day with an upbeat, cheery manner, then I could manage. But it was futile, and my skin wasn't thick enough. Nor was my patience. I don't profess to be a saint, and I started to give her a piece of my own mind, which only made matters worse, causing arguments.

Gary asked why I couldn't leave – a question that I wrestled

with most days. On some level, I understood that frustration
over her limitations had turned to an anger that she could only
deflect outward. And, as miserable as it made me, the kid from
Barnehurst still clung to the thought that I should be there to
help my mum and sister, and that if I wasn't around, everything
would implode. There'd be no one to do the treatments. The
business would go under. Then what? Plus, it wasn't Mum's fault,
I told myself; it was a consequence of her illness; it was not who
she truly was.

'Okay,' he said, 'then you have to take ownership for staying.'

Gary has this way of shooting arrows that go straight to the
heart of the matter, keeping things black and white, and we both
knew I was hanging in there out of a sense of obligation – roots
that would hold me in place for the longest, unhappiest eighteen
months. I never felt strong enough to leave, to sever the attachment. Not until the day Mum crossed the line.

I had arrived at the house around 8.30 a.m., as I did most mornings, and donned my white lab coat, resolving to start the day
with my best foot forward, without ill-feeling, and be focused on
the clients. My 9 a.m. appointment arrived – a beautiful model
called Helen – and I greeted her cheerily before leading her to the
treatment room upstairs.

I applied the face mask, then left her to relax as I returned to
the kitchen – potting some orange skin food and adding extra
oil, mixing it into a white jug for the second stage of the massage.

That's when I heard Mum's hurried footsteps approaching from
the hallway. '*What* are you going to do with all that? Why are
you making so much?!'

I ignored her.

'It's such a waste of materials!' she snapped, and she shoved the
jug across the countertop, like it was a plate of food being rejected.

I threw her a glare that I held, and meant, for a few seconds. 'Mum, *don't*. I can't have a whole day of this . . .'

And then, inexplicably, like a child throwing a tantrum, she started screaming and ranting incoherently. I thought of my client Helen – she'd hear everything. I rushed to Mum. '*What* are you doing?! Ssssh! SHUSH!' And in an instant, faster than I could click my fingers, she stopped. I could see the confusion in her eyes, and she surely saw the horror in mine.

'Right,' I said, 'I'm going upstairs to finish my treatment.'

I grabbed a small pot of orange skin food, leaving the remainder in the jug, and picked up a kettle of hot water with my other hand. I brushed past her and walked into the hallway. And then, as I neared the stairs, *VVVOOOP!* – a huge dollop of face cream came flying through the air and splodged diagonally across my face. Mum had grabbed the jug and hurled it at me. Bull's-eye.

Pot in one hand, kettle in the other, I looked at her, and in the face where I had just seen anger, I saw sadness, maybe a tinge of regret.

'That's it,' I said, calmly. 'It's over.'

She said nothing as she turned back into the kitchen.

In my heart, I felt something snap, forever broken.

Upstairs, I washed my face and returned to finish Helen's treatment. 'Everything okay, Jo?' she asked. I forced a smile but I think she noticed that I was on the verge of tears, and it was hard to disguise my shaking.

Mum came upstairs and stood in the doorway but I didn't give her a chance to say anything. 'Get. Out,' I said.

I actually finished the rest of my appointments that day, and Mum stayed out of the way. On the train journey home, the sadness weighed on me. 'If I stay a moment longer,' I thought, 'this will be my life.' I also heard Dad's voice in my head. A distant echo. 'It's okay, Jo's here – she's got it!' But I couldn't make this neat and tidy. It was unfixable. It was too big. And yet, as much as I knew what I needed to do, I struggled with the idea of letting go.

I lay curled up in bed for two weeks solid, either sleeping or crying, and constantly ruminating. Mum and Tracey didn't call. Neither did Dad, but I didn't expect him to. Even if he knew what had happened, it wouldn't have been like him to get involved. Gary picked up the pieces and gave me the room to mourn, mourning the loss of the mum who never really returned from hospital. The imposter who threw that face cream at me wasn't Mum; she was a stranger that the illness had created, a mean-spirited and irascible stranger who hadn't previously existed. I don't know whether it was the bang to the head or the illness that had placed her in the Maudsley. But as much as I was cognisant of the trauma she had been through, the switch in her character was no less hurtful. And it hurt. It hurt like hell.

I'm not one to mope and, after about two weeks, it reached a point where Gary had seen enough. He brought me a cup of tea and sat on the side of the bed one morning and proceeded to issue a gentle kick up the arse. 'Okay, this has gone on long enough,' he said. 'I'm going to go to work and you are going to get up and make a decision: are you going to dust yourself down and build again, or are you not? When I return this evening, we will have dinner, you will have made a decision and we'll talk it through together.' He stood up, kissed me on the forehead, and left for the day.

Nine hours later, he arrived home to find me in the kitchen, showered, dressed, and cooking coq-au-vin. I offered him a glass of white wine and clinked mine against his. 'Okay,' I said, 'I've dusted myself down. I want to rebuild.'

PART TWO

Wings

ELEVEN

The story of Jackie Pullinger remained a burning torch of inspiration, and I remembered how she packed up her world, left behind her comfort zone, and arrived in Hong Kong with something like ten pounds to her name. But regardless of her limited funds, she had trusted her instincts and taken a leap of faith.

I hadn't known how to leap until circumstances, and Gary, provided the forceful shove. I didn't even know what I was going to do. All I knew was that I was good at one thing: making face creams and giving facials. 'That's where you start,' said Gary. 'You're going to do what you've been doing for your mum, only now you'll be doing it for yourself.'

His building surveyor's wage would cover our mortgage payments, food shop and utility bills, but if we were going to do more than exist, I needed to book appointments quick and make my business work. It's a pressure any entrepreneur will be familiar with when weighing the pros and cons of any launch: we have those moments when we think, 'What can we lose and what can we gain?' As I saw it, Gary and I had *nothing* in reserve so we had nothing to squander. I couldn't lose him or our marriage, and they were the most precious things in my life. If my solo venture went south and we lost the flat, so what? We had rented before, we would rent again. And if work truly dried up, I would find a job somewhere. A funny thing happens when you mentally paint the worst-case scenario: the risk doesn't feel so loaded and the leap not as daunting. That's the thing about the fear of failure – it stems from the height from which you can fall. It is a long way down for established entrepreneurs who have built brands, mini-empires and reputations. But at this juncture, in early 1989, I could only fall the height of the kerb. Moreover, having emerged from such a bad experience with Mum, I didn't see how much worse things could get. I had reflected enough. It was now time to get going again. And how does anyone get started? Easy. You start by getting off your arse and making difficult calls.

I took out my pocket-sized address book, sat at the kitchen table and wrote down the names of the women I had personally brought to Mum's business. Twelve names. That was my starting point. I called each one, explaining that Mum and I had gone our separate ways. 'I have no clinic and nowhere for you to come for a treatment,' I said, 'but if you are still happy for me to do your face, I'd be happy to come to your home. If not, I will completely understand.'

Without hesitation, they each wanted to follow me. I placed a tick against their names and started crunching the numbers with a calculator. With a single treatment costing £45, if I did two treatments a day, five days a week, I could earn a maximum £450 in a week. I figured that I'd clear at least £800 a month because some women would come fortnightly. It might not have been the clientele from Balfern Street, but it was better than nothing. Moreover, the backing of these women made me feel that I was worth something, after a period of feeling worthless; it breathed life into the hope that I could actually do this and start anew.

Next, I took stock of the basic tools and apparatus I'd need. I had four white Egyptian cotton bed sheets from Peter Jones, so I took a pair of scissors and slit them down the middle to create eight covers for the treatment bed, meaning there would be enough for four people a day (two sheets per person per treatment). But I still needed a bed. I applied for a £100 overdraft facility at the NatWest bank that afternoon ... and got turned down. That rejection was no bad thing. It started a lifelong rule that still hasn't been broken to this day: I've never had an overdraft on any personal account. Mum's debts, Dad's gambling and the bank manager's refusal taught me not to spend money I don't have.

In the end, I sourced a portable, fold-up bed that came in its own suitcase-style cover and cost £50. I already had two holdalls from Marks & Spencer: one for the sheets; one for the face creams. All that was left were the fundamental tools of the trade: the canisters, jugs and raw materials that I had left at Mum's. I called her, remained civil, and explained that I would need to retrieve my belongings. She put the phone down, giving me no choice but to visit Balfern Street one final time.

Gary drove me there but stayed in the car – I didn't want to drag him into this unholy mess any more than necessary.

Tracey opened the door and I walked into the sitting room to find Dad on the sofa, cup of tea in one hand, newspaper open across his lap. 'Jo!' he said, looking surprised. Mum appeared in the doorway, calm, indifferent, watching me as I moved toward the big wooden dresser where I knew the jugs and oils were kept. The silence was awful and I couldn't wait to gather my things and get out of there. But the dresser was bare – Mum had already cleared it out. I turned around and she just stared at me. As for Dad, he didn't know where to look or what to do with himself.

It was unfair that he was caught in the middle, and I felt sorry that he had been placed in such a position. I kept looking at him even though he couldn't look at me. He sighed. 'I don't know, Jo. I don't . . .'

And then, in my head, from nowhere, an instinct came shooting out of my mouth. 'Oh my God, Dad. Everything's in the boot of your car, isn't it?!'

He shot up, picked around his pocket, tossed me his keys and ran out the house, shouting, 'I don't want any part of this!'

I picked up my bags and walked outside. I flicked the boot to Dad's red BMW and my hunch was spot-on: all the ingredients and oils and ten canisters – my half, if you like – were there. I loaded it into the boot of Gary's car before returning inside to find Mum standing in the hallway.

'I'm your daughter! Why are you doing this, Mum?'

'No, Jo. Why are *you* doing this?' she sneered. 'Breaking everything up.'

The notion that I had done anything other than try to keep everything together was preposterous but there was no reasoning with her. I turned and walked out the door. Before I even reached the pavement, Tracey came rushing out, holding a single plastic bottle.

'I think this is yours, too, Jo,' she said. The poor girl was so torn, and that one item was her offering. I gave her a hug and told her to look after Mum before returning to the car, with tears streaming down my face.

Back at the flat, and in the days that followed, I partly hoped that the phone would ring, but it never did. Not for two weeks. Eventually I decided to be the brave one. Mum picked up, heard my voice and put the phone straight down again. We wouldn't ever repair this break. I splintered from the family then, and Dad and Tracey drifted away with Mum. I wanted Dad to drive over and be there for me, but he chose not to be, probably because he knew it was a choice between Mum and me. By staying away and making no contact, his loyalties were painfully clear. The pull from Mum and Tracey proved too great. I wanted him to do more than he did but that had been the story of our life. And I think I knew back then that something had snapped in our relationship, and things would never be the same again.

The reality about splits in families is that time, fortified by stubbornness, wedges itself between people and makes the gap wider, leading to an estrangement that becomes unbridgeable. That's what happened. My parents and sister effectively disappeared from my life. There would be the odd telephone call now and again but each one amplified our distance. Mum couldn't forgive me for going it alone and, when resentment sets in, it can erode relationships.

As I stepped away, Tracey very quickly replaced me at work, and she and Mum became a team, continuing on with the business. They had enough clients and materials to continue trading and earning a living.

I have never stopped loving my parents, but there comes a time when enough is enough. I had no energy left for the continual fighting and the bitterness that was making me miserable. Having hung in there for so long, I had to leave for reasons of self-preservation. I had to leave to focus fully on Gary, me and *our* survival. I had to make my own choices now and that meant moving on, preserving the past – the days we laughed, the struggles we overcame, and the memories we shared – as something treasured.

I actually believe that this sorry state of affairs fuelled my drive and will to succeed, determined as I was to put as much distance between me and the struggle that seemed to define my childhood.

When I deliver talks to young entrepreneurs today, I point out that our individual backgrounds, adversities and struggles are part of life's tapestry. Each stitch – every memory, emotion, lesson or heartbreak – is woven into a complex design that is not necessarily of our choosing. Pull one thread – try to change, fix or remove one aspect – and the whole thing would come undone. We wouldn't be who we are. And maybe we only find meaning in events when we look back and see how every thread weaves together, and why it was weaved a certain way.

I didn't think that way at the time, of course. I thought more about Jackie Pullinger's example, and how she had left behind everything that once felt safe, albeit in drastically different circumstances. But she inspired me to let go of what scared me – not having stable foundations beneath my feet, not feeling safe and, ultimately, thinking I wasn't that bright. I had previously doubted whether I could go it alone, whether I was even good enough to go it alone. But I picked up a bottle of rosemary oil, unscrewed the lid, placed it to my nose and breathed in its aroma, as if it was a reviving smelling salt. I closed my eyes and leapt into the unknown with my husband holding my hand. And I started to do what I wasn't very good at – I started to believe in myself.

I laid out the jars and oils on the countertop of my kitchen and placed them alongside the lemons, avocados and yoghurts bought from the supermarket. Using my four plastic jugs and two saucepans, I got to work that first day after returning home, making a face cream while simultaneously cooking a casserole. By the time Gary walked in through the door, I had twenty-four face creams in the fridge and dinner on the table.

My first appointment was forty-eight hours later with a lovely lady called Alicia Castillo, who lived in a street near Sloane Square. I felt strangely nervous ahead of that first Monday morning treatment, probably because the stakes felt so high.

Gary had dropped me off early so I headed to a nearby sandwich shop, Angelo's, to order a cup of tea and a cheese and tomato toastie. I sat outside, squatting down, leaning back against the window, with my portable treatment table and two holdalls to one side. And I gave my twenty-five-year-old self a pep talk to quell the nerves. 'You're bloody good at this ... nothing has changed ... everything's going to be fine ... this is how you start.'

As soon as I stepped into Alicia's flat, I wondered what I had been fretting about. She, like the other eleven clients, reminded me that the service – the facials – was simply on the move instead of being confined to one place. To prove the point, she had lined up three friends to follow her hour, meaning that I had four back-to-back appointments.

Another staunch supporter was former British Olympian Gina Sopwith, who had known me since the Airlie Gardens days. If ever there was a sober voice of reason, it was Gina, who was one of my most trustworthy and honest sounding boards.

My original clients would recommend me to friends and spread the word. In essence, they were not only my 'founding clients' but my organic marketing and PR team. Thanks to them, I would have ten new clients by the end of that first week. Twelve had become twenty-two, building a head of steam as I was simultaneously finding my feet. And one supportive call that I didn't expect would come from Buckingham Palace.

The Duchess of York's name was on my scribbled list of twelve, and I had left a message on her answering machine. She called me back one evening and listened with great interest as I explained everything, even my trepidation about starting from scratch.

'I have an idea,' she said, 'why don't you come to the palace, we'll have a cup of tea, and we'll work all this out.' Of course, I didn't only want to go over for a cup of tea, so I agreed to take my treatment bed and give her a facial at the same time.

Any natural nerves about going to the palace were eclipsed by the fear I had about *driving* into central London. I wasn't going to go by taxi, lugging my gear around, so I felt there was no choice but to take the one car we owned – Gary's cobalt blue Ford Escort. The problem was that it would only be my second time behind the wheel since passing my test at the age of nineteen.

Driving is not one of my strong points but, in my defence, my dyslexia sometimes makes me pause for thought on certain lefts and rights, and my sense of perspective isn't helped by my lazy eye. It's not surprising that Gary suggested we do a dry run the night before 'so that you feel confident about the route'. I suspect it was about giving him confidence, too!

He drove and I wrote down the lefts and rights at this set of lights and that roundabout. Doing the dry run definitely made me feel better, as did the fact that I didn't have to worry about what to wear. My white lab coat, worn over a black shirt, black tights and matching shoes was the only uniform I needed.

Upon arriving outside the magnificent frontage of Buckingham Palace, two police officers checked my identity at the main gate, noted the folded treatment table in the rear seat, and waved me through. 'If you can park over there, madam,' said one of them, pointing to the right of the gate in front of the palace.

I pulled up and was in the middle of taking out the bed when I heard a commotion and the sound of steps running across gravel. I looked up to be confronted by the startling sight of three policemen hurrying towards me. 'Not there! You can't park there!' said the most stern-looking bobby. 'You were told to park *over there*,' and he gestured to a spot where all the other vehicles were parked. I had driven on to an area where there must have been some kind of concealed pressure plates, triggering an internal alarm. I was mortified. 'I need you to reverse and park in the correct spot, madam.'

'Could you do that for me?'

'I beg your pardon, madam.'

'It's just that I'm not very good at reversing.'

He looked flabbergasted. 'No, madam. I will need you to do it.'

The fact that I was actually admitting to a police officer that I wasn't confident in manoeuvring the very vehicle in my charge was perhaps not the smartest move.

'You do have a driving licence, madam?'

'I do. Yes, I do ... but I've only driven this car twice, today being my second time.'

Thankfully, at that merciful minute, I saw a suited gentleman walking towards us – a member of Sarah's staff who had come down to greet, or possibly rescue, me. Once the officers recognised him, the policeman kindly reversed my car while I profusely apologised about the palaver I had caused.

I was taken to the second floor, where we walked down the widest corridor I'd ever seen, carpeted in scarlet red, in between walls papered with forest-green silk, and lined with gold-framed art. Everything felt so Victorian and opulent and there was a museum-like hush. Halfway down the corridor, the suited gentleman knocked on a solid wood door and we walked into an apartment which had a commanding view of the Queen Victoria Memorial and the avenue of The Mall.

Sarah greeted me with her usual effusive warmth and a flash of red hair, and we sat down to talk through the previous eighteen months. Apart from Gary, I hadn't spoken to anyone about what had happened and she let me talk, and cry, and get it all out. She listened with great sadness because she had known our family of old. As I laid out the treatment table for her facial, she took a pen and paper and wrote down ten names, just as Gina Sopwith, Alicia Castillo and many others had done. 'These are the people I'm going to call,' she said. 'I'm going to help you as a friend, and you are going to build this business, Jo.'

*

As I looked ahead to the future, the past was determined to hang on to my ankles, as illustrated by the legal letter that arrived in the post.

In the week I had walked out of Balfern Street, a lawyer friend had advised me to send a letter, formally severing the business relationship with Mum. Boy, did that elicit a response from her lawyers! I hadn't read the small print when we signed the agreement, so I didn't know the implications of extricating myself from a partnership. That's also when I learned the true scale of the debts that Mum had kept hidden: £30,000. Moreover, as a partner, this debt was my shared 'joint and several liability', the lawyer said.

I had inherited a debt that wasn't mine and there was nothing I could do. I had to find a way to pay back that £30,000. I was informed that I was the only one who had the means to pay. *Don't worry, Jo's got this.* I don't know how it was deemed that I, the one with a business that was yet to get off the ground, was in a better position than Mum with the established client base, but what was I going to do? I didn't contest anything. I simply shouldered the responsibility and made an arrangement with NatWest, agreeing a payment of £450 a month, which was as good as a second mortgage.

Launching a business with an albatross around my neck wasn't the ideal start, but I refused to let it hamper me. Since the days of Bible school, Gary and I had a saying: 'Keep turning the page.' No disagreement, problem, worry or amount of yesterdays should bleed into tomorrow. Clear the air. Deal with it. Move on. And that's what we resolved to do. I accepted the reality and vowed to chip away for as long as it took to pay off the loan. There was not a cat in hell's chance that I was going to allow the past to derail me.

Over the following months, something amazing started to happen with my business as word of mouth led to my phone ringing nonstop. My appointment book was chock-a-block in no time as twenty-two clients mushroomed into about fifty, and they were a cosmopolitan bunch, too: Britons, Americans, Indians, Greeks, Russians and Middle Easterners.

Gary would drop me off in London around 9 a.m. and I would jump in a taxi throughout the day and bounce from house to house – from Belgravia to Knightsbridge, Chelsea to Kensington – until he picked me up around 6 p.m. I would continue in this vein for the next six months, building a platform, becoming established, and counting on this expanding network to keep putting my name out there. But Gary and I could see that the business was growing so quickly that we had no choice but to match its pace and move into the heart of the city. There was only so long we could do the back and forth from Crystal Palace. 'Something good is happening here,' he said, 'and you need a base.'

We knew that it would require a financial risk because we'd need to find somewhere central to our clientele, and that would mean high rent, while still paying off the inherited debt, not to mention the mortgage in Crystal Palace – we deliberately kept the flat as our safety net should all else fail. But Gary had it all worked out. Think of how much we'll save in taxi fares and petrol, he said; think of the extra facials you could fit in working from one home-based clinic, instead of dashing all over London. He cal-culated that by increasing the price of a treatment by £5 to £50, we'd pretty much break even initially. A move to London made sense on every level. Besides, the business, not us, seemed to be dictating matters. We decided to follow her lead and see where she took us. We did what every entrepreneur must do when they are in the fortunate position of being able to harness momentum – we decided to leap again, trusting in what we had.

And we kept turning the page.

TWELVE

When the estate agent opened the door to a one-bedroom rental flat a mere stroll from Sloane Square, I instantly knew I had found my castle.

It didn't matter that it looked drab, with grey walls, purple furniture and a kitchen the width and length of the interior of a black cab. I saw beyond all that. The front door opened into a hallway that connected the only two rooms of this third-floor flat: a rear double bedroom with en-suite, and a large living/dining room with a bay window that overlooked a residential street lined with red-brick, five-storey, Victorian mansion houses. I parted the filthy net curtains and spent a minute or two watching the world go by, imagining us living there. I spun around. Gary was right behind me. 'This is it – this is where we'll start,' I said, emphatically.

It was October 1990 and he had searched everywhere for a place that *felt* right. My husband's nose for the right property is almost as good as mine with fragrance, and he had unearthed a gem. We would never have known the kind of security and happiness that we would go on to experience over the next decade in this flat – the place where we would build the Jo Malone London brand.

Its location was ideal, north of the King's Road, tucked behind the Peter Jones store. Life seemed intent on leading me to Chelsea: from living with the Sewells and my job at Pulbrook & Gould, to that first appointment with Alicia Castillo, almost as if I had walked these streets in the past to ready me for the future. Maybe that was the 'click' I felt on walking in.

Our estate agent, an accommodating, nothing-is-too-much-trouble Australian called Sandra French, agreed to remove the hideous purple furniture as we arrived with a round dining table, a bookcase, a two-seater apricot-coloured sofa, a television, and two French dressers for either side of the central fireplace. Unfortunately, due to stretched finances, we had to keep the net curtains and still use our piece of blue foam as a bed.

Sandra also agreed to two modifications in the lease: firstly, the deletion of the clause that said tenants weren't allowed to conduct a commercial business from the premises; secondly, the addition of a break clause that if things didn't work out with the business, we could vacate without penalty. Gary insisted on *everything* being above board, otherwise he'd never be able to sleep at night.

The layout of the flat meant it was easy to visualise how the at-home clinic would be divided. We'd use the front room as our living quarters, flopping down the piece of foam on the floor each night before rolling it up and storing it in the hallway closet. The back bedroom, with a bath in the attached en-suite, would be the treatment room, and the 7 x 5-foot kitchen would be our somewhat cramped mini-lab. After a lick of white paint the flat looked as good as new, if a little stark, but we could add more furnishings and curtains later.

On our first proper night there, Gary and I popped open a bottle of white wine and sat cross-legged on two cushions in front of the fireplace eating a Chinese takeaway. Because that's what

I still did when there was a special occasion to celebrate, as Dad and I used to do after a good day at the market.

The flat was not luxurious by any means, even if the address may have been, and it was there that I discovered how much the sense of smell could bring luxury into even the most sparsely decorated room. Often, when I talk about scents, I refer to my fondness for the crisp smell of something clean and fresh; think newly laundered, pristine sheets in a hotel room; think of the effervescence of a slice of lime dropped into a fizzy glass of water. Think of the memory and sense its smell – that's what I do. I wanted the sense of luxury to permeate the whole flat, for my benefit and that of the clients. So I'd go to the nearby Crabtree & Evelyn, buy a spiced lemon cologne and spray the sheets and towels, even the net curtains, leaving a gentle scent of deliciousness. I'd place twigs of rosemary on a baking tray and turn the oven on low. I'd burn different types of scented candles, infusing the flat with clean, relaxing aromas that brought me a sense of security. I did all this instinctively at the time; the idea that I would one day create my own fragrances hadn't yet crossed my mind.

We had a good bunch of neighbours in the building and, over time, we'd get to know them well. On the ground floor, there was a young Italian lawyer called Mario whose chirpy character brightened up my mornings whenever I saw him. There was never a dull moment with him around, with the stories of his social life and the property law cases he covered. The second floor belonged to a lady in her sixties. 'Mrs P' I called her, and she had strawberry blonde hair lacquered into an immoveable bun, and she wore the brightest red lipstick that was applied as generously as her face powder. She was a bit of a sticky-beak who, whenever she heard a noise or conversation on the stairs, pulled her door ajar, with the latch on, not wanting to miss a thing.

'Morning, Mrs P!' I'd say, running down the stairs.

'Morning, dear,' she'd say, and she'd slowly, reluctantly, close the door.

Above us, on the fourth floor, were two beautiful, party-loving Italian sisters in their twenties, and their glamorous presence left Gary's eyes out on stalks most of the time. I remember the day when they had a plumbing issue and he rushed upstairs to be their knight in shining armour. The 'quick fix' seemed to be taking an age. After leaving it an hour, I stepped out on to the communal landing. 'GARY!' He shot down those stairs faster than a rabbit out of a trap.

Gradually, it dawned on them that I was a beauty therapist working from home. The foot traffic up and down the three flights of blue-carpeted stairs was hard to disguise, and I'm sure Mrs P had never spent so much time at her peephole. But not one of them complained, probably because they learned that there were perks to having me as a neighbour: each Christmas, I'd make up little gift bags of product and leave them outside their doors – my small 'thank you' for our happy co-existence.

My main focus when we moved in was transforming the dreary bedroom into a treatment room, and I wanted to create the kind of space where clients could unload their troubles and stresses and step into a calming bubble for body and spirit. I wanted to go beyond anything I had previously seen with Madame Lubatti and Mum. It had to *feel* sensational, like nothing anyone had known.

I still used my fold-up treatment bed, and we purchased a white stool for me to work from, a white chaise lounge for the client to relax on, and a small round table to place a white-shaded lamp on, for when I needed low, moody lighting. Gina Sopwith made me a rectangular, birdseye maple mirror as a house-warming gift and I propped it against a recessed wall to make the room look bigger. And my time working at two florist's taught me that nowhere is complete without a vase of flowers, and so I bought white roses to finish off the heavenly theme I was going for.

Before the first day of business, I sat, wearing my little white lab coat, at the head of the treatment bed, taking a moment to myself. A summer's breeze travelled through the flat because the windows, front and rear, were wide open, and the door that led into the bedroom was also open, which allowed me to look straight down the hallway towards the sitting room. I heard the distant din of London in the background: the chugging of an idling black cab in the street; the horn of an angry motorist; and the banter of some builders working nearby. But my calm was uninterruptible within those four walls. I had captured what I set out to achieve: a simple, all-white haven that hovered somewhere between serenity and indulgence. And in that peace, when I gave myself the chance to pause, I knew that this was the beginning of something special.

Such stillness and time for reflection would be hard to find in the coming years. From the moment the first client pressed the buzzer at the main entrance, the weeks and months would blur into one due to the ongoing, ever-accelerating momentum.

My hamster-wheel days would start at 6 a.m. in the tiny kitchen, making face creams and setting aside oils for my back-to-back, ninety-minute appointments – one hour and fifteen for the actual treatment, and fifteen minutes for clients to ease back into reality. My diary, from Monday to Friday, tended to look like this: from 9 to 10.30 a.m., 10.30 a.m. to noon, noon to 1.30 p.m., lunch, 2.30 to 4 p.m., then 4 to 5.30 p.m., and finally 5.30 to 7 p.m. I'd do a maximum of six clients a day at £50 a treatment. I'd clean up by 8 p.m., make a quick dinner (or throw a frozen pizza in the oven) and then tackle the orders for customers who had left messages on the answering machine, requesting anything from two to five pots of face cream.

I bought small, white paper bags and laid out the orders every Monday, Tuesday, Wednesday and Thursday with Post-it notes stapled to the top. Customers quickly discovered that pick-ups were strictly between 1.30 and 2.30 p.m. With Gary at work, there was only one of me, so I had that hour-long window and that was it. If anyone – famous or not – buzzed the door at 2.32 p.m., I'd have to answer through the intercom and explain that I couldn't serve them because I had a client with me. It's amazing how punctual people learn to be when face creams are at stake.

Over the years, many people from all walks of life would trot up and down our three flights of stairs: from celebrities – actors, pop stars, TV hosts, supermodels, and members of royalty from around the world – to clients who would save up to afford a facial every three months.

The beauty of working with such a variety of people was that I didn't really know what to expect. One week, a supermodel client told me that she had recommended me to 'some friends'; in the following days, our stairwell resembled a vertical catwalk that could have rivalled London, Paris or Milan fashion weeks. And then there was the day I heard the blaring of horns outside, followed by a few disgruntled profanities. I hurried over to the living-room window and there below, stopped slap-bang in the middle of the street, was a row of four black SUVs – the security detail of a client who was stepping out of one vehicle and walking to my front door. 'The neighbours are going to love me!' I thought.

Another time, Special Branch had to carry out a recce of the flat to evaluate the floor plan and exit points for a visiting foreign dignitary, but, short of someone shimmying up a drainpipe, there was only one way in and one way out. And the anonymity of the building meant that celebrity clients could come and go without being spotted.

Had any journalists cast their eyes on my appointment book, they would have thought they were reading a beautician's version of *Who's Who*, and yet I wasn't fazed by anyone's status, calibre or fame. Skin doesn't recognise class, and there is something about the intimate space between 'the face girl' and client that is a great leveller. The treatment room is a good place to realise that we're all human, with the same skin issues, same emotions, same flaws, and that fame and wealth aren't character traits. I took the privacy of each client seriously and, in time, everyone came to understand and value that my discretion was assured. I'm pleased to say that in the ten years we were there, not one newspaper or member of the paparazzi traced anyone to my door.

Conveniently, a Safeway store was just around the corner on King's Road, meaning we could pop there and back within five minutes whenever we were short on supplies. One morning, in those first two weeks, I nipped out because I needed more plain yoghurt to make up a face mask. On the way back, at the zebra crossing on the corner of our street, I recognised a woman on the opposite side of the road – one of Mum's longest-standing clients, a member of the 'old guard', as I used to call them. As soon as she saw me, she marched over and spat at me, leaving a spray of saliva on the lapel of my white beautician's coat. She spat out her words, too. 'What *you've* done, to *your own* mother, is disgusting!' With that, she stomped off, nose in the air, no doubt feeling satisfied that she had made her point, albeit while demonstrating it with the actions of a lout.

I stood there and wiped away her spit with my sleeve. It stunned me that this 'lady' had acted in such a way, and it hurt, too. Being spat at in the street made me feel like dirt; it also told me that wild gossip was spreading a narrative that I had somehow treated Mum badly and left her in the lurch. The more successful I would become, the more this myth would grow legs, running around London's high society until it became a Chinese whisper. Only one person spat at me, but I would face sly remarks and disapproving

looks from those who didn't know or care for the facts. No one had
the balls to have a direct conversation and ask what really happened.
No one had a clue about what had really gone on, or how much I
had loved my mum, or about the debt I was paying off.

I tend to view this sorry mess the same way I viewed it back
then: human nature is divided between those who thrive on, and
get easily distracted by, gossip and they tend to go nowhere; and
those people who know their purpose, know what they want,
and won't give weight to the chirpings of misinformed tittle-
tattle because they know that such things are a waste of focus and
energy. Once back at the flat, I had a little cry, dried my tears, and
then got straight back to work, making more product.

Our kitchen was smaller than the smallest cell, devoid of any
obvious inspiration. It had a single sash window that offered a
view of rooftops and chimney pots receding into the distance,
beyond Sloane Square. And yet I loved nothing more than being
in that confined space, whisking and mixing into the night, trying
to adapt and improve my treatments, constantly playing around
with different ingredients and essential oils.

Of course, the thing about experimenting is that not everything
will turn out perfectly. One week, I made a papaya mask with
sandalwood powder, set in a cool jelly. But three women's faces
broke out in a rash and I had to hurriedly apply plain yoghurt
as a soothing balm. Ironically, it was those flare-ups that led me
to a breakthrough: the creation of a nourishing gel that calmed
everything from rashes to sunburn to blemishes. Before I knew it,
clients were raving about this 'wonder product', saying how much
softer and fresher their skin felt after using it. I made fifty pots
of this gel – and it would go on to be a bestseller in the future –
leaving me with the lesson that some things are born out of the
very problem you are seeking to solve.

Masks, creams and gels were one thing, but I also wanted to develop my own lotions, so I bought gallon containers of unscented body lotion bases and mixed in different oil combinations, such as lemongrass, rosemary, lavender and jonquil. I also called on the help of a tall, bespectacled, softly spoken man called Derek, who I had come across while working for Mum. He headed up the British office of the Paris-based Lautier Florasynth group which, as well as supplying essential oils and fragrances to half the cosmetics industry, was a stable for some of the finest perfumers in the industry, hence why I valued his expertise. I'll only use his Christian name because, as Dad used to say, never let daylight in on magic, but Derek would be a linchpin to my future success, helping to pave the way for the next phase of the business.

He stopped by one week and I told him about my ideas for lotions, saying that one combination of ingredients intrigued me: nutmeg and ginger. As we talked, he said he could supply 'the juice' (*le jus*) – the concentrate of a fragrance that gives any cream, lotion, gel, oil or perfume its name. 'I'll tell you what I'll do,' he said, 'I'll put one kilo through as a sample and see how you get on.'

Within a week or so, a small box of miniature, brown glass bottles arrived – one batch was nutmeg, one ginger – and my experimenting went into overdrive. I wanted to create a lotion with power and punch, so I'd add ten, twelve, fourteen drops into the base, then I'd whisk up a lotion until I was happy with the texture and scent. I had no idea how popular the combination would be until I first massaged it on to the forearm of a client while their face mask was setting.

'That smells and feels unbelievable. What is it?' asked the first woman I tried it on, and the longer the lotion lingered, the more she raved. Other clients had similar reactions so I started giving them a scoop to take home in a pot, at no extra charge.

Once the lotion had proved a hit, I set about making an accom-
panying bath oil, because I had long believed that the sensual
experience of taking a bath required more than ambient warmth,
steam and a few candles dotted around the edges. It demanded the
luxury of fragrance. 'How beautiful would it be if women could
bathe in this same scent?' I thought. And so soluble bath oils were
added to my repertoire.

Nutmeg & Ginger Bath Oil actually became a gift to those clients
who had been with me from the start, presented in my plain, white
gift bags – my small way of saying 'thank you'. In my mind, this
gift formed only a sample of limited stock, and that's when things
started going crazy. Clients didn't only order one bottle of bath oil
but five, and then ten. But the tipping point came in one mad month
after different people ordered the bath oil and lotion in bulk – as
gifts for employees or dinner-party guests – leaving us with orders
of fifty, eighty or one hundred at a time. I had to pull in Gary every
evening that month to meet this spurt in demand. He'd do a full
day's work as a surveyor and then join me on our mini-production
line as I provided on-the-job training, but he never once moaned.
'You're working late. Why shouldn't I?' he said.

He'd also help with the labelling. I had a roll of sticky labels
that we fed through a second-hand typewriter we'd bought for
£25. Using two index fingers, I'd stab out the name of the product to be affixed to the back of the bottle; on the front, I'd use
pre-printed stickers from Prontaprint bearing my initials, 'JLM'.
With our first big orders out of the way, we didn't think we'd face
another rush like that for a while. How wrong we were!

As a result of those bulk orders for different events, more than
one hundred new people returned to buy more, saying it was 'the
best thing we have ever smelled'. This was the moment when I
believe Jo Malone the business truly took off.

Things became so busy in the run-up to Christmas that I pulled in a friend whose sole job was to answer the front door to the passing trade we had never envisaged – a whole new clientele only wanted product and we were swamped with hundreds of orders through December.

By the time our days finished at gone midnight, rows of gift bags filled one entire side of the living room, as well as the space between the bay window and the back of the sofa. Each morning, the eight shelves of our pine bookcase were fully stocked with product. By the end of the day, they were half-empty.

EMI Records had started referring us to its people – artists, agents and producers – and one female executive came to the flat one morning, looked at those shelves and said: 'I need to buy something for the team. I'll buy the lot.'

How tempting that was, but I didn't have time to replenish the stock for the rest of the day's clients, so I agreed she could take half and I'd make up the remainder of her order within the next forty-eight hours. I hated turning business away. Indeed, I can remember only one other occasion when I had to do such a thing. Robert Redford was shooting the movie *A River Runs Through It* on location in Montana. Someone connected with the production called to say they wanted me to create a fragrance 'to keep the mosquitoes away while Mr Redford is filming'. I didn't know where to start with that time-sensitive request, and I certainly didn't know how I'd find the time, and so I had to leave Robert Redford to fend off the mozzies by himself.

Not everything I made would become a commercial product. As I kept trying out combinations of ingredients, many creams and lotions would never go beyond the treatment room and my circle of clients.

Since that first batch, Derek had sent me a bunch of different fragrance samples, and I happened to pick out a vial of peach concentrate – to imagine this scent, think about placing a peach to your nose and smelling the blush of its skin. That same week, another client had brought me a pot of honey from a beehive in the country, and, as I looked at the vial and pot side by side on the kitchen countertop, I decided to give that pairing a try. I heated the honey, added some oil with the peach, created a paste and then mixed it all into a body lotion base.

The first client who sampled this concoction was Jennie Elias, an interior designer and one of my original twelve clients. The moment I massaged a small amount on her arms, she was sold. She couldn't get enough of my peach and honey lotion but the only problem was that, as the honey solidified, it sometimes sent tiny crystals rising to the surface. One shake of the bottle would mix everything together again but it was a flaw I wasn't happy with. Jennie didn't care, and I struggled to prise those bottles away from her. 'It's fine, it's fine, don't worry,' she'd say. She wasn't the only fan, either. Little bottles of that lotion would visit two or three royal palaces throughout Europe, too. Peach and honey – good enough for certain royals but, in my mind, not good enough for general sale; forever to be a secret shared with a limited number of clients.

Gary and I held our 'board meetings' in bed on a Sunday morning – the one time we had a proper chance to catch up with each other, as well as air anything about the business. He'd get up, nip to Piccolo's on Sloane Street and buy two bacon sandwiches while I brewed some coffee; we'd then crawl back into bed and sit there, leaning back against our pillows, with notepads on raised knees, and discuss where we went wrong and what we could improve. And then, at the end of each month, we'd sit in the living room and spread our bank statements on the floor, cross-referencing them with my Ryman's duplicate-page invoice book to calculate what money we had left over.

Eventually, we earned enough to throw out the foam 'mattress' and buy a sofa bed – talk about going up in the world! But the most satisfying financial moment would come in 1994 when I received a letter from the NatWest bank, acknowledging receipt of my final £450 payment and confirming that the debt inherited from Mum had been cleared. It had taken almost five years.

We bought a bottle of champagne that night and, you guessed it, a Chinese takeaway, pinching ourselves about how far we had come. 'Can you believe this is happening?' I asked Gary. He laughed – one of his snorting laughs that twitches his nose. 'Believe it?!' he said. 'We don't have blinking time to believe it!'

We would come to realise that success begets success, and I think many entrepreneurs will associate with this: once you begin to feel successful, and embrace the natural momentum of the business, you tend to manifest a confidence that magnetises more success until it snowballs. Not that it makes it any more believable. Gary and I found the pace of our success almost preposterous – the speed of growth, the dizzying amount of orders, the volume we were shifting. I just wish there had been a pause button that could have allowed us to stop, step back and savour it more than we did. But we had to keep moving on to the next, and the next, and the next thing to do. From the outside, it may well have appeared that our lives were work, work, work, which was true. But there was a 'quality of life' in being side by side, sharing this incredible adventure, growing together, in our element.

Ask any mountaineer about climbing a summit they never thought they'd get the chance to ascend – they won't recount the fatigue, only the thrill of the experience. I would go back and relive every single hour of the climb Gary and I were attempting, without knowing the height of the mountain, or how capable we were. We decided to neither look up nor down. We simply kept looking at each foothold, kept focused, and kept powering on.

THIRTEEN

In Columbus, Ohio, in the 1860s, a chemist called Dr John Pemberton owned a laboratory where he manufactured medicines and photography chemicals. He was renowned for his innovative use of drugs, mixing this with that to invent some new tonic. One such experiment led to the creation of a hugely popular fragrance he called 'Sweet Southern Bouquet'. But, as healthy as those sales surely were, nothing made him as famous as his next product.

After moving to Atlanta, he was tinkering with his recipe for French Wine Coca – comprising Peruvian coca and the kola nut – when, in response to a prohibition on alcohol, he cooked up a caramel-coloured sugar syrup in a brass kettle. He replaced the wine with the syrup, added carbonated water and, hey presto, he had the formula for Coca-Cola, a drink he initially advertised as a refreshing 'nerve tonic'. His bookkeeper registered the brand name in 1886 and Dr Pemberton would go on to make a small fortune. In the first year alone, he sold twenty-five gallons of his syrup. Ultimately, he would sell ten billion gallons globally.

I love stories that inspire me, and nothing inspired me more than this account of a chemist who took a departure from the norm, dabbled with something new, and created a product that changed the world.

In the early summer of 1993, I had face creams, lotions, bath oils and gels, but my instincts suggested that I needed to go in a different direction. I felt the business needed something more; that a hole needed filling. I smelled the memory of Madame Lubatti's lab and the aromas from Fields & Co. I saw Mum's favourite fragrances on the dressing table in her bedroom. And then a light bulb came on: 'I wonder if I could take the fragrance from lotions and bath oils and turn them into an *eau de cologne*?'

The thought alone excited me; moreover, it felt like a natural evolution for the business. But I had no idea where to start. My elementary understanding of *Harry's Cosmeticology* certainly wasn't going to cut it. Skincare creams, lotions and bath oils were one realm, but fragrance-making belonged in a faraway, artisan's galaxy.

As much as I could rely on my sense of smell, I wasn't a perfumer – one of those technicians that the industry calls a 'nose' (*le nez*). That's a whole other craft, the DNA field of the industry, where master craftsmen break down scents to a molecular level and turn concepts into compositions into product, drop by drop. When it came to making fragrances, I was in the dark without so much as a torch. I needed to find a perfumer who would be willing to collaborate and, for that, there was only one place to go.

On the British Airways flight from London Heathrow to Charles de Gaulle, Paris, I was under no illusions about the scale of this undertaking. On the face of it, I can see why my plan looked a little overambitious: a one-woman band, working from a flat, with limited recognition and zero training, wanted to build a fragrance that, in her mind, had to be wholly original. I'm not sure even Dad would've taken those odds.

What's more, I was acutely aware that my feet would be walking in the crater-sized footprints of giants. After all, Paris was where the perfume house of Galimard supplied fragrances to the court of Louis XV; where Guerlain created a scent for Queen Victoria; and where a perfumer called Ernest Beaux developed Chanel No.5 in 1921. Since then, from the 1920s through to the 1960s, other legends established themselves, such as Givenchy, Christian Dior, Hermès, Lancôme, and Yves St Laurent. But I didn't have any pretensions about competing with, or being like, the big brands. To me, they were the shiny, polished monoliths that were part of the landscape, not my considerations. I was in the embryonic stages of a creative exploration, finding my feet. I knew my place – a tadpole in an ocean – and I think that very perspective was the reason I didn't feel daunted.

At that stage, my only motivation was the love for our little business and the development of our product line, as if led by some mission statement written by my creative soul: 'Forget what everyone else is doing, go in your own direction, get it right but, most of all, be original.'

And yet I felt bold enough to walk up the gravel driveway of an industry, approach its French doors, pull back the big brass knocker and ask its experts to show me the way. To some, that might seem audacious but all of us have to start from the beginning, in whatever we do. Instead of asking, 'Why me? Who am I kidding?!', I prefer to switch it around and ask, 'Why not me?' Sometimes, you have to bowl into certain situations, and I was unafraid of bowling in anywhere or approaching anyone.

I'm sure this attitude stemmed from having high-profile, hugely successful clients who made me feel their equal. Once you've seen beyond the masks of celebrity, it's easy to see beyond the facades of the great perfume houses. But I also never doubted that I could make fragrances, hence why I never felt inferior. All

I needed was one door to open and one person to show me the way, just like Dad had with face creams. That would be the key to unlock my future.

My great difficulty was that I hadn't been a voracious student of perfumery and I didn't understand, let alone speak, the vernacular of the industry, nor did I know the technicalities of odour structure. One journalist wrote that I arrived in Paris with a fixed composition that was *'considered so unorthodox, it required a protracted pilgrimage to find a perfumer who would collaborate'*. I wish I had been that prepared! I actually arrived with no 'brief' – the written concept that people in my position usually pitch to perfume houses – and not a single idea in my head. Starting lines didn't come much greener than that, and walls not much higher. Yet, some deep sense of knowing kept pushing me forward, undeterred. And there was one other factor – my old friend Derek, the only friend I had in the industry, whose guidance would steer me.

When we first spoke about my plans to create a fragrance, I threw a stream of questions at him. How do I go about this? Which perfumers will work with me? How do I get an 'in'? In my naiveté, I thought that working with a perfume house would be like having a direct relationship with old suppliers like Fields & Co. and Baldwins. 'It's not as easy as that,' Derek said. 'And I'm going to be honest – you're too small for them, Jo.' Kind and candid – that's why I liked him. He had a valid point, too. I was the face girl who had recently ordered one kilo of nutmeg and ginger; the big brands were ordering thousands of kilos of compounds from his company. But as much as I heard and respected what he said, it didn't put me off. I wasn't going to be told 'no' under any circumstances.

The next time I spoke with Derek on the phone, I said, 'I've thought about what you told me, and I accept that I might be too small for them, but I've had some further thoughts and you might think differently if—'

'Jo, me thinking differently won't change the reality. I'm sorry. I'm not sure we can help you in the way you are asking,' he said, or words to that effect.

But in my mind, there had to be *someone* willing to help. And I had a sneaking suspicion that if I kept pushing my luck, Derek would relent and at least introduce me to one of the perfumers at Lautier Florasynth. 'When are you next going to be in Paris?' I asked him one day.

'Why?'

'Because I want to make fragrance and I'm going to see you there,' I said.

He laughed. 'Okay, but I can't promise that your trip will lead anywhere.'

And that's how Gary and I ended up boarding the plane to France.

The trip coincided with our wedding anniversary, so it would be part work, part pleasure, allowing me to justify my audacity at least should we run into dead ends. But regardless of the outcome, Gary and I were grateful to have time away from the business. We couldn't remember the last time we had properly unwound, and we hadn't visited Paris before so we were going to enjoy a four-day break.

We stayed at the Hotel Princesse Caroline, on a street just north of the Arc de Triomphe and I instantly liked how Paris didn't feel as hurried as London; less rat race, more laissez-faire. Locals strolled, they didn't scurry. The city seemed to breathe creative air, and every turn of every corner opened up a new enchanting street or architectural beauty.

Gary and I visited the sights and museums, and treated ourselves to the famous chocolate cake at Angelina's on Rue de Rivoli, overlooking the Jardin des Tuileries, with the Eiffel Tower in the distance. The tearoom alone symbolised the grandeur and aristocratic nature of Paris and, as I people-watched from our window table, it felt like I was observing a scene pulled from a 1950s movie. 'Mum would love it here,' I thought – the energy, the unapologetic femininity, the chic style, and the confident but demure manner with which the ladies carried themselves, leaving behind a waft of the perfume they wore so boldly. Mum had never visited Europe, yet she would have absolutely fitted in, a swan among swans. She and I hadn't spoken but I knew from Dot that her business was ticking along and they were doing fine, and that was all I needed to know from a distance. I was happy that she and Tracey had found their way after the dissolution of our partnership.

On our second day in Paris, I took a break from being a tourist and changed into my make-a-first-impression outfit: a little navy trouser suit. I left Gary at the hotel and walked to the offices of Lautier Florasynth, where Derek had agreed to meet me. As soon as I entered the lobby, lined with glass cabinets filled with bottles of perfume, it felt like a museum of fragrances, thick with the scent of jasmine. Everyone who walked by me was dressed in black and wearing an intense look on their face, moving about the place in quiet reverence but with great purpose.

I took up my position on a black leather couch and waited for Derek. As I did so, I looked through the glass into one office and noticed a man pegging thin strips of paper to a table's edge – he was, as I found out later, drying fragrance strips. I could have stayed there all afternoon being a sticky-beak but I saw Derek striding over. As I stood to greet him, an immaculately dressed, studious-looking man was crossing the lobby floor, holding a bottle and a paper, looking every inch the master perfumer.

'Derek! Derek!' I whispered. 'Do you think that man can help?'

'Ab-so-lutely not, Jo. That's Monsieur Jean-Louis Sieuzac.'

Without realising it, one of the great 'noses' had just crossed my path. Monsieur Sieuzac was a true genius who had most notably created fragrances such as *Dune* and *Fahrenheit* for Christian Dior, and *Opium* for Yves St Laurent.

The only audience I'd be granted that day was with Derek, who took me into a room and effectively invited me to lay my cards on the table – the 'Okay, let's hear what you want to do' moment. No chummy chat between friends; this was professional and, if I was serious about making fragrances, he wanted to hear my plans in detail.

I'm not sure I drew breath as I proceeded to gush about how I'd trusted my nose since being a young girl and how certain scents made me feel alive. I reeled off a list of different childhood memories and the smells they evoked, and how these smells were the palette I wanted to explore to create fragrance. I reminded him about my belief in the business and how I'd progressed from face creams to body lotions to bath oils, and how I foresaw the same success with perfumes and colognes.

'I'm passionate about this, Derek. And I can do this . . . if you can help me.'

I think that was the moment he started taking me seriously, or maybe he thought, 'This girl isn't going to quit.' Either way, he spent the next two or three hours with me, providing a crash course in how perfume houses worked, how scents are extracted from flowers, and how a fragrance is constructed. Then there was a whole new language to grasp, such as *the accord* that happens when individual ingredients blend to become a unified scent; or *the notes* that make up a fragrance's composition – a top note (the first impression; the accent that soon fades), the middle (the core and most distinguishable scent), and the base (the longest-lasting essence; the truth left on the skin). And don't forget the tiers of the creation process: clients (the brand) consult with an evaluator who acts as the bridge to the perfumer ('the nose'). The evaluator, he explained, expresses a detailed concept to take to 'the nose', who then sits in a lab, surrounded by a palette of hundreds of aromas, and weaves together notes – drop by millilitre drop – to create different variations of the fragrance outlined.

'What you need to know is that only the evaluator can work with the perfumer, not the client,' he stressed. 'Those masters won't work one-on-one with you.'

Derek emphasised that point. I noted it as 'a rule' to be addressed later.

But at this meeting, and others that would follow, I appreciated every insight and piece of knowledge he laid out like building blocks placed in front of a child learning the alphabet for the first time. Derek was the most patient teacher and, through him, I came to understand the alchemy and wizardry involved in fragrance-making. The more I heard, the more I wanted to dive in.

He was the one who made me realise that while we may work with chemicals, compounds and molecules, it is not a science but an art – the art of fragrance, complete with its own sculpted structure and musicality. If music is an art emitted by sound waves, then perfumery is an art emitted by olfactory vibrations. And it has kept evolving ever since the creation, in the 1300s, of the first alcohol-based product called *Hungary Water*, a rose and orange flower infused perfume made on the orders of Queen Elizabeth of Hungary.

As I wrapped up that initial meeting with Derek, my head was spinning from all the knowledge, and I couldn't wait to get back to the hotel room and spill it all out to Gary. But before I left, and after agreeing to meet next in London, he turned to me and asked, 'Have you ever been to Grasse?'

'No,' I said. 'What's there?'

*

Grasse, in the south of France, one hour's drive from Monaco, sits on the hilltops north of Cannes, and is *la capitale mondiale des parfums*. It's where perfumers have flocked since the end of the eighteenth century. This genteel town is the heart and soul of fragrance; the cosmetic floor of nature's chic department store that is the French Riviera. The minute you arrive, the fragrant air engulfs you – the rose, jasmine, orange blossom, lavender, and wild mimosa that are all hand-plucked and collected in wicker baskets.

Gary and I stayed at Hotel des Parfums, located on a hill overlooking the old town. We strolled down a winding road into a quaint, ancient square surrounded by cafés, *boulangeries*, and compact townhouses that were a watercolour wash of ochre and peach, with turquoise-green shuttered windows and terra cotta tiled roofs. A bell tolled from its twelfth-century cathedral, momentarily interrupting the buzz of the daily market packed with flower stalls, adding to the dreamy scent drifting through the narrow cobbled lanes. Even the Victorian, hinged lamp posts offered flowers, geraniums spilling from hanging baskets. I thought I had died and gone to heaven.

We found a table beneath a beautiful tree outside a brasserie, and we sat there, in the dappled shade, enjoying *steak frites* and a carafe of rosé wine, taking in the local scene, a scene that my dad could have painted. In that spot, in that square, I fell in love with fragrance. Head over heels for life. In the evenings, all I wanted to do was sit outside and breathe in the heady air, pulling in every sight and smell.

That week, my education continued as we visited two of Grasse's perfume houses: Molinard, established in 1849, and Fragonard, dating back to 1926. But the real spectacle was the International Perfume Museum where we wandered its three floors – passing giant brass kettles, decanters, steel vats, and nineteenth-century copper stills, with elephantine pipes looping in an arch into boiler-sized centrifuges. That's where I realised I had come home.

If my time in Paris involved Derek *telling* me about the basics, then the visit to Grasse was about artisans *showing* me the meticulous process, from collecting petals in the fields to distillation, absorption, extraction, blending, and the finished fragrance captured in crystal bottles. I had never seen anything quite like it. I had never seen jasmine and tuberose pressed into a layer of cold animal fat spread across plates of glass in wooden frames (the fat soaks up the odour and the pomades are then washed in alcohol to eliminate the fat, leaving behind fragranced alcohol). I had never imagined such a thing as an orange blossom garden, or halls of jasmine packed into bundles of sackcloth.

Each evening, before and after dinner, I couldn't wait to get back to the hotel room and experiment with some of the sample 'notes' Derek had sent me before my trip. They were in 10ml brown and green bottles that had a pronounced lip around the top of the neck, to help measure out one drop at a time. He had given me some teat-pipettes and I'd pinch one drop, two drops, three drops on to my own fragrance blotter strips, trying to compose something from this note and that. I was playing around, getting carried away with different aromas, jotting down combinations that I thought worked, scratching the ones that didn't, listening only to my instinct: 'Try more complex jasmine here . . . a touch more lavender there.'

I've heard it said that the definition of joy is being immersed in something in which you lose yourself. For me, that was, and remains, the transporting effect of fragrance. Gary was somewhere in the room, on the periphery, on some earthly plane that I had left behind in order to explore a safe dreamscape that would only ever be accessible to me and fragrance. That was what Grasse did for me – it opened up a fifth dimension. I've always said that those four days felt like a spiritual experience, connecting me to my purpose in life. Never before had I seen a reflection of myself so clearly and realised who I was.

Once my amateur compositions were ready – I'd use wooden pegs that I'd bought to clip fragrance strips to the table's edge, mimicking what I had seen at Lautier Florasynth – I'd then wait, with eyes on my wristwatch, because, like any great drama, a fragrance unfolds in three acts as the alcohol evaporates during the 'dry-down' period. Act One comes in the first minute, teasing the scent to come; Act Two kicks in after about five minutes, when the molecules react with the skin and the fragrance starts to reveal its story; and Act Three, ten minutes in, provides the crescendo when, after full absorption, the evocative essence truly settles on the skin. That's why I advise people never to make up their mind about a fragrance based on the first spray. No one at any perfume counter should expect a purchase after Act One. The earliest time to reach for your purse is Act Two; though it is preferable to wait until the finale when a fragrance's sincerity fully blossoms.

I learned everything there is to know about fragrance in Grasse, and I would soon have the opportunity to apply this new-found knowledge. In the following weeks, Derek would go to his superiors to argue my case, effectively saying, 'Let's give her a chance.' Whatever he said, and however he pitched me, it must have been convincing because he invited me into the Lautier Florasynth stable as a client – the break I needed.

I would now be able to utilise fully my sense of smell, and nurture my relationship with creativity, getting to know its rhythm and timing, soon learning that ideas will come when strolling down the street, or sitting in a coffee shop, or on a plane. Once unleashed, this creativity would be boundless, opening up a whole new avenue of possibilities. And a series of inspirations would lead to the fragrance that would truly put me on the map: Lime Basil & Mandarin.

FOURTEEN

When I start to develop the idea for a fragrance, I am, in my mind, creating a unique character that breathes on its own, with a heartbeat, soul and personality: whispering to me its capabilities, strengths and weaknesses; hinting whether it will be dominant in a room or more reserved, and whether it will turn heads or slowly grow on people. But however it behaves socially, one thing is guaranteed: each one will make its charm and presence felt, stirring moods, memories, emotions . . . and our senses.

At the risk of sounding a little odd to the non-aficionados, fragrance, to me, is not a shapeless form that evaporates into thin air; it is a living beauty that, once out of the bottle and on the skin, comes alive in its invisibility. I tend to personify a fragrance, and if I could issue gentle guidance to each one before it steps out in public, I would say, 'Be bold and make your presence felt. Never be generic. Forever be unique. Evoke emotion. Connect. Trigger memories.'

Personally, the most rewarding moment is when a fragrance proves its worth and starts communicating, using the different notes of its composition to express itself. And then, when everyone starts buying it, raving about its qualities and how its essence makes them feel, I can sit back and feel like a proud parent.

I want a fragrance to ignite not only our sense of smell but our four other senses. If I were developing a fragrance with Grasse as my inspiration, I would pull the memory from a mental photographic library: I'm in the square of the old town, sitting outside the brasserie. Okay, so what do I smell, see, feel, taste and hear? I *taste* the berries of the rosé wine. I *smell* the tarragon from someone cooking in a nearby kitchen, and the flowers in the market. I *see* a dog lying in the shade beneath a tree. I *feel* the sun hitting my skirt and the warmth I want to bask in. I *hear* the clang of the bells from the cathedral and the chatter of people all around.

I'll stay immersed in that scene because each memory unlocks another, and then another, firing like a fast-moving montage, allowing me to whiz through every recall and sensation, selecting the smells that resonate and eliminating the ones that don't. How can I create the smell of burnt clay on terra cotta tiles? What's the note that evokes geraniums? What scent is warm like summer? How do I recreate the cold rosé on my lips? My mind continues in that vein, ten to the dozen, racing through images at a million miles an hour, kicking up and spraying around different memory associations in order to pluck just one or two notes that I can then start to experiment with.

For me, everything returns and speaks to me via my nose. In its simplest form, removed from the complexities of the technical process, that's how my creative process begins. This scattered, disorderly, untrained approach might not be the conventional way a fragrance is designed, but, then again, nothing I do is 'conventional'. Yet the perfumers with whom I work trust that, no matter the tangents I explore, I'll ultimately take them to the desired destination. And that's exactly what happened with Lime Basil & Mandarin.

*

In the months since Paris and Grasse, I had continued to experiment with different samples sourced from Derek and, for the first time in my life, I started to believe I could excel at something. Fragrance not only flooded me with ideas but it made me feel complete, fuelling an almost obsessive drive of creativity.

When Lime Basil & Mandarin first arrived as a spark of inspiration, I didn't know it would turn out to be as big as it was. Nor did the idea come in one burst; it gradually percolated over many weeks until a series of loose thoughts and memories coalesced.

If I remember the order of those thoughts correctly, it was the random memory of me sucking on a lime-chocolate sweet as a kid that first made me think of lime, and so I started from there, playing with a whole host of different lime notes in my kitchen, initially mixing them into a body lotion base. Matters of structure and composition didn't even enter the equation within this rudimentary process, though it is no surprise that my experimentation began with a citrus note – the signature theme that would underpin, or be laced through, everything I'd create.

Other memories or observations then came to mind, one triggering another: me squeezing a lime in the kitchen – the idea for a sharp, cologne-like character; dinner at the Sambuca Italian restaurant in Symonds Street where I enjoyed a pasta in pesto sauce – the smell of basil with its aniseed twists. I thought about that herb which made me think of summer, and summer made me think of orange groves, and orange reminded me of the orange and cinnamon wreaths we used to buy for the flat in Crystal Palace. But oranges weren't sweet enough. What's sweeter than oranges? Mandarins. Go with mandarins. And from that foundation, I was off and running, snatching an hour with my pipettes and weighing scales, laying out the notes in front of me, waiting for a rough sketch of the smell to form.

Once I felt I had pinned down the general idea, I called Derek and briefed him verbally that I wanted to create a Lime Basil & Mandarin fragrance, outlining which notes I wanted to emerge first, which should hover in the background, and which should linger. And that's what sent me into true fragrance development with a perfumer in Paris in 1991, although I still had one small hurdle to overcome.

As much as Derek had forewarned me about industry protocols – clients consult with an evaluator who liaises with the perfumer – I didn't like the idea of being one stage removed. I understood an evaluator's value in tracking tests and generally managing a project, but I couldn't bear the idea of not brainstorming one-on-one with the actual 'nose'. How could I put my name to something if it was created at arm's length, with me outside the room? It made no sense. 'Derek,' I said, 'I have to be part of the creation process. I can't work any other way.'

I told him that I needed to *learn* from the perfumer. Why did orange blossom smell floral one minute and then like a masculine cologne the next? Why can lavender smell like dog pee on a bush and then the cleanest soap? Why can liquid honey smell offensive at first but then come across all velvety when mixed with alcohol? I was like a child armed with a thousand 'whys' and only the perfumer had the answers.

Derek was fast realising that doing things the conventional way wasn't my style, and Gary laughed when he relented and removed the evaluator from the equation; of all people, my husband wasn't surprised that I had gotten my way. And so, within months of travelling to Paris as a debutant, I returned to the city to go behind the curtain and sit down with a perfumer in a lab of a thousand scents, sitting with him at a table scattered with vials, going through an exhaustively microscopic but rewarding process.

Within this collaboration, then and now, I felt as though I truly came alive. Nothing feels as magical as that zone when it's me and the perfumer side by side. On this first occasion, the French gentleman, who spoke good English, was gracious enough to give me the room to paint my olfactory vision, trusting the randomness of my intuition. In turn, I respected his mastery, as he set about constructing a fragrance that was *an exact* translation of the idea swimming in my head. For me, the preciseness of that translation is everything. I have to sniff the blend and know that he has delivered an interpretation faithful to the scent I have in mind, not 'close' or 'there or thereabouts' but spot-on.

These interpretations hinge on the tiniest, finely measured fractions as the perfumer creates different variants of the same fragrance; a teeny bit more juice in variant 'A', a smidgen less in variant 'B', a different molecule in 'C', and so on and so forth through variants D, E, and F. When seen up close, this craft is something to behold. Sometimes, there may be 250 submissions before we get there; sometimes, only ten, and I'll haggle with myself, back and forth, inside out, until I know we've nailed it.

Up until this point, I'm not sure I had fully appreciated the capabilities of my own nose, but the more I used it, the more agile it became. Of course, my heightened sense of smell had been there since childhood – ever since the age of ten when I first alerted Mum to when her oils were ready on the stove – but I had never considered that it would help transform my life. I had no philosophy, only intuition – that's all I had, and that's all I'll ever have. It may be a cliché but I have built a career by literally following my nose, trusting this most primal instinct the same way a bloodhound tracks a scent to match the 'odour image' in its brain.

I *see* smells in colours and memories, and I *hear* tunes when conjuring a scent. Some have said that my sense of smell borders on synaesthesia, a condition where 'the production of one sense impression relates to another sense being stimulated', as though the senses have got their wires crossed. I like to think it's some kind of neurological compensation for my dyslexia, giving me an edge in adulthood because I never caught a break at school. In my mind, I'm like a conductor pulling in different instruments and musicians to create a symphony. I'll hear a woody note – dun-dun-dun-dun, dun-dun-dun-dun; or the more high-pitched operatic note of white rose – laaaaahh! Or maybe a dash of jazz (orange blossom) – din-da, din-da, din-da; or a faint brush across the cymbals (lemon leaves). After hearing the notes, my brain then switches to *seeing* the composition, discovering where the void exists – the hole that cuts right through the centre of a fragrance. 'Okay, what is needed? What can I pour in there that will bring this alive? A wood? More citrus? Floral?' I'll see red, as if I'm dripping red notes down a white canvas. I'll see greens splashed against a wall. I'll imagine splashes of all sorts of colours to see what smells those mental images conjure.

Conveying this somewhat abstract process probably makes it sound more structured than it actually is, but I hope it goes some way to illustrating, in a simplified nutshell, how the different strands of my creativity pull together. I've never really had to explain this sacred process in detail before. I find it hard enough explaining it to myself. I think the best description I've ever read about my work and the fragrances I create came from *New York Times* scent critic Chandler Burr in his 2008 book *The Perfect Scent*. Like a perfumer translating what's in my head, this is what he wrote:

'Her genius is the fingerprint she leaves on each scent, a marvellous quality that is not weightlessness – it's something much more startling: Weight that floats, hovers in the air. Solidity shot through with light . . . like the revolutionary new-technology translucent concrete that architects have just begun using, a recipe of glass gravel mixed with optic fibres.

When poured, this concrete forms slabs of luminescence, and the outlines of people inside the walls of buildings using it are visible to those outside at night, against the glow of the light inside . . .'

If only Chandler's words had been available in 1991 – they could have acted as the written brief that I never had.

Once I made my first fragrance, the doors were flung open to a whole new universe, and I wanted to sprint, not walk, into making the next one, and the next, fearful that my ideas would somehow run out, like a tap running dry. I felt the preciousness of a newly discovered resource and didn't at first trust it to be limitless, so I kept pushing myself, trying to hurry along a process that requires patience.

But that was part of the beauty of what we were doing – we didn't know the rules or the norms, so we made up our own. There was a lot we wouldn't know and came to learn, but the biggest gap in our knowledge was the expectation that every fragrance needed to be married with a strong marketable image.

Throughout the 1970s and 80s, the trend was all about 'power fragrances'. A bit like the shoulder pad, these scents made a bold, fashionable statement, as depicted in multimillion-dollar ad campaigns that used sultry models and dramatised TV commercials to tap into the psychology of escapism, sex, passion, and mystery. Consumers bought into the promise of a certain alluring lifestyle. Image leads, scent follows.

I walked in the opposite direction, probably because my focus was more about the artistry than any marketed persona. My life-long association with beauty and cosmetics had been steeped in natural ingredients ever since I walked into Madame Lubatti's lab and so, for me, the ingredients *had to be the hero*. I didn't want to promise anything other than a beautifully constructed fragrance, and I wanted my notes to be front and centre, reflecting a truth of human interaction: we smell a fragrance, our attention is drawn, and *then* we see the wearer. Scent leads, image follows.

Buying a perfume or cologne can't suddenly make you sexier or more powerful or more successful. You can only enjoy its notes and *feel* good. And call it by its name. Lime Basil & Mandarin is Lime Basil & Mandarin, a composition that doesn't need to hide behind psychological fluff and slick marketing campaigns. With me, what you see is what you get. It's the same with my fragrances – they stand on their own and speak for themselves.

Lime Basil & Mandarin certainly did that, surpassing all expectations – outselling anything else. I think Derek felt vindicated in taking a chance on me after that, and I would be eternally grateful for the education and opportunity he provided. Over the next ten years, I would go on to create fifteen more fragrances, complete with matching lotions and bath oils, and each would build their own fan base.

Back at the flat, I started offering four scents during a treatment, and each client couldn't wait to find out the 'fragrances of the day', which, in turn, led to more local buzz and more sales. Our flat started to resemble, and smell like, a lab. Product seemed to fill every available shelf, table and corner. And, honestly, had things stayed that way, I would have been content, even on the nights when I flaked into bed and didn't think I had the energy for another dawn start, or when I felt overwhelmed and didn't think I could make another face cream, whisk up another lotion, or devise a new scent. I could have happily remained there, doing treatments in the back room, forever.

But Gary couldn't say the same.

Inevitably, when a flat doubles up as a skincare clinic and becomes overrun by a booming business, there will be domestic challenges. One day, I filled the bath with seashells that I was trying to scent with lavender – scented seashells from the seashore sounded like a good idea. The problem was that I got so immersed in making more face creams that I forgot to forewarn Gary when he arrived home from work.

'JO!' I heard him say from the hallway.

I popped my head out of the kitchen and there he was, not looking best pleased. 'I can't take a bath!' he said.

The words 'Sorry, Gaz!' were often heard in our flat, almost as often as the sight of him throwing his hands into the air in part-surrender, part-despair. The poor guy barely had enough room in the kitchen to make a cup of tea, due to all my stuff cluttering the stove, sink and counter. Or he'd come home early to find he was unable to use the toilet because I was still with a client – and the en-suite was our only loo. He'd have to go down the street to the nearby bistro, telling Joseph the owner that 'Jo is doing one of her faces again!'

One Saturday night, pre-Christmas 1993, it all became too much.

We were on our sofa bed, eating pizza at 2 a.m., talking about the unremitting pace of our life and speculating about how much longer it could continue. I was saying something when Gary put a slice of pizza in his mouth … and gagged. 'Oh my God, this tastes like nutmeg and ginger!' He dropped the slice on to his plate. '*Everything* tastes of bath oil. We can't keep living like this. We just can't.'

I could see he wasn't happy but I didn't know what options we had. 'What do you suggest?'

'You need a shop.'

'I don't want a shop. Somewhere bigger maybe, but a shop? That's not me. This is me – a clinic, working from home.'

In previous months, well-meaning individuals had attempted to steer us in business, perhaps thinking that we needed assistance,

but none of the advice or direction – which had included the suggestion of moving into retail – had resonated, and it still didn't,
even when my own husband recommended it. But he had clearly
been thinking about it for some time.

'Look,' he said, 'I'm prepared to give up my job and dedicate
my time to you and the business. But you need a shop. We've
outgrown here.'

I didn't see it. All I heard were alarm bells as anxiety led me
into thinking that the stability we had built would be squandered;
that our winning hand and good fortune would turn against us
if we changed a single thing. I saw Dad struggling along with
magic shows and market stalls. I saw Mum borrowing my birthday money for extra funds. I saw me as a child having to eke out
what food remained in the cupboards. I saw the teacher telling
everyone that I'd make nothing of my life.

I saw myself and didn't want my head above the parapet.

Fear – the enemy of any entrepreneur.

We had food on the table and bills that could be paid, including our rent and mortgage payments. 'You realise we could lose
it all?!' I said, quickly becoming flustered. Owning a business
isn't rocket science; it's about courage, creativity and faith. And
I don't mind admitting that I temporarily mislaid two of those
prerequisites for a moment.

Gary, ever the gentle and patient one, took my hand. 'We find
a shop, give it a year and see if we can survive; like we did when
we found this place.'

'And if it doesn't work?'

'I go back to construction and you go back to faces.'

When it comes to fragrance and creativity, I have the nerve and
vision. When it comes to strategy and the business side of things,
the nerve and vision is all Gary. I wasn't entirely convinced but
I trusted his judgement. And so, over a pizza with a topping of

bath oil, we agreed to turn a kitchen countertop operation into a retail business.

One of my facial clients was renowned PR expert Deborah Bennett who, in her time, had managed major publicity campaigns. I used to see her most weeks and, when I had time, we'd snatch a coffee, too – she would become not only a dear friend but one of the unsung heroes of our business.

A cross between Audrey Hepburn and Dorien from the BBC series *Birds of a Feather*, Deborah is glamorous, well-put-together, tremendous fun, and a great friend. I can hear her now as she used to arrive in our flat for a treatment. 'Darling! Darling!' Gary and I both adored her.

When we first met, we were keen to meet her boyfriend Henry because it was clear from the way she spoke about him that he was the love of her life. For ages, we were dying to meet him, and then she brought him to one appointment. That's when we discovered Henry was a dog who stood barely a foot off the ground.

'Flippin' heck!' said Gary. 'Henry's a schnauzer!'

Deborah was a wise sounding board for us both, so, while I was doing her face, I talked to her about opening a shop, still voicing some lingering reservations, probably because I wanted her to talk me out of it. But she didn't; she thought it a marvellous idea. In fact, she was so onboard that she offered to help get my name out there.

Gary and I had never previously promoted ourselves but I now understood the need for visibility in the marketplace. Word of mouth only went so far. So, Deborah said she'd start making some calls.

Admittedly, not everyone was keen on progress. I had built a somewhat exclusive club of ladies – I had around 750 clients at this point – and one or two frowned at the prospect of me opening a shop. I think human nature likes being in on secrets, and some women liked wearing a fragrance that wasn't commonly available.

'Why would you jeopardise all this?' one lady asked, and she almost made me believe my fears again, until she added, 'If you set up a shop, who's going to do our faces?! And will the prices of the fragrances go up?'

Meanwhile, Gary, who quit his job to become the managing director of our company, had been busy searching for the best retail location and had lined up Sunday appointments at two separate premises in Walton Street, within walking distance of our flat. When we turned up, I disliked both, mainly because their exteriors appeared too polished, in an artificial way.

'Nope. Not for me. Come on, let's go,' I said, starting to walk home.

Gary thought I was being a pain. 'Slow down a second. It will look better when we've renovated and put your name above the door.'

But I wasn't having it. As we continued down Walton Street – which the *New York Times* once described as the place 'where the elegant meets the ordinary' – he and I proceeded to have a terrible row. He said I was being difficult, deliberately trying to avoid opening a shop. I said he didn't understand the risks involved.

'And guess what, Gazza? It's not your name above the door if this fails, it's mine! If this all goes wrong, the egg's on my face, not yours!'

My married name is Willcox (which is how my family, the taxman and immigration control know me) but I had only ever traded under Jo Malone, so I felt the reputational risk was all mine, which, again, was silly but I wasn't thinking straight. So I flounced off, leaving Gary standing there.

Walton Street is tucked away from the busyness of Fulham Road at one end, and Brompton Road at the other. Over the years, it has managed to keep a certain charm with its mix of two-storey townhouses and independent, fashionable shops. In 1994, one young woman had a first-floor shop selling the most amazing handbags – her name was Anya Hindmarch; chef Brian Turner owned a restaurant there; the pharmacy Santa Maria Novella was renowned for its own potions and scents; and Joseph was well established with his legendary fashion store. But my attention was on none of those businesses, because I had stopped walking and was now staring at the premises at No.154.

Gary caught up with me.

'This is it – this is the one,' I said.

He took one look at the bombsite that was a 300-square-foot, gutted shell showcasing nothing but exposed brickwork and steel beams.

'You've got to be blinking joking.'

FIFTEEN

The more I thought about it, the more I grew accustomed to the idea of running my own shop. The prospect of getting up, *going out* to work, putting in a shift, and interacting with customers started to give me the same tingle I'd felt when selling Dad's paintings at the market, and when working for Justin de Blank in Elizabeth Street.

If I could have told my young self that she would one day take the keys to premises in London, she would have disbelieved it in the same way she would have disbelieved the press coverage that would start to trickle in, using epithets such as 'elite beautician' and 'fragrance queen'. Those tags amused me, because the cap that fit best was the one nobody but myself used: 'shopkeeper'. I was going to be a shopkeeper, and was proud to regard myself as such.

While I focused on my creativity and making product, Gary handled the nuts and bolts of the business, and negotiated a five-year lease with the landlord. We picked up the keys at the start of July 1994 and set an opening date of 19 October, firstly to take advantage of the pre-Christmas trade but also because we now had serious overheads and needed to be earning revenue. This meant we had three months to get everything in place: transform the unit, find suppliers, design a brand, interview candidates to be our two shop assistants, and find a factory to make the creams, lotions and bath oils in bulk. The days of four plastic jugs and home-made products were over; we now had to adhere to stringent compliance regulations that came with opening a shop.

Gary, for one, was delighted to reclaim the kitchen. He had improved access to the en-suite, too, because, with so much going on, and because I wanted to be on site at the shop from mid-afternoon, I cut back my treatments from six to four a day.

The first major task was to transform 154 Walton Street from a dusty shell into a beautiful, classic studio. For that, we turned to one of my face clients – an American woman called Sandra Ankarcrona, who ran her own interior design company. It turned out that she had previously worked as a director at Clinique, so she brought industry appreciation as well as artistic flair. We sat down one afternoon and I explained how we needed to repeat the look and feel of the treatment room – pristine, elegant, unfussy, soothing. She worked wonders, creating a design that blew me away: an all-cream interior with black trim, exuding a classiness that was accentuated by varnished wooden floors. But she also managed to capture a luxurious mood, stepping into a space that felt harmonious and sensual all at the same time.

As for our brand imagery, no longer would plain white bags and plastic bottles with typed labels be enough; we now needed to make an impactful first impression on the public stage, and I must have obsessed about this one aspect more than any other. In this area, Gary's savvy input would prove invaluable.

He may have started out in life wanting to become a vicar before moving into construction, but this diversion into retail was when he flourished. I could make product all day long, but I would never have known how to run a business without him.

Not only did he bring gusto to the operation, he brought a natural understanding of branding and the marketplace. 'We're building a brand,' he said, 'and we have to build it from the top; we can't be shy, we can't build from the bottom and hope to climb. You start high in the marketplace, establish yourself, then move down. Everything we do now from this point – the first impression we leave, the manners of our staff, the packaging we use, the style of the shop, the interviews we give – has to reflect the elegance of not only our product but our target audience.'

He could still be the boy from Beckenham, and I the girl from Barnehurst, but the brand had to be in a different class. With that in mind, another client, and another unsung hero, stepped forward – Isy Ettedgui, the wife of Joseph, he of the eponymous fashion store and one of the greatest retailers of our time. If anyone understood minimalist branding and understated but arresting aesthetics while still managing to convey glamour, it was Isy.

We sat down and brainstormed one Friday afternoon at the flat and she prompted and prodded my design preferences. 'What do you like?' she asked. 'Let's start there.'

'Lines. Straight, sharp lines ... and borders. Not too bold, though.'

'What about colours?'

'Nothing too loud. I like cream, black, gold.'

Within the week, after engaging the help of a designer friend called David, she returned with a simple but striking design: cream box, pencil-thin, black borders with a parallel gold line running on the inside, and 'Jo Malone London' across the label. The whole look was clean, classical, understated, and devoid of embroidery. I loved it. Clearly, the customers loved it, too: more than twenty years later, Isy's iconic design lives on.

*

It would be a while before our production line required giant conveyor belts manned by ladies in blue outfits and white hairnets, so we found two decent-sized laboratories that were sufficient for a small business like ours: one in Hampshire, the other in Devon. Our suppliers, for ribbon to gift bags to plastic bottles to glass bottles to lids, were dotted around the south of England. There was nothing centralised about our operation and we faced a few logistical headaches in the initial weeks, which was one reason why Gary had to hire a van to pick up our bottles and then transport them to the manufacturer for our first batch of product. My biggest concern, now that the hand-made days were over, was ensuring the quality of the end product wasn't affected by switching to a factory operation.

On our first on-site meeting at the lab in Devon, where body lotions and bath oils would be made, I was impressed by the smooth-running set-up, though I'm not sure the manager could say the same. 'So, all I need are your signatures and formulations and we'll be good to go,' he said.

I looked at Gary. Gary looked at me. 'Oh, I don't have the formulations for my product written down,' I said. 'They're all in my head.'

I think he thought I was joking, because he half-laughed, half-frowned. 'But you can't get the same results with product if you don't measure it out?!'

'Oh, I do. Every time. I just pour until it feels right.'

'So how many drops of juice do you use?'

'I don't really know – until it smells right.'

I had never seen anyone look as dumbfounded, not then, not since.

Only when we worked there and then on a couple of formulations did he believe it, having seen it with his own eyes. Over the next week, I undertook the laborious task of committing my recipes to paper for the first time. It took me hours but it was worth every minute when the first samples came back. This man's team got it closer than I imagined anyone would. Not 100 per cent – some didn't smell right, some were too thick, too thin, too waxy – but, after a few tweaks, the factories were soon delivering a consistent product with the most amazing texture.

As all the necessary pieces of our operation dropped into place and the shop continued to take shape, I found myself dashing from the flat to Walton Street whenever time allowed, because I didn't want to miss a thing. I snatched glimpses of every extra touch and new addition, from the shelving, to the cream-coloured cupboards, to the round table for the middle of the floor, to the glass desk for the tills, to the spotlights for our street-facing window. The highlight, though, was watching the awning go up.

I was unpacking product one late afternoon when Gary rushed in, grabbed my hand and led me outside. 'You're not missing this!' he said.

From the opposite side of the street, we watched as our little shop – with the door to the left of the main window – was christened with the words 'JO MALONE' in black on cream. No matter the number of times this name-above-the-door moment would be repeated over the years, it would never feel as special as that 'first' in Walton Street.

Gary squeezed my hand. I could see what it meant to him because he had tears in his eyes, which started me off, which, in turn, started him off some more. We stood there, half-crying, half-laughing, feeling elated. It felt like we were staking our flag into a personal summit, bringing value to every ounce of struggle, doubt, worry, fear and exhaustion.

I was going to love being a shopkeeper.

*

Deborah Bennett proved as good as her word on the PR front, lining up a piece in the *Financial Times*, in the 'FT Weekend' section, which was some start as far as we were concerned. Its associate editor, Lucia van der Post, widely regarded as the 'style queen', only features the crème de la crème of the luxury goods industry in the 'How to Spend It' pages, so it felt like a bit of a coup. Indeed, her article couldn't have been more supportive or positive. But this silver cloud had one dark lining: the opening date was mistakenly printed as Monday 17 October – two days early, and two days away.

As anyone in retail will confirm, the week prior to opening can be frantic. For as long as there is a date circled on a calendar – and ours was 19 October – perfectionists like me will utilise every second up to the sixtieth minute of the eleventh hour. So it is perhaps understandable why I felt a cold, clammy sweat creep up my back as I read that one typo. We still had interior alterations to complete, walls to paint, and stock to transfer from a rented office we were using as our mini-warehouse at the Old Imperial Laundry in Battersea. In the ensuing crisis call with Deborah, she effectively said, 'Stunning piece of publicity, one big error, and you now have no choice but to open on Monday to avoid customers turning up to an unfinished shop.'

For the next mad forty-eight hours, and with the help of friends who answered our SOS, we worked with the speed of whirling dervishes, fuelled by nothing but adrenaline, from Saturday mid-morning into the wee hours of Monday. Brian Turner supplied meals for the sustenance of our team as we painted the walls and then stood there with turbo hairdryers, trying to accelerate the drying process.

We finished around 3 a.m. but, as exhausted as we were, the place looked amazing, with the meticulously displayed collection of product in every corner, on every wall, and in the window:

face creams, body lotions, bath oils *and* the new addition of shower
gels, together with small huddles of fragrances in their glass bottles, with polished silver tops glinting under the spotlights. We
had gone to the wire, we'd made it and we'd be opening in seven
hours, at 10 a.m. sharp.

In daylight, the shop looked *and smelled* magnificent. Different
pockets of scents emanated from the assorted fragrances which,
overnight, and together with the orange and cinnamon potpourri
on the tables, had combined to mask the whiff of fresh paint:
jasmine, lavender, vetiver, lime, mandarin, ginger, basil, rose,
and coriander – it was like walking into the sweetest-smelling
orchard.

We had by now employed two shop assistants – both called
Amanda – and I had purchased a uniform of navy Armani suits,
a splurge shaped by my husband's sound advice that every first
impression made had to speak to the class of the brand. I was
standing there, near the till, soaking up the ambience when
an overeager customer started banging on the door, forty-five
minutes before opening. She couldn't wait until ten so asked if
she could buy some bath oil. Not one to turn away a customer,
I went to grab a bottle but it wouldn't budge from the shelf. I
tugged harder and, with a kind of gloopy, sucking sound, it came
free ... but not without leaving a print of paint on the bottom
of the bottle.

I tried another – same thing. Then another, and my heart sank.
'The bottles, Gary!' I screamed. 'They've all stuck to the paint!'

There's nothing quite like a last-minute hitch to get the blood
pumping. I looked at the time: 9.15 a.m. Gary and I rushed around
every newly painted surface and used palette knives to slide under
each bottle and flick them free, accepting that the resulting marks
on the shelves were flaws we'd have to live with on day one.

We made it with five minutes to spare, at which point Gary opened the front door, took a strip of black grosgrain ribbon – the type we'd use for gift wrapping – and tied it to either side of the frame, leaving it taut across the entrance.

As we started to count down to opening, the latest edition of *Tatler* was hitting the news-stands, announcing our arrival to a wider audience, courtesy of Deborah Bennett's continued efforts. 'Scenter of the Universe', said the headline in a two-page spread written by the magazine's fashion director Kathy Phillips, and I couldn't have asked for a better write-up: *'Jo Malone's discreet labels are already seen in the smartest bathroom cabinets. Now, with a new shop in Walton Street, her delicate, natural unguents will be making a splash all over . . . You might feel you know her name already. It has been whispered among media, fashion, society and even royal households for some time. Seen through the keyhole, bottles bearing the discreet Jo Malone label have long adorned the bathrooms of the ladies who latch on to the latest good thing . . .'*

In the coming weeks, that article would help turn word of mouth into a media buzz that would lead to a demand that, on the first sedate morning, we couldn't possibly have imagined. Outside, on an unremarkable day, the skies were London grey and the pavements damp. No locals turned out. No press. No fanfare. But, in front of a handful of friends and our two shop assistants, the occasion felt momentous in its own small way.

Gary stood beside me and presented the scissors. As the clock struck ten, I cut the ribbon to inaugurate the opening of our little shop in a little quiet street in our own backyard.

SIXTEEN

On our first morning of business, we had taken a team photo before the ribbon cutting. The two shop assistants and I posed by the central table filled with product, and we wore our biggest smiles and Armani suits. I wish I could find that picture today because, while it depicted the giddiness of a debutant shop-keeper embarking on an adventure, it also captured a naiveté that I miss. There is something magical about beginnings, about the challenges that come with territory not yet conquered, about being the underdog. I think I'd far rather stand at the beginning of something, looking up, rather than at a summit, looking down.

In that first week, we held a celebration party at Mosimann's in Halkin Street, inviting not only our friends but all my clients. There must have been more than four hundred people present, and we shared such a magical evening. It was the first time I had ever given a speech in public and I remember saying that none of us knew what the journey would entail. What's more, we didn't *need* to know. Our strategy, as I told everyone, was to put one foot in front of the other, take it day by day, and enjoy every moment.

Having already built a sturdy client base, we launched from a stronger position than most, but, above and beyond our modest revenues, we couldn't know how long it would take for sales to take off. But Gary had crunched the numbers and he reckoned that we'd be doing well if, with the increased overheads, we broke even in the second year. That was our realistic hope as we opened on that wet October morning.

What we certainly weren't expecting was an offer for the business.

Five hours into the opening day.

I had spotted the diminutive gentleman walk in as I boxed and bowed one woman's fragrance. Dressed in a dark navy, pinstriped suit, he was suave but looked out of place as he dawdled around the shop, giving the lotions and bath oils a cursory glance. He then brought a big, fat cigar to his lips and prepared to light it.

'I'm sorry,' I said as I finished serving the customer, 'you can't smoke in here.'

He apologised and approached the till. He was American; his accent East Coast. 'I'd like to speak with Jo Malone.'

'You're speaking with her,' I said.

He smiled. 'Congratulations on the shop.'

'Thank you. It's been a lot of hard work.'

'I bet,' he said, taking a beat before adding, 'I'd like to take you to lunch.'

Initially, I thought he was flirting. 'I'm sorry, we're busy, so thank you but—'

'I am acting on the instructions of a client who wishes to make you an offer for your company.' He raised his eyebrows, as if to say, 'I'm serious.'

He said no more than that and offered no business card, but he had my attention and it was obvious he wanted somewhere discreet to talk. 'I'm nipping out for a coffee,' I said to shop assistant Amanda Lacey. 'Won't be long.'

Joe's, the café owned by Joseph, was my coffee spot in those days and where I'd do press interviews, just around the corner in Draycott Avenue. The American gentleman bought two cappuccinos. We sat at a small square table facing one another and, after the exchange of a few pleasantries, he didn't beat about the bush. 'My instructions today are to offer you one million dollars for your company.'

'One. Million. Dollars?' I said, making sure I'd heard him correctly.

He nodded. 'And should you agree, our condition is that you walk away without any further involvement in the business.'

'Can I ask who your client is?'

'I can't divulge that, I'm afraid,' he said.

If it sounds bizarre now, then that's because it sounded bizarre then. As he kept a straight face, awaiting my response, I wondered if someone was setting me up, and yet everything about this man's appearance and demeanour smacked of a professional.

I stirred my coffee, buying a few seconds, trying to work him out in the way Dad used to work out if a poker opponent was bluffing, but I couldn't get a good read on this guy: he was expressionless. The first thought that came into my head was the piece of blue foam that Gary and I no longer slept on, presumably my mind's way of contrasting the years of blood, sweat and tears with the easy way out. When you've come from nothing and you hear the word 'million', human instinct is to lean in, however briefly. But faced with the value of an experience yet to begin versus the value of the first offer that comes along, I knew my answer.

I looked up. 'Thank you very much. I'm flattered but not interested.'

He looked surprised. 'Can I change your mind?'

'No, thank you.'

'I'm not sure I'll be making this offer again.'

I stood, shook the man's hand and bid him a polite farewell before walking back to the shop, never to see or hear from him again. I didn't know how serious or credible he was – fifteen minutes in his company hardly constituted due diligence – or whether he represented some unknown rival who didn't want my business to take off. That night, Gary and I laughed about the ridiculousness of it all. 'Well,' he said, 'you know your value now!' We agreed that the only time we ever wanted to hear the words 'one million' again would be the day we turned over six figures. But the prospect of that happening seemed many moons away.

That November, I was looking forward to my thirty-first birthday, mainly because it would be the first time in a long time that I'd get to mark the occasion properly, instead of being elbow-deep in plastic jugs and face creams. Gary had the night planned out: take in the fireworks at Battersea Park, then grab a bite to eat afterwards.

During lunch hour, and in between treatments, I had nipped over to the shop. He was out back, unpacking a consignment of bath oil before pouring it into 200ml cubic glass decanters.

'Remember, don't overfill them,' I said. 'Don't go all the way to the glass stopper. Fill only to the bottom of the neck.' If I had learned one thing from working with a formulator, it was this: oil expands and creates gasses in heat and therefore pressure, so it's important to leave air in the bottle neck, just in case.

I watched him fill the first decanter a little too generously. 'Too much, Gary!'

'Jo, we're charging people a lot of money for these – we've got to give value for money.'

Moreover, he cited our compliance with 'weights and measures' regulations which meant if we promised 200ml of bath oil, 'then we better sell 200ml of bath oil or we'll be in trouble'. I left to do another treatment, trusting him to strike the balance.

By the time I returned for the final hour of business, Gary had filled dozens of the decanters and placed them on one of the high shelves. He had gone to run some errands, leaving Amanda Lacey in charge, which we often did – that girl was not only a grafter but could sell ice to an Eskimo. I took over from Amanda around 4 p.m. because the lovely Mya Waters, the PA to Giorgio Armani, was picking up a collection of product that her boss was buying to give as corporate gifts.

She can't have been in the shop for longer than a couple of minutes when we heard a loud *WHOOSH!* followed by a crashing sound.

'What was that?'

WHOOSH! Another one.

And that's when I saw it – a gooey waterfall of bath oil so thick it cascaded in slow motion, flowing from the high shelving and dripping over the cupboard beneath, pooling on the floor. The oil in those bloody decanters had started to expand under the heat of the non-halogen spotlights, and the pressure was ejecting the glass stoppers.

I'm not sure Mya spotted it as I guided her to the door, muttering something about an electricity fault blowing the light bulbs. I ushered her outside, saying it was probably best she return the next day, and I flipped the sign in the window to 'Closed'. I rushed to the back to grab whatever tea towels were lying around. But it was too late – the Jo Malone version of Tchaikovsky's *1812 Overture* was about to reach its crescendo. One by one, the decanters started erupting in rapid, almost choreographed succession – the third, the fourth, the fifth, the sixth – tipping over the decanters and spilling more bath oil. All I could do was look on helplessly until the performance was over.

Gary, like a man who turned up late and missed the orchestra's main number, walked in. He looked at me, looked at the floor and knew straightaway what had happened. I could have throttled him.

We didn't make the Battersea Park fireworks that evening. We were too busy on our hands and knees – not talking to each other – cleaning up the whole mess until 4 a.m. But I would soon see the funny side, and it has since become a standing joke in the family whenever my birthday rolls around.

'What are we going to do for your birthday this year?' Gary will say, before completing his own joke. 'Want to fill some bath oils?!'

I could probably write a whole other book on the mishaps, comedy of errors, late orders, last-minute panics, and little disasters that felt huge at the time. And Gary certainly wasn't the only one who occasionally slipped on our steep learning curve.

When it comes to being creative and interacting with customers, leave it to me. I love nothing more than engaging people in the product, massaging a lotion into someone's arm to familiarise them with the texture; or giving someone a spritz of fragrance before walking them through the inspirations of a fragrance, the same way a sommelier would point out the different flavours in wine. But when it comes to anything that involves numbers, like tills and running credit cards for example, my dyslexia will hold up its hand and apologise in advance. On one particularly busy Saturday, I temporarily forgot about this limitation. I forgot what the doctor had told me – that when under pressure or stress, my dyslexia can sometimes lead to confusion.

A queue had formed at the till, so I told Amanda to stay on the shop floor while I ran people's payments. We had one of those manual, credit card imprinters, and I kept inserting people's cards into the flatbed tray, sliding across the roller, and taking a carbon copy of the receipt, processing about ten customers in succession.

The following day, I received a call from one of those ladies, a long-standing and extremely wealthy female client. 'Jo,' she said, 'I'm wondering if you can help me. I'm in Harvey Nichols and I've been pulled aside by management who are asking some rather uncomfortable questions. It seems I've been trying to buy some tights using a credit card belonging to XXXX' – and she said the name of someone famous. 'The last time I used my credit card was in your shop and she was there. I think there's been a mix-up.'

To my mortification, I had given her the wrong card, and it would transpire that I had also swapped the cards of two other customers. To make matters worse, when Amanda checked the payment slips, I hadn't taken a single signature. 'Jo, you're not only meant to take the imprint, the customer has to sign for the product, too!'

I spent most of that day tracing and calling about ten customers, making sure they had the correct credit cards and asking if they wouldn't mind popping back to sign the payment slip. Most returned – one or two didn't – but Gary was relieved that I hadn't frittered away £200 worth of product. Not surprisingly, I wasn't allowed near the till again.

Another time, I thought it would be a good idea to create an autumn-themed display. We had put a tree trunk in the window but it looked unfinished and so, during a walk with Gary in Oxfordshire, we picked up a bundle of twigs, broken branches and two-foot logs that were lying around. On paper, recreating a pocket of the English countryside in Chelsea, and tying bottles of fragrances to the 'tree', sounded like a great idea; in reality, not so much.

The earwigs, centipedes, and beetles we found crawling all over the shop were not the problem. I walked in one morning, detected a burning popcorn kind of smell, heard a low humming buzz, and then spotted the mini-swarm of wasps. Attracted by our woodland theme, these wasps had come in from upstairs via one of the light fittings but, instead of finding a tree, they had found an array of scents and were having the time of their lives. Cue the emergency arrival of a pest controller.

Mistakes are the essence of being an entrepreneur; without them, we wouldn't have the kind of instructive experiences that make us better. I'm not sure what we would have done had we not kept laughing; in fact, not a day went by without a good old belly laugh. And the biggest hysterics came when Gary had what I call 'one of his Del Boy moments'.

Sometimes, when I was doing a treatment, and when the shop assistants felt stretched, he would become a stand-in salesman. With his sunny disposition and charming manner, it could be argued that there wasn't anyone better suited to meet and greet the customers. But, after years in the construction industry, it's fair to say that it took him a while to master the subtle art of selling.

One morning, a French lady walked in and the ever-helpful Gary asked if he could be of any assistance. 'Yes, I am looking for a new fragrance,' she said, in her exquisite accent.

'And what kind of fragrance are you looking for?'

'I don't know. Is there one that you can suggest?'

'Oh yes!' said Gary, taking a bottle from one of the shelves. 'This one is just knicker-dropping!'

And, with that, the French woman put her hand to her mouth, turned on her heels and fled without saying a word, leaving Gary standing there, fragrance in hand.

'What on earth possessed you to say such a thing?!' I asked him later.

'That's how I've heard you describe it!'

'But that's what I say to *you* – it doesn't mean we say it to customers!'

The best bit about that story? The woman returned an hour later, when Gary wasn't there, and bought four bottles of that 'knicker-dropping' perfume.

Becoming a shopkeeper didn't mean I stopped creating. Far from it. If anything, I wanted to diversify and keep making things, and the addition of scented candles was chief among them.

I always burn a candle in my home. It is one of the great affordable luxuries, and can fill a room just as much as a bottled perfume. It has the ability to lull us into a whole other state, be it relaxation in the bathtub, romance at the dinner table, remembrance of a loved one, meditation for the mind, or the pure enjoyment of the scent alone. There is something decadently mesmerising about a flickering flame. For that reason, and for the first year only, we bought an outside brand of jasmine- and cinnamon-scented candles.

Meanwhile, I started experimenting back at the flat, looking to make my own collection. After melting wax with different fragrance compounds, I took my ideas to the manufacturer in Devon. The hard part of working with fragrance is transferring it into another medium, and candle-making proved the trickiest of them all – the wicks didn't stand straight, the aroma burned out too quickly, and the wax wasn't the right quality – but, after much trial and error, we got there, and our patience paid dividends in sales. Indeed, our line of scented candles would prove to be almost as popular as the bottled fragrances.

Beyond the staple product lines, I sold big cellophane bags filled with home-made orange and cinnamon potpourri and priced them up at £49.50. 'No one's going to spend that much on a bag of dried flowers!' said Gary. I made fifty bags on a Sunday and they had sold out by Tuesday. I did the same with scented seashells, as tried and tested in our bath. I bought little silver caskets and filled them with amber crystals. I used foam oasis balls to create a scented artichoke 'tree' soaked in orange and cinnamon. I felt like a glorified *Blue Peter* presenter, turning nothing into something and seeing if people would buy it.

Of course, what the customers never read about are the products that go awry, like the discontinued skin toner I created, only to discover that all the bits floated to the top; or the lime-based body lotion that, no matter how much we tweaked it, constantly thinned out and poured like water; and then there was my 'Send a Scent' initiative – a kind of Interflora service where a man in a van would drop off a mini-bottle of fragrance – which I thought was inspired but no one really grasped the concept and, within two years, had died a death. There were dozens of attempts to find the next big thing, and dozens of times we fell short. Mercifully, the products we did get right were selling better than ever before.

Occasional days of hectic trade had now become an everyday occurrence. Within a month of opening, our 340-square-foot space proved too small to handle everyone, so customers had to queue outside. If there is one truth about queues – other than the mystifying capability of the British to tolerate them – it is their magnetic effect. When people see a line, it creates intrigue; when you have intrigue, you attract custom.

People have asked me if there was one moment when I first realised that the business was starting to explode. The answer is one Saturday, three weeks before Christmas: the shop was rammed; I stepped outside, and the queue must have been twenty-foot long. Author Malcolm Gladwell describes the tipping point as 'that magic moment when an idea, trend or social behaviour crosses a threshold, tips and spreads like wildfire'. Witnessing that line outside, I sensed that we were crossing some kind of special threshold.

Inside, you'd have thought we were holding an over-subscribed cocktail reception. Gary, Amanda Lacey and I were swamped, and the shrill of the phone in the background was relentless. And so began the start of an amazing first Christmas, when our little street crackled with festive spirit as every business owner did their bit, from festive-themed windows, in-shop decorations, mince pies for customers, and carols playing in the background. Brian Turner was a star on those Saturdays. When he saw the queues forming, he brought out trays of mince pies, laughing and joking with our customers. That man was a joy to be around, and he exemplified the community and love that we would never have known had we stayed in the safety of our third-floor flat.

There were no exceptions when it came to queuing. Once, the security guard for one famous person came into the shop and dropped a heavy hint, saying his client was waiting in the car and didn't have long.

'I'm sorry,' I said, 'but I'm afraid she's going to have to queue like everyone else – those people outside have been waiting a long time.'

It didn't matter to me whether you were a VIP, a member of royalty or a dowager from Belgravia, everyone was treated the same. Did that mean some security guards had to line up and hold their client's place? Possibly. But not one single person was allowed to queue-jump or receive preferential treatment and, to be fair, no one ever complained, at least not to me. Although there was a funny moment when David Linley, the son of Princess Margaret, stopped by to purchase a gift for his wife Serena.

He had queued patiently outside with my dear friend Ruth Kennedy, who was the managing director of his furniture design company. Ruth had been supportive of the business from the start, and understands retail from the boots up. Over the years, I would often fall back on her wise counsel – and we would often laugh about this one particular day.

The shop was once again heaving and, as David shuffled along the line and approached the entrance, he was a true gentleman, holding open the door for a lady who was leaving . . . followed by another . . . and then a stream of ladies . . . and then a couple. The steady stream of comings and goings meant he was standing there for a good minute or so. David, dressed in a black jacket and matching polo-neck sweater, was graciously thanked by each customer, who had clearly mistaken him for the Jo Malone door-man, rather than a member of the Royal Family.

As the tills kept ringing all the way up to Christmas Eve, we realised that we were woefully ill-prepared for the festive crowds that flocked to Walton Street each year, and we certainly hadn't anticipated demand on the scale we experienced. We found our-selves replenishing the shelves four times a day. Six months of product sold out in six weeks. By the time we reached the end of the financial year in April, we had in those six months essentially already hit our five-year goal. But, as incredible as that was, I derived most fulfilment from knowing that my fragrances were making a positive difference to people's lives.

Nothing beats the feeling of a customer, in person or in writing, raving about a fragrance: how it smells to them, the emotional connection they feel, the memories it evokes, and how they can't imagine wearing anything else. Like fashion and music, taste in perfumes and colognes is such a subjective thing, and yet the fondness with which people talk about my fragrances – and the way newspapers report how each scent built its own 'cult follow-ing' – will always mean the world to me.

Occasionally, I would hear about a fragrance's unexpected benefits, too. Ruth Kennedy was once standing in line at a pharmacy in New York when one of my scents proved too much for a gentleman she passed in one of the aisles. 'He came up behind me and asked me to marry him because I smelled so good!' she laughed. 'That's when you know you have a great fragrance, Jo!'

Such stories were gratifying, because, in that pre-social media age, Gary and I had no way of tracking how the product was being received, or how far the ripples extended outside London. A customer made a purchase, walked away with a bag bearing my name, and that was the only context we were afforded. I had no idea how the product was being talked about by my peers in the fragrance industry either.

I remember when someone first said to me: 'You're changing the language of fragrance, Jo. Everyone's talking about you.' My first thought was, 'Am I? Are they?!' I was immersed in my own bubble, enjoying the experience of watching our little business grow. I didn't even think about the bigger picture; not straight-away, at least.

Of course, I had read about the kudos we were receiving but at no point did I think that our little operation would ever – could ever – get noticed by one of the perfume houses in Paris. Just because a singer-songwriter sells out a local music venue most Saturdays doesn't mean that a record label will come knocking. I wouldn't know it at the time but, in later years, I would hear the story from one perfume house in Paris that a big brand sent its people to check out the shop discreetly 'to find out what you were doing so differently'.

In my mind, I wasn't necessarily being 'different'. I was simply following my intuition and naming fragrances after their ingre-dients – a trend that most brands appear to adopt today but, back then, I suppose that simplicity made me stand out. 'Simplicity' sums up my approach. I believe that the hallmarks of quality and luxury are discernment, not fuss, not razzmatazz, not bells and whistles. Understated. Subtle. Like a scent that gradually makes itself known and quietly commands attention.

I can reflect on everything now but, in the mid-1990s, I had no time to consider the impact of what we were doing. All we could do was carry on throwing coal on the fire to keep the operation rolling along. But I was never too busy to create, and that's what I was asked to do when I was invited to collaborate on two fragrances: one for French Connection, the other for McDonald's.

Understandably, Gary had a bit of a wobble over both approaches, and his concerns went something along these lines: 'DON'T YOU THINK WE'VE GOT ENOUGH GOING ON?' But Alisa Green, then married to French Connection founder and chief executive Stephen Marks, was a facial client and she asked if I'd ever be interested in helping create their first fragrance.

As the company's creative director, she was someone I admired enormously. Furthermore, it was an opportunity to be involved with Stephen, an old-school retailer who had established the fashion brand in 1972, and had caused a stir in the mid-1990s with a masterstroke of marketing, using the company's initials – FCUK – for a now-iconic ad campaign.

As busy as the shop was, I viewed opportunities to work with greats like Alisa and Stephen as educative experiences that held their own value. Here was a chance for me to challenge myself: could I create for another brand? I think any self-respecting entrepreneur can challenge themselves outside the boundaries of their own business.

The end result was a clean, citrusy, grapefruit-scented cologne with a wonderful woody note running through its centre, and I was as proud of that fragrance as any. I can say the same about the one I designed for McDonald's UK to mark its twenty-first anniversary since opening in Woolwich in 1974 – a unisex fragrance that we called *First Generation*.

Some people asked at the time why I'd work with McDonald's when my brand was high-end luxury, but I felt that enquiry spoke more to a very British obsession with class than it did to my reason for doing the project. Whatever I do, and with whomever I work, my creativity is never compromised – the beauty and luxury lies within the bottle, not the point of sale. In the same way I don't look at people on a different level, nor do I grade opportunities that arise. Working on a market with Dad had taught me that much.

Besides, one of my chief considerations in weighing up an opportunity is the people I'll be working with, and CEO Paul Preston, whose wife Mary was a face client, was someone I respected. I also liked the motivation behind the fragrance – it wasn't for general sale; it was a 'thank you' gift for staff to mark the anniversary.

Going into McDonald's UK was my first experience of stepping into an all-male boardroom as I presented my samples to executives. I could tell a few of them were thinking, 'We're McDonald's, why is this woman here?!' but I did derive enjoyment from watching those fourteen or so suited men from a fast-food empire take the A, B, and C sample bottles, sniff them and give their opinion on the lime and verbena fragrance I had created. I like to think that I wasn't the only one who learned from the experience.

What few people knew at the time was that the fragrance proved so popular with staff that those same executives agreed to use the scent for their sachets of hand-wipes throughout the country. So, if you ever went to McDonald's in 1995/96 and used their mini-towelettes, you were among some of my early customers.

These commissioned projects were all part of a busyness that made me understand the imperative of employing a PA for the first time. When Cherie Fullerton came along, I didn't know how I had coped without her; she proved to be a godsend, able to read my mind before I'd even asked her to do something. I never thought I'd ever require an assistant but I couldn't have kept on top of things without her, especially since she also oversaw the running of the warehouse, plus the mail-order business we had also established.

Nor did I ever imagine that I would have to stop doing facials, but I had less and less room for ninety-minute treatments. At first, I tried reducing my facials, going from ten a week to five and then two, but, eventually, the appointments petered out and found their natural end. Treatments had provided the foundation from which we had grown, but the business was now dictating the direction we needed to go, and our exponential growth was sometimes hard to believe, no more so than when Christmas 1995 rolled around.

Our first full year of trading had been incredible. At the end of each day, Gary would write up a daily takings report and shake his head. 'You aren't going to believe what we've done today,' he'd say. It reached the point where we were close to breaking the one million barrier in turnover – a goal that would have sounded ludicrous had we dared contemplate such a figure twelve months earlier, but now, as we prepared to turn into 1996, it seemed oddly realistic.

We had two new shop assistants by then. Amanda Lacey, who was always ambitious and full of ideas, moved on and, I'm delighted to say, went on to become a facialist in her own right and launch her own brand. Instead, Vicky Martin and Lorna Trevelyan joined the team.

Those two might as well have been sisters: blonde, beautiful, tall and, more importantly, smart and retail savvy. However frantic things became, they were the level heads that kept the ship steady, while being able to keep it fun at the same time. Laughter was around every corner. I had known graft, hard work, creativity and stress but we laughed every single day and the shop was a joy of a place to be. That atmosphere matters in a small business. Camaraderie, team spirit, and keeping things light, even in the intense moments, are ingredients for success, because everyone then wants to work hard and pull in the same direction.

On Christmas Eve around noon, as trade started to slow, we let Vicky and Lorna go home. One hour later, Gary and I were thinking of closing early, so he started to go through the day's receipts before heading to our own festive lunch at San Lorenzo.

'How have we done?' I asked. 'Good,' he said, tapping away on the calculator. 'So what does that mean we've accumulated over the year?' 'I don't know,' he said. 'Let's work it out.' And so he scanned the books and ran the numbers.

'Wow,' he said. 'We're £362 short of our first million!'

'There's no way we're closing now,' I said. 'We stay open until we make that last £362!'

Over the next two hours, a trickle of customers, mostly men looking for last-minute gifts, passed through. At around 3.30 p.m. that trickle became a steady flow and I didn't look up again for the next hour. I turned to Gary. 'How we doing? Are we close?'

I can't remember the exact amount but it was less than a fiver.

The shop was now empty but a lone businessman walked in and didn't really seem to know what he was looking for except to say he needed a stocking filler. 'What's the cheapest thing you have?' he asked.

I picked up a 100ml bottle of shower gel. 'This would be ideal,' I suggested.

'How much?'

'Eight pounds ninety-five.'

'Perfect. Just the job,' he said.

Gary suppressed his whoops of delight as I finished serving the gentleman, gift wrapping his box and placing it inside a bag filled with black tissue paper. And before he could take the bag, I reached under the counter for a bottle of champagne that a customer had gifted us earlier. 'Happy Christmas, sir,' I said.

He didn't know it, but his stocking filler had just made us our first million – fifteen months after I had been offered that same amount for the business.

He was a little taken aback by my generosity. He studied the Dom Pérignon label, looked at the two smiling faces in front of him, and said, 'Happy Christmas to you, too, but may I issue a small piece of advice – you'll never make your business work if you're giving things like this away!'

The following year proceeded along the same upward curve, and it was around this time that our first overseas interest made itself known. America came knocking with a call from Harpo Productions. When my PA Cherie rang the shop to pass on the message, I had no idea who they were. 'It's Oprah Winfrey's production company – they want you to take part in a special they're doing.'

Oprah had become the queen of daytime television in the States with her Chicago-based talk show, but it wasn't until 1993 that the rest of the world knew her name after she landed a live interview with Michael Jackson and it became the most-watched interview in television history, attracting a reported global audience of ninety million. So, three years on, it felt like a pretty big deal when one of her producers invited me on her show for a segment entitled *Million Dollar Businesses*.

I can't remember how they heard about our story, but I assume I must have been quoted somewhere talking about our million milestone. Regardless, Gary and I were on a plane to Chicago one month later, which felt surreal because I'd not even done any local television at that point.

Oprah was famous for celebrating the entrepreneurial spirit in people, and our segment focused on small businesses that started at home and had built from nothing. Other guests in the green room were a schoolgirl who had created a product that guaranteed crispy bacon in a microwave; someone who made designer hairclips; and the man behind Jamba Juice, which was proving all the rage in California.

I didn't see Oprah backstage, so the first time we met was 'on air' as I walked out to the all-cheering, all-whooping, contagious energy of a studio audience. As I took my spot on the sofa, I looked out and saw two or three television cameras – a bright red light atop each – and a haze of lights. Strangely, I didn't feel nervous, probably because Oprah made me feel instantly at ease, but I also discovered that I felt confident when talking about my fragrances, as if I was their best ambassador as well as their creator.

The interview couldn't have gone any better, but I don't think I fully appreciated the scale of that show's influence until we returned to London. It had been business as usual for maybe a month, until one Saturday when Gary looked out of the shop window and saw a coach had parked directly outside – so close that its front end nudged and damaged our awning. But Gary's consternation over that slight hit soon faded when he saw more than fifty American tourists disembarking and headed our way.

In the coming weeks, more coachloads of Americans would stop by and we came to realise that it didn't only bring another spike in sales, it meant that each of those customers returned home to their different states, armed with product and bags bearing my name. Each tourist was a walking advertisement, spreading a scented ripple across the Atlantic, coast to coast, from New York to California.

I suppose that's what they mean by 'the Oprah effect'.

SEVENTEEN

The period 1996–99 felt like being on a merry-go-round going faster and faster, while still having to reach out and spin plates on the sidelines. A million and one good things seemed to happen at the same time, and I started to wonder if life would ever slow down again, which was ironic when you think we had opened the shop to provide us with a little bit more breathing space.

Sales rose day after day, month on month, boosted by the mail-order business that Cherie oversaw from our office at the Old Imperial Laundry. With more than twenty staff now on the payroll, we knew that we were outgrowing Walton Street. But one place we didn't want to outgrow was the flat in Chelsea, so instead of paying rent, we started paying a mortgage after the landlord agreed to sell.

We stopped trying to second-guess what would happen next. Indeed, I seemed to say the same thing in every press interview. 'Who knows what tomorrow will hold?'

What we couldn't know was that our story in the mid-1990s still had some unknown twists and turns to come. So much of the brand's future would be influenced by matters of fate, and by the people who would walk into our lives – and our shop – and open up a whole new chapter.

In the previous eighteen months, and long before my appearance on *Oprah,* almost every department store in the world had come knocking, offering to stock our product as 'a niche brand'. We hadn't proactively pursued any of those approaches because we felt we were still learning the ropes of retail, without having to grasp the more complex intricacies and territories that come with the wholesale marketplace.

When you're the new kid on the block, tasting success and attracting attention, it is perhaps tempting if a big-name department store arrives on your doorstep with an offer. Today, it seems we live in a more entrepreneurial age with start-ups and television shows that can bring investment and fast-track growth. But Gary kept urging caution, saying we were setting out to build a brand with longevity rather than be a flash in the pan. Many first-time entrepreneurs can fail if they go too wide too soon, especially without the proper foundations and seeding in place, so we chose to bide our time and wait for the right offer.

One such offer arrived in September 1996 during London Fashion Week – the year when designers Alexander McQueen and Julien Macdonald bossed the catwalk, and someone coined the term 'Cool Britannia' to capture the cultural renaissance in fashion, music, and retail. Twice a year, designers, stylists, and buyers from the department stores descend on the capital, so we had become used to the extra footfall as they heard about our shop.

Different retail scouts operate in cities around the world, looking for the next new talent or brand that's trending, and an agency called Agal UK Ltd had alerted its clients to our success. And that tip-off is what led to an approach we couldn't resist.

A fair-haired gentleman, looking dapper in a pinstripe suit, walked in and held open the door for a tall, strikingly elegant lady wearing a glamorous brown coat; it was obvious from their appearance that they belonged to the fashion world. What I didn't know, until they introduced themselves, was that they were two of the biggest names in retail: Dawn Mello, president and chief merchant at Bergdorf Goodman, and her creative director Richard Lambertson – a duo who had recently relaunched Gucci before returning to helm Manhattan's most prestigious emporium.

Dawn was an industry icon. At a previous stint at Bergdorf in the 1980s, she had discovered Donna Karan, Giorgio Armani and Michael Kors. Now there she was, standing across from me, the epitome of feminine grace and smelling amazing – always a good sign in my book.

There was something else she did that I noted, too – she chose a lot of product and insisted on paying. She was Dawn Mello; doubtless she received freebies wherever she went, and yet she didn't expect something for nothing. Of the many flattering things she and the utterly charming Richard said, only one sentence stuck in my mind: 'What an amazing space you have created,' she said, looking around. 'Have you thought about coming to New York?'

And that was the question that opened the door into our partnership with Bergdorf Goodman, a store that understood luxury like no one else, and believed in brand-building not just brand-placing. It felt like the perfect fit in every respect. But as great as the opportunity undoubtedly was, Gary wanted to strike a deal that was right, hence why negotiations lasted a good twelve months, into the autumn of 1997.

When it came to deal-making, my husband would prove to be one shrewd, tough negotiator who held his ground. On the other side of the negotiating table sat the equally shrewd Vicki Haupt and she, as the general merchandising manager, had been charged with doing what was right for Bergdorf. The great thing about

Vicki was that she didn't flex any corporate muscle and treat us as the minnow. She remained conscious of how big this deal was for us, while also aware of the points where she could concede ground and where she couldn't budge. Gary, too, had his no-compromise points – and that was how we reached a potential deal-breaker.

'We want to use our own packaging and gift bags,' said Gary.

'I'm afraid we can't give you that,' said Vicki. 'We've *never* done that at Bergdorf Goodman. It has to be your product in our bags.'

But this opportunity was about increasing our visibility and Gary held firm. 'I understand the history and prestige, Vicki, but we have one chance to get this right. You'll have other chances, we won't. The department store that allows our packaging will be the one we sign with. That's our non-negotiable; otherwise we can't proceed.'

He wasn't bluffing. This was our only means of self-promotion outside of London. We could picture it: shoppers walking down Fifth Avenue, carrying our cream-coloured bags tied at the handles with a bow, emitting a hint of the scent inside.

We were confident that other stores would come knocking if this deal went south, and therein lies a key point for any entrepreneur entering into negotiations: the worth of your brand, and the vision and principles you hold dear, should not be diminished by the size of the giant sitting opposite.

Vicki offered a compromise. 'Okay, we'll agree to put the product in one of your bags which we'll then slot into a Bergdorf bag. How does that sound?'

Bearing in mind that it was a concession no one else had previously won, we were happy because we suspected that once customers had our bags then they wouldn't be too concerned with the store's, possibly even dispensing with them – and that's what transpired after the first few months.

Gary never once thought small on our behalf, and that

belief – together with the product – is what got us into Bergdorf
Goodman. He negotiated the whole deal, including floor space,
commissions, the lot. Come spring 1998, we were ready to take
the quantum leap from Walton Street to Fifth Avenue.

Bergdorf Goodman sits in all its gilded splendour on one whole
city block in Midtown Manhattan, between W 57th and W 58th,
a site once occupied by the Cornelius Vanderbilt II mansion. A
majestic store – nine storeys high, with mansard roof and a marble
and stone-clad facade – it is one of retail's ancient monuments. I
hadn't fully appreciated that truth until I first stood outside. Only
then did it become obvious why, in 1952, *Time* magazine called
it 'Fifth Avenue's finest' – and it still is.

I looked behind me and saw Tiffany's across the street, and
immediately pictured Audrey Hepburn as Holly Golightly,
window shopping, peering into a glamorous new world through
her own reflection, realising who she was and what she wanted. As
a big fan of *Breakfast at Tiffany's*, and the non-conformist Holly, I
took this location as another positive sign. I had only ever viewed
America through the television screen so it felt quite surreal to
be standing on the street where they filmed a scene from one of
my favourite movies.

Gary and I stepped inside Bergdorf Goodman, and the whole
place seemed to shine, from every reflective surface to the crystal
chandeliers; its opulence conveyed a captivating charm, and its
sense of history, fused with modern-day luxury, was breathtaking.
This was the store where every luxury brand longs to sit, and no
wonder.

On our first visit, Vicki, along with Pat Saxby, the vice president
of the cosmetic and fragrances division, provided a tour and that's
when we first saw the spot from where we would trade: a little
windowless rotunda at street level. It was only a 100-square-foot

space, much smaller than Walton Street, but it was 'a land grab' that we would maximise. In the year it took for the deal to be finalised, though, we had some serious work to do to put us on the radar of the American consumer before launching.

Through a PR agency, we secured some great coverage in *Vogue, Harper's*, and *Town & Country*, but we were acutely aware that a few well-placed articles — even my favourite one, calling me 'The Wolfgang Puck of Fragrance' — were never going to trigger sufficient demand when we were essentially coming from a standing start. Unlike London, and outside of the Oprah fan base, we didn't have a pre-established client base or any word-of-mouth wildfire burning. Very quickly, we realised that we had to get product into people's hands — 'seeding'.

Via my network of clients and friends in London, I had about fifty names of people in the fields of entertainment, business and politics on the East Coast, so I spent one evening writing to and calling each of them. I offered ten or twenty bags of product and asked if they would be willing to give them to friends as hostess gifts or birthday presents. Each person I approached agreed to help. Fifty 'influencers' distributing product among their social circles was a subtle way of getting our brand talked about. I hadn't forgotten how clients in London had placed bulk orders for corporate events and dinner parties, leading to an influx of new customers — and that was the kind of seeding we were looking to replicate, albeit less organically.

Another plank we laid, with the help of our friend Susan McCone, was a trunk show held at her shop Jonal and Co. in Madison Avenue. Today, Susan is a reverend who runs a church in Connecticut but, back then, she was a fashion designer. She promoted the event and I pitched up with a trunk filled with product — the equivalent of a pop-up today — and I sold out after a week. Long before our gift bags started walking out of Bergdorf

Goodman, they were walking out of a little shop in the Upper East Side.

The next thing we did was wow the media, but not with a press conference or a lunch with me. A fancy restaurant and quotes wouldn't have impact; the clincher would be the product. Our shop assistant Vicky Martin flew over for this mission and I struck a deal with the New York Palace to book a two-bedroom suite in exchange for some positive PR and product. From that hotel on Madison, and over a five-day period, I greeted and spritzed around sixty journalists. As I familiarised them with the collection, I shared the story behind each fragrance: how it was made, what memories inspired it, and what each ingredient is meant to express. For a select few, I went further and conducted a full facial. Among those 'clients' was Pamela Fiori, the editor-in-chief at *Town & Country*. Pamela, a woman of effortless style, was someone I would come to know well, and she was a great support, then and in the future, raving about my fragrances . . . and my facials. *'I was given a treatment by Jo and felt as if I were in a trance for several hours afterward. And my skin looked years younger. In fact, I felt years younger,'* she wrote.

Our good press, and our concerted push, would continue for a good year, through to the following Christmas, and I think that was when Gary came to understand the exhausting nature of this groundwork.

We had booked into The Carlyle, which I chose deliberately because this kind of discreet, sophisticated hotel was exactly the kind of place where a Bergdorf customer would stay, and I agreed a deal with management that everyone in residence would receive a product-filled Christmas stocking.

'How many are we doing?' Gary asked as I collected our room keys.

'Only four hundred and fifty.'

'FOUR HUNDRED AND FIFTY?!'

'Not as many as Santa has to do!'

We became busy elves that December of 1997 – one fragrance, one bath oil, one candle per stocking. But the morning after checking in, I heard from Queen Noor, a long-standing client who often visited London, that her husband, King Hussein, was sick. This wonderfully big-hearted man had become a dear friend along with his wife. She explained to me how he had been admitted to a clinic in Minnesota, and she invited me to go see him, so I dropped everything, caught a plane, and left Gary with the Christmas stockings.

I returned late that night and walked into our room to find him supine across the bed, barely able to open his eyes. He didn't even lift his head when he heard the door go, but he did say, 'I did them all . . . never again.' Everywhere I looked, on the bed, on the chairs, on the floor, were filled stockings. I don't think Gary had ever been so pleased to return to London. Sowing such seeds can be a slog; it requires graft and patience, and there's no real way of knowing how effective it will be, but we could do no more. We could only hope that all these different efforts would come together and translate into demand for our March 1998 launch.

We were raring to go by the time the big day arrived. Gary, Vicky and I returned to New York two days ahead of time to single-handedly stock the shelves within our little rotunda. We didn't stock our entire line in New York – we started with six of the fourteen fragrances, together with bath oils, scented candles and a skincare range. And this time, we waited for the paint to dry!

I answered any last-minute questions from the four American staff we had trained up during previous visits and we went on to enjoy a brisk day's trading, leaving us feeling hopeful but realistic about the way ahead. We were under no illusions that we had entered a fiercely competitive market, because the industry itself was experiencing a challenging time. As a write-up in *Women's Wear Daily* made clear at the time, 'When it comes to the fragrance business these days, the sweet smell of success isn't wafting over all department and speciality stores.'

On the night of the launch, I don't think anyone was looking too far ahead. But Dawn Mello pulled out the stops to celebrate our in-store arrival, hosting an amazing black-tie dinner for two hundred guests, including some of our British friends who had flown in. The venue was The Galleria building, a fifty-five-storey high-rise between Lexington and Park Avenue, and the moment we stepped foot inside its glassed entrance, into the vast atrium, we sensed the setting was going to be impressive. We took the lift to the Sky Room on the 54th floor and walked out into a restaurant with an all-glass exterior that offered 360 degrees of a twinkling Manhattan. All around the room, skirting the floor and on the tables, there were dozens of candles. Dawn hadn't overlooked a single detail, even down to the bespoke menu of my favourite foods, including the yummiest of them all: soufflé.

And when the sheepish-looking maitre d' explained that there had been a power failure in the kitchen – putting that very dessert course at risk – Dawn was not to be thwarted. 'Here, take my keys. Go downstairs and use my kitchen,' she said. 'We shall deliver Jo's soufflés!'

She allowed the chefs to use her private apartment in the same building, meaning a troop of servers ran up and down the back stairs carrying plates. I liked Dawn – a woman who always had a solution to a problem. She delivered the soufflés, and our presence in her store would put us on the map in America, adding rocket fuel to our seeding.

Every three months, I'd return to New York, sustaining a promotional push with in-store appearances. One Christmas, more than one hundred women lined up, which definitely felt like a breakthrough moment. And so I grew used to the transatlantic back and forth, and my body clock learned to adjust to the endless 'red-eye' flights.

The switching between time zones also taught me to be flexible within our new topsy-turvy lifestyle: days in London may have ended at 5 p.m., but New York still had five hours to go, so we would often find ourselves on the phone until 10 p.m. In reverse, when in Manhattan, we'd be up at dawn dealing with matters back home. That's when I taught myself three things about constant air travel: set your watch to the time zone you are travelling to; eat to that timetable on the plane; and always have a pre-flight face mask to keep the skin hydrated.

One thing we soon discovered about our American consumers was that bath oils weren't popular. As one New Yorker told me, 'You Brits bathe; we Americans shower.' But, bath oils aside, early indications at the end of our first quarter were encouraging as Bergdorf reported a double-digit increase in the fragrance market 'and part of that boost can be attributed to interest in London perfumer Jo Malone', said a report in *Women's Wear Daily*.

Gary, quite rightly, wanted us to keep our foot on 'the gas'. One evening in New York after closing, we were about to head back to our hotel when he took out three of our gift bags and handed them to me ... without slotting them into a Bergdorf bag.

'What are you doing? They're empty!'

'Nobody else knows that,' he said, with a wink.

My husband never does miss a trick. He had fought damn hard for those to be seen all over town, and, in those early days, we had to be flag-bearers, too. So every time we set foot on a Manhattan street, carrying those bags became as necessary as an umbrella in

London. Only Gary didn't call this 'seeding', he called it 'walking the dogs'.

New York is a go-getting city full of make-it-happen people, and the fashion and beauty industry is not necessarily for the faint-hearted. It is a fast-moving environment where the pursuit of excellence has never involved easy roads, and the standards and expectations can be fierce. But, at a time when we were finding our feet, Gary and I were lucky to be given time with some of the leading players in retail. Dawn Mello and her team were as helpful and down-to-earth as they come, but another gem was Rose Marie Bravo, then the president of Saks Fifth Avenue, who helped steer us through the unknown quantities of the vast American marketplace.

Gary and I might as well have been Lewis and Clark, the explorers Thomas Jefferson sent out to discover how far west America stretched beyond Mississippi. The size of the continent represented a daunting challenge for us – we didn't understand the diverse characteristics of each state. New York was a world away from Florida. Texas was a different planet to California. And we had no idea how to build on our success and reach the Pacific Ocean. Rose Marie was the one who literally got out the map and showed us the way.

We had received an invitation out of the blue to meet up at her offices at Saks. We didn't know the purpose of the meeting but you don't ask why when you get a call from such a respected figure in the industry; you just go. When we walked into her office, we realised that she was a fan of our brand – hundreds of our gift bags, filled with product, were huddled in one corner, waiting to be given as presents to friends and staff.

'You've got more inventory in here than I've got back in London!' I said.

Rose Marie, a natural, olive-skinned beauty thanks to her Italian blood, laughed at my observation, flashing a set of pearly white teeth that matched her signature pearl-drop earrings. 'Well,' she said, 'that's why I want to talk to you. I want to see how we can do more with your product throughout the United States.'

Over the next hour, we would receive the benefit of her golden insight, explaining where all the 'critical locations' were around America, and what made them so different. She knew the market from east to west, having previously been chairman at both Macy's in New York and I. Magnin in San Francisco. She had started out in 1974 as a sales manager in cosmetics and fragrances at Macy's; more recently, she had built Saks' fashion and fragrance lines, so the advice she imparted was invaluable.

I had to leave for another meeting, but I left Gary to continue the geographical plotting, and he later shared with me how Rose Marie rolled out a map of the US on the floor, got down on her hands and knees and stabbed her finger at the cities where we would need a presence in order to grow: Chicago, San Francisco, Los Angeles, and Dallas.

Gary was blown away because, until then, he hadn't been able to picture the way forward and his surveyor-trained mind needed to see some kind of architectural drawing. Afterwards, as he and I enjoyed a hot chocolate back at the hotel, he kept shaking his head. 'I cannot believe how lucky we are ... these people ... I mean ...'

There we were, two green kids from Kent, fresh from a meeting with a genius of a woman who had decided to guide us, despite being one of the busiest people in Manhattan. Of course, she did so in the hope that we would link up with Saks one day, but she certainly didn't have to help us plot the way ahead like she did. This was one of many wonderful moments we'd share with Rose Marie, and she would soon take over the helm at Burberry, mastermind its rebirth, and discover the talent of designer Christopher Bailey, the Yorkshireman who would go on to be the brand's CEO.

We found a friend for life that day in New York. And when she moved to London to join Burberry, we were able to show her the way in our home city. Or, as she once put it, 'You were my first call and first friends in London!'

Dawn Mello and Rose Marie Bravo played pivotal roles in our growth across America, but there was also another major player waiting in the wings, someone we had been talking to for quite some time, as he monitored our growth and bided his time. But that relationship was still developing in the background, and it would be a little while longer before that interest led anywhere.

As an employer, it is important to me that work doesn't feel like one constant grind of graft, graft, graft. Whenever small victories happen for any entrepreneur – hitting a weekly sales target, or setting a new quarterly sales high, or reaching a milestone that once seemed out of reach – we should step off the treadmill and take time to acknowledge the partners or personnel who have played a part in that accomplishment. The team that surrounds us is the team that will determine what levels of success are reached. I expect a lot from my staff because you do not succeed in the luxury goods industry if there is an ounce of complacency. By 'complacency', I mean not accepting one brilliant day in sales as anything other than ordinary, because *every day* needs to be brilliant. And once you hit consistently brilliant days, the question then has to be, 'How can we make it better?' That's why I need people whose work ethic and standards mirror mine because, where there is synergy, there is often success.

Since recording that encouraging first quarter in America, we had not had a chance to celebrate properly as a team, so I threw a party at the Nicole Farhi store in Bond Street, where we had the downstairs restaurant to ourselves, free to let our hair down with some good food, a good DJ, and have a good old knees-up.

It seemed fitting then that this turned out to be the Friday night when I received a phone call on my mobile from across the pond. It was some time around 11 p.m. when I nipped out to speak with Vicki Haupt.

When I returned to the room ten minutes later, my assistant Cherie said she knew it was good news judging by the smile on my face. I walked over to the DJ and asked him to turn down the music, because I had an announcement to make. I took the mic, gathered everyone together and said, 'I'm glad we're all here to share this moment because I've had some news from New York – we've just hit our first million dollars in America!'

I swear that our screams and cheers would've been heard across London. What a high that was, and how wonderful to mark that milestone as a team. We ordered champagne and I asked the DJ to play *New York, New York*! And in that moment, as we gathered in a circle, linked arms and sang our hearts out, I think everyone in that room believed that if we could make it there, we could make it anywhere.

As time zipped through 1998 and into 1999, we had to turn our attention to new premises in London. Our five-year lease in Walton Street was almost up, and the landlord had other plans for the unit – it was the nudge that we needed. I was sad in a sentimental sense – we were leaving a shop full of memories and a street full of good people – but the business was crying out for more space. If our time in America had taught us anything, it was that we had to step up and think bigger.

Whenever Gary scouted for a new location from this point on, he wouldn't go anywhere without a clicker-counter. He'd tuck this golf ball-sized gadget into the palm of his hand, stand outside a shop, and each time someone walked by, he'd press the button with his thumb, standing in one spot for hours, monitoring foot traffic to ensure the street was consistently busy. By the time he presented me with a property brochure, I knew that he would have done the necessary homework and research. But still, I wasn't expecting him to turn up with an address in Sloane Street.

The two-storey unit at No.150, then Sketchley's cleaners, was nearer Sloane Square than 'the cool part' of the street – the Harvey Nichols end – but that hardly mattered. Why shouldn't we be the first luxury name on the block? Lure the chic crowd from one end to the other? The likes of Tiffany's, Cartier, and Chloé had not yet arrived, but the Peter Jones store at the end of the King's Road was within spitting distance, and Gary's clicker-count was impressive. The foot traffic alone offered potential, not to mention the loyal customers who would follow.

But the feature that sealed it for me wasn't the 2,500 square feet over two floors, or the fact that we had a basement to convert into a small boardroom, staff dining room, and kitchen. No, the clincher was the back stockroom and office, because, in my mind, I was already knocking down walls and turning it into a luxurious treatment room.

For the refit, we hired a Canadian called Steven Horn, who is like the brother I never had. We had got to know him when he booked our holidays while working as a travel agent. In him, we saw a hard worker who was super-organised and, as became clear in our conversations, had a passion for design. So we appointed him to be our operations manager, and Sloane Street would be his first project.

The great thing about Steven is that he moves hell and high water to get the job done, and I'll never forget the morning I dropped in to check on progress, only to find his twelve builders asleep on racks and shelves with bubble wrap used as pillows because they had worked until four in the morning. He drove them almost as hard as I drove Sophie and Emma, the two girls I trained up to be our full-time facialists.

I'm sure those poor girls went to bed most nights with my voice ringing in their ears: 'No, not like that, like this!' And when they couldn't get it right, I fell back on my own training. 'Right,' I said, 'we're doing this with our eyes shut. Close your eyes! It needs to be instinctual, not visual. Okay, let's start again . . .'

In the end, it proved time well spent, because my girls would, in my opinion, go on to provide the best service in London. And Steven created a luxurious treatment room: low lights, log fire, and candles, where clients would be cosseted and wrapped in white blankets and white cashmere, spritzed with fragrance, and massaged from head to toe.

The rest of the premises were coming along nicely, too, but there was only one snag: as much as Steven's team worked around the clock, he informed us that there would be a ten-day gap between Walton Street closing and Sloane Street opening.

'That's it, then,' said Gary. 'We can't trade – nothing we can do.'

'We can't go *ten days* without selling anything, Gary!' I said.

'What choice do we have? The shop isn't going to be ready!'

'What choice do we have?' He was talking to a girl who once worked on the markets. 'I know exactly what we're going to do,' I said. 'Steven, come with me. I need help with a table from the flat . . .'

I don't care if you're standing at Crayford market or in Sloane Street, a merchant is a merchant who cannot allow the chance of a sale to slip by. I had watched my dad set up a stall even when he didn't really want to. I had watched him think on his feet, which is what every entrepreneur must do, and that had stayed with me. Each day of business, then and now, I wake up feeling the chase within me. *What can I do to make it happen today?* And that was the voice that made me set up a wooden trestle table – my stall – on the pavement, manned by shop assistants-turned-market traders, Vicky and Lorna. Gary was dead against it, saying we'd get into trouble and that 'this was not how a luxury brand should operate'. I gently pointed out that luxury brands operate by making money. 'And that is what we are going to do – you'll see!'

Vicky foresaw only one problem with my plan. 'We haven't got any product, Jo. What happens if someone wants to smell a fragrance?'

'You tell them stories: how I made it, what inspired me, what the fragrance is meant to conjure.' *Dad, standing at the stall, telling the tale of the clipper he'd painted, describing its history and the voyage it was embarking on.* 'Stories have the power to connect, so let's tell the story behind the product.'

Without a website and because our phone lines weren't yet connected, we had to think of a way of diverting our customers from Walton Street. We hadn't put up any 'we are moving' notices at the old shop, so we knew they would still head there. We decided to arrange a chauffeur service, hiring four cars and four drivers, to pick up each customer, ferry them to Sloane Street and back, and then deliver the orders later. As I pointed out to Gary, if a chauffeur-driven car doesn't equate to luxury, I don't know what does.

His initial embarrassment over this impromptu street trading soon fell away when he realised we were earning almost the same as we would have done in the shop. To any passers-by, it probably looked like we were signing people up or taking names for a petition; certainly, no one complained and we didn't receive a visit from the council.

I don't think Vicky and Lorna ever expected to be so busy as they stood there, day in, day out, taking orders. Out of all the memories that we'd amass in our new premises, I don't think anything topped those ten days when our makeshift market stall in Sloane Street turned out to be our first triumph.

The shop opened in September 1999, complete with limestone floor and shelves in bays along the walls. And there was one innovative touch that we had been keeping under wraps – 'scent booths'. Not dissimilar to a bank of telephone booths in a luxury hotel, they had touch screens allowing customers to select any kind of note they desired. Each selected category brought up a list of my fragrances; with one press of a tab, a vent released a quick spritz of that scent.

I was probably more excited by this addition than the customers but, naturally, not everything would go smoothly. Four days after opening, I discovered that none of the screens worked – the vents only released shots of air, minus the scent. Clearly, no one had dared tell me or, worse still, no one had noticed! Every customer up until that point had selected their scent and walked away saying, 'Oh, I love it! Oh, it's wonderful!'

'Well, they're still buying the fragrances!' Vicky pointed out.

I'm pleased to say that we fixed the technical hitch and the 'scent booths' were a great success. Free 'Fresh Air by Jo Malone' would be available for a limited time only.

Unlike Walton Street, we wanted to announce our arrival in style – you don't arrive at either end of Sloane Street with a whimper. We hired a lighting guru called Charlie Fisher who brought pizzazz to any event, and pizzazz was what he provided, beaming a projection of 'JO MALONE' not only on to the pavement but high into the sky.

We threw a cocktail party for three hundred guests, inviting every loyal client, friend and supplier who had supported us since the beginning. Of all the riches that success can bring, nothing is greater than the riches of friendship, and I think that's why that night felt so important – it was our 'thank you' to so many.

One special 'thank you' was reserved for Steven Horn, who had created a shop worthy of flagship status. Without his craft and guidance, I honestly don't know where we'd be, so, before anyone else arrived, the three of us disappeared to the boardroom downstairs, leaving our maestro of catering, Johnny Roxburgh, of The Admiral Crichton event planners, in charge.

Behind closed doors, and with a few teary words, we presented him with an engraved Cartier watch to commemorate the occasion. Meanwhile, as we heard the footsteps of guests on the shop floor, Johnny's shrill voice started telling us to hurry up.

I went to the door and pulled the handle. Locked. *Wait, did I lock it? No, I didn't lock it.* Gary tried, thinking I was being weak. It was when Steven couldn't open the door either that we realised it had jammed. Johnny was by now outside, wondering what was taking us so long.

'JO! JO!'

'JOHNNY! JOHNNY! We're trapped in here!'

I could have taken the Cartier watch off Steven and gifted it to Johnny when he got us out of there, using a hammer and a screwdriver to jemmy the door.

Gary said the night felt like the big wedding celebration we'd never had as kids. And it did. I felt such overwhelming love and gratitude for every single person in the room, but what none of them knew was how much was shifting behind the scenes, and the secret that Gary and I had been harbouring for almost four years.

As we opened Sloane Street, our business was growing faster than we could accommodate, galloping at such a rate I didn't know how we would keep up. There had been days when I worried about finding ourselves in a place where we'd be out of our depth. We had built the great ship *Jo Malone* and steered her into waters we didn't think were possible, but now we needed a new crew and fresh navigation to help us set sail around the world.

And so, in October 1999, we made an announcement that nobody saw coming.

We'd sold the company to Estée Lauder.

EIGHTEEN

Informal discussions had actually been taking place in the background since 1995, twelve months after opening Walton Street and before Bergdorf Goodman's approach. We hadn't told a soul because Estée Lauder had recently become a public company, so confidentiality was imperative. And, as someone who likes to keep her cards close to her chest until there is something to say, that suited me, too.

One journalist would later note that the cosmetic titan entered our lives under the radar, 'slowly but quietly' – and that aptly describes the tempo of our unhurried dance as they courted us and we weighed their intentions, long before active negotiations began.

Acquisitions are a bit like marriages: regardless of the instant attraction, you need to think with your head as well as the heart. You need to feel a synergy and you need to trust the other party implicitly, because the union is supposed to be for better, for worse, for richer, for poorer, in sickness and in health. Estée Lauder looked attractive and promised an exciting future, but Gary and I were in no mood to rush in; we wanted to explore every detail to the nth degree, which was why, with everything else going on, it turned into such an elongated process.

Our dance had started as most interactions do – with a business card.

Four suited executives entered the shop towards the end of business one day in the winter of 1995. One of them, a tall, bespectacled, grey-haired gentleman, did all the talking but didn't exactly make the purpose of his visit explicit. They, too, were checking us out, placing a toe in the water. The most he said was how they had been watching our growth with interest, and how they would be 'interested in having a conversation at your convenience'. With that, he slid his business card, face down, across the desk.

I didn't turn it over in front of him. After all, this wasn't the first confident suit that had wandered in – we'd had buyers and venture capitalists in before, not to mention the mystery man with the million-dollar offer on day one. But once they had left, I looked at the card: *Bob Nielsen, Head of Prescriptives Division, Estée Lauder Corporation*.

My heart went *boomph!*

I rang Gary. The next day, he made the phone call. Within a week or two, Bob returned with another of the executives from that first visit – Pamela Baxter. When you think of the humanness behind a corporation, you think of someone like Pamela, a bob-haired, Coco Chanel look-a-like, who I loved the second we were introduced. She had recently overseen the launch of two Tommy Hilfiger fragrances – *Tommy* and *Tommy Girl* – so it was clear that Lauder was exploring different avenues in fragrance. I assumed Walton Street to be one such avenue, but both Pamela and Bob, and various other executives who came through our doors over the coming months, never went beyond expressing an interest in 'ways we could work together'. They made all the right noises but we remained none the wiser. Did they want to invest? Were they going to ask me to collaborate on a new fragrance? Or was this a buyout?' 'However we fit into this whole equation,' Gary told me one night, 'we aren't rushing in feet first. Remember, they have come knocking on our door, not the other way round.'

Ultimately, Lauder's team extended an invitation to visit their headquarters in New York. We flew in on 6 January 1996, to be greeted by the beginnings of a blizzard as a record nor'easter dumped two feet of snow. Our flight was the last one to land before all airports closed. As our car crawled its way from JFK into Manhattan, all I could think about was the magazine article I had read on the plane as we came in to land: an interview with Bobbi Brown, talking about her brand after selling to Estée Lauder the year before. In the quotes attributed to her, she mentioned how 'incredible' her experience had been with such a 'phenomenal partner', and how it was leading to steady growth overseas. I knew that this was our flashforward, as seen through another's eyes.

By nightfall, New York City had virtually ground to a halt, in unison with the rest of a paralysed East Coast. More than twenty inches of snow fell, whipped up by wind into deep drifts. Buses didn't run, the subway stuttered to a halt, and the only thing moving along Madison Avenue was the odd pedestrian skier. But our meeting at Estée Lauder would go ahead. In the face of a storm, it was business as usual, which I suppose was an encouraging sign.

Our welcome couldn't have been warmer inside the General Motors Building, on Fifth Avenue, almost opposite Bergdorf Goodman. In the boardroom, about twelve smiling faces had gathered, making us feel like visiting dignitaries. Bob Nielsen joked that he was glad to see 'a little bit of light snow' hadn't stopped us. I reminded him that it takes a lot to deter weather-hardened Brits. That opening gambit sums up the tone of the relaxed exchanges throughout the day, though some soft balls were lobbed into our court: did you really start this from your kitchen? What are your inspirations? What do you think makes you so different? How have you found your first year in retail? Without a doubt, we were being vetted as well as wooed. But still, no one fleshed out 'the ways' we could work together. It seems that was being left for another time, one year down the road, when we would finally get to the meet the king of the industry himself.

We met the ebullient Leonard Lauder at his penthouse apartment in the Upper East Side. A breakfast meeting, over eggs, smoked fish and toast, illustrates how relaxed everything was. By now, we assumed he had received every ounce of feedback from the executives who had visited the shop and seen our Saturday queues for themselves. So the fact we were sitting there, in his home, told us something.

What was instantly obvious from the way he spoke was his love for the industry; he talked about it with the passion of youth, not a man of sixty-two, and I knew there and then that there was something special about him. He understood the entrepreneurial spirit, having witnessed his mother build her eponymous company in 1946. This background perhaps explains why Leonard, the one-time delivery boy turned CEO, seemed to understand so much of our journey. Few people we'd met had understood the challenges involved, but he knew what it took to find your voice, build a brand, and keep evolving. He also reminded me of my dad in many ways: the charm, the pristine suit, the storyteller and, as we would discover in the coming months and years, the consistently engaging company.

Looking back, if ever there was a moment when I thought, 'This is where I'll feel safe', then it was at that breakfast meeting. And yet, however relaxed we were in each other's company, we still skirted around the edges as two noncommittal parties sounding each other out, exploring boundaries, playing the long game.

We wouldn't meet again for another few months, this time in London on Grand National Day, at the Mirabelle restaurant in Mayfair.

In the cab, I was incredibly nervous, suddenly worried at the prospect of someone spotting us with Leonard. We were nowhere near the stage of active negotiations but the situation felt so secretive, and so loaded with possibility, that I felt twitchy. 'Relax!' said Gary for the umpteenth time. 'No one's going to see us and, even if they did, they wouldn't twig.'

As we took our seats, Leonard's calm demeanour soon put me at ease, and we continued from where we had left off in New York, although the conversation centred on our product lines and vision and what we foresaw for the business. There was clearly a desire to move the dialogue along to a more formal footing.

Before coffees arrived, I excused myself to go to the bathroom. My head was spinning. Everything Leonard said made me foresee a deal that would send our brand not only around America but around the world. As slowly as the wheels were turning, I felt the promise of such an enormous opportunity and it was a lot to process, so I took a few moments to gather myself before heading back.

As I walked out of the ladies, I heard a familiar woman's voice. 'Jo!'

Oh God, no. I turned around to find a journalist friend heading my way.

'Fancy seeing you here!' she said. 'Who are you having lunch with?'

I panicked. And when I panic, convincing white lies are the last things that come to mind. 'Oh, that's my uncle! My uncle from Ireland, he's a horse trainer . . .'

'Ohhhh,' she said, with mock surprise. 'How odd that he's sitting here with you on today of all days – Grand National Day.'

As I scrambled for another desperate lie, she moved quickly to save me from further embarrassment. 'Jo! I know exactly who that is!' she smiled. 'Good running into you. Enjoy your lunch.'

Rumbled. Well and truly rumbled. I hurried back to the table, terrified that our secret was out. 'Leonard! Leonard! A journalist has spotted us. And I told her you were an Irish horse trainer!'

He and Gary couldn't stop laughing, which at least made me feel better because I honestly thought the cat was out of the bag. As it was, I fretted about nothing because the journalist had the decency not to print a word, not even a social gossip piece. Indeed, we managed to keep all our future meetings, which were held primarily in New York, under wraps. As time marched on into 1997, our deal with Bergdorf Goodman actually helped provide the perfect cover for our regular presence in Manhattan.

The more due diligence we did, and the more we discovered about Estée Lauder – from their team and members of the work- force – the more sure I became about the fit. We were introduced to Leonard's wife, Evelyn, who was beautiful, smart, funny, and able to put her finger on any issue at hand. In meeting her, I real- ised that we shared the same kind of values, both in business and in family, and another part of the jigsaw fell into place.

There were many nights when Gary and I tossed and turned, throwing around the pros and cons of an acquisition. The heart said 'yes' but the head pondered whether we'd be swallowed whole and lose control of everything we had built. Change was inevitable but releasing my grip on the reins wasn't proving so easy to do. I wanted everything to change, and everything to stay the same. I think what eventually convinced us to enter into active negotiations were the assurances from Leonard and others that 'staying the same' was exactly what would happen, and that

I'd retain control. John Larkin, their financial director, and one of the team we trusted and loved the most, assured us from day one that, 'We will keep everything as it is – you'll carry on what you've been doing.'

It seems amazing to me now that our dance with Estée Lauder went on for a good couple of years before negotiations even began, sometime around mid-1998. And it would then be a further year before a deal was struck. In that time, and because we had no experience of global organisations and global deals, Gary and I had sounded out many friends who worked at that level, and Ron Dennis was chief among them. He knows as much about the mechanics of deal-making as he does about Formula 1 and we came to rely on his wise counsel.

By this stage, our business had grown into a far more appealing prospect, with the success of Bergdorf Goodman. In addition, we opened three more shop-in-shop units: at Holt Renfrew, Toronto; and at Saks Fifth Avenue in Chicago and Troy, Michigan. Overall, we were in a far stronger negotiating position than when Bob Nielsen first walked into our shop.

Gary and I stepped back at that point and left it to the merger-and-acquisitions professionals: our lawyer and lifelong friend Jeremy Courtenay-Stamp, who brought in deal-maker extraordinaire Peter Hansen. People have long been intrigued about the deal we struck but what goes on in the negotiating room should be treated the same as that which goes on in the treatment room – it should stay behind closed doors.

There would be many clauses, technicalities and points to wade through but, for me, four points were important: that I retained creative control; that my loyal team were kept on; that we built the business with Lauder within a shared vision; and that the financial terms were worth it. As Gary said, 'They're not just buying stock on the shelves and a shop on the street, they're buying your expertise and the future of the business which exists in your head.'

I've never revealed how much money was involved and I don't intend to now, suffice it to say that it was not as much as some reports speculated but it was more than some had predicted.

By the time the paperwork was ready to sign, we were already scheduled to be at the Holt Renfrew store in Toronto, where I was doing a personal appearance. So we spent the weekend in Canada before flying to New York to execute the deal on a Monday morning, at 9 a.m. sharp, in front of a phalanx of lawyers in a huge corner room of a law firm inside the General Motors Building, several floors below Estée Lauder. The news was publicly announced on 25 October 1999.

Much would change further down the line – circumstances that I couldn't foresee as we approached a new millennium – but I couldn't have been more delighted at the time, as my published quotes from the time reveal: *'I'm a very happy woman . . . I feel like a weight has been lifted and I am free to be creative again . . . I want to push the boundaries of this industry and make a difference in cosmetics and fragrances. I was reluctant to sell until I met Leonard. He's an entrepreneur and a real kindred spirit. I know my business is safe in his hands.'*

The morning after we'd signed the papers, I went for a quiet stroll around Central Park, wanting to be alone with my thoughts. It's important for my well-being that I can step out of the city and into green, open space where I can feel grounded amid nature and collect myself, especially after such an intense period. As I crossed Madison Avenue towards the park, all I could smell was chestnuts – a smell that I'll forever associate with the Big Apple.

I strolled through the park and headed to Bow Bridge where I stood at the centre of its hump, overlooking the lake. The sun was out and the wind was up, whipping across the water's surface. I'm sure it wasn't the case but it felt as if there was no one else around as I disappeared into my own zone, taking stock of what had just happened. I thought of Mum and Dad and wished that things could be different; that they could have been sharing this moment instead of being at arm's length. Whatever had gone on between Mum and me couldn't diminish the fact that only she could have known what it meant to be joining forces with Estée Lauder because, at one stage in our lives, Madame Lubatti was *our* Estée Lauder. I didn't want to call her up and say, 'Look what I've done . . . look at me.' I wanted to call her up and feel her pride in me. I stood atop the highest mountain and realised that I had spent my whole life longing to hear Mum and Dad say how well I had done. Who knows, maybe that is *precisely* the reason why I was there.

The wind started to chill the back of my neck. Winter was on its way, and I smiled. I remembered me as a little girl, standing at my frosted window, not wanting to feel the cold and vowing never to live in struggle ever, ever again. And now, there I was, in a position where I would never have to worry about money again. I felt a huge swell of emotion, not only because I felt gratitude and happiness but because I felt my own pride in that little girl who had never given up on her dream – and maybe, in the end, that's the only pride worth chasing.

NINETEEN

L eonard Lauder's credo is that they are not a family business, but a family *in* business. This theme of 'family' was a golden thread that ran through the philosophy I heard in private, and the talks he gave in public. As chairman, he never lost sight of the fact that he was once his mother's delivery boy. He also knew the value of people at the grass-roots level of any company, and that was why he, not an executive, flew to England to meet our staff and put them at ease about the future, wanting them to know that they still worked for Jo Malone London but were now also regarded as part of the family. I thought it spoke volumes about the man.

On the morning he arrived, I, too, wanted to provide a personal touch – bacon sandwiches and mugs of tea for everyone, including Steven Horn, who wanted to walk Leonard through the interior design. Our twenty-odd employees convened on the shop floor and Leonard, sartorially immaculate as ever, stood in front of the counter, thanked everyone for being there, and was about to commence his speech when the fire alarms started screeching. The bacon sizzling in the confined kitchen was giving off too much smoke.

Steven and I darted downstairs and, by wafting arms and tea towels, we managed to kill the alarm. We returned upstairs. 'Sorry, Mr Lauder!'

'Don't you worry, Jo. So, as I was saying—'

But the alarms erupted again.

Everyone laughed uncomfortably. Leonard smiled politely. And Steven and I rushed back down again. 'You begin, Leonard!' And so the CEO and chairman delivered a speech that I didn't get to hear because I was running around like a headless chicken, constantly wafting tea towels to prevent another rude interruption. When I heard applause, we returned upstairs only to be greeted by the sight of two fire brigade trucks rolling up outside, blue lights flashing. That was when I realised that our smoke detectors were monitored through the burglar alarm system. 'Never a dull moment, is there?' said Leonard.

'Welcome to my world!'

Estée Lauder acquired our business because, like us, they saw the potential for global development. But the wonderful thing about the transformation that would follow was how little it changed the essence of who we were. As promised. That was the beauty of what Lauder did at the time: they bought the DNA of an entrepreneur and the only tinkering that took place was to engineer a growth spurt that improved distribution, made the brand more visible, and prepared us for the world stage.

Leonard didn't wish to change the way I worked personally, either. He recognised the individuality that had created my line of fragrances and so I was given the space to develop more with my chosen perfumers. I don't think I could have felt happier. As I told one reporter in 2002: 'The Lauders have allowed me not just to continue to be who I am, but they've given me the rein to be more than I ever thought I could be.'

Together, we put into action a five-year strategy, covering brand, tone, voice, finances, and projecting our growth through to 2005 – where the new domestic stores would be, what international presence we would have, and how we would build a website. Online and in-store, they wanted to take my concept of storytelling – the stories behind each fragrance – and use it store by store, country by country. Now, the inspirations I had shared with customers in Walton Street and Sloane Street would be written up and used as part of the worldwide marketing.

Gradually, year on year, we would see our small business grow rapidly into its own empire. Domestically, we would open in the Royal Exchange and Brook Street in London, followed by Edinburgh, Leeds, Glasgow, and Guildford; and then, via shop-in-shops in Europe, in Paris, Dublin, and Munich. In America, we would launch in Boston, Boca Raton, San Francisco, and Los Angeles via Saks of Fifth Avenue, and then Atlanta, Palm Beach, Houston and Dallas via another department store, Neiman Marcus. In February 2001, we would finally achieve our first free-standing site in New York, inside the Flatiron Building on Broadway at 23rd. And after that, we would push east to the other side of the world: Sydney, Australia; Tokyo, Japan; and, of course, 'The Fragrant Harbour' of Hong Kong.

This was the rocket fuel that Leonard had promised during our initial talks. 'I know you can do this on your own,' he said, 'but we can make it happen faster.'

Whichever new shop or in-store site opened, Gary and I would ensure we were there for the launch. First and foremost, I was a facialist-turned-shopkeeper. Getting lost in a corporate labyrinth wasn't me. I wanted to maintain a daily interaction with the customer. And while I couldn't be in fifty places at once, I wanted to touch base with each location as much as I could.

We'd string together mini-tours because personal appearances and bottle signings were one way of ensuring I met as many customers as possible in one burst. At home, we'd do Edinburgh-Glasgow-Dublin-Leeds. In the States, we'd do an East Coast leg (Boston-New York-Palm Beach-Boca Raton) and then the West Coast (San Francisco-Los Angeles-Dallas-Houston).

I think a few people at Lauder wondered if Gary and I would eventually flag from the travelling, but how can you get tired of your own magic carpet ride? All these amazing things kept happening that we couldn't quite believe were actually happening. I was doing the very thing I loved on a scale that I could never have dreamed of.

We also started noticing a difference in how we were treated: when dining at restaurants, management started referring to me as 'Miss Malone', and courses would arrive 'compliments of the chef'; when checking in at hotels, we were automatically upgraded from an ordinary room to a suite; and when boarding aeroplanes, we started turning left. When you've grown up in the back of a bus, so to speak, the appreciation of these perks wasn't lost on us. Gary and I felt privileged and lucky, and took none of it for granted. I didn't feel spoiled and didn't feel that we were worthy, either. But, like Gary said, 'We've earned it so let's enjoy it.'

He and I had each other to keep ourselves anchored in reality; although there was one time when he couldn't have been blamed if his feet temporarily lifted a few inches off the ground.

We were in Tokyo, one of the most amazing, vibrant cities I have ever visited, and our hosts threw a dinner in our honour as we negotiated a deal to launch in Japan. The hilarious thing was that as we entered the private room in a restaurant, Gary was swept away to the top of the longest table by all the bigwigs, while I was left to take my place at the other end, sitting with two men who were in charge of the stockroom and boxing product. I didn't mind that. I had a great evening, talking to each of them, listening to how they had started and the passion they had for their respective jobs. But I kept a beady eye on my husband as he lapped up the attention, sitting like a king at the top table, holding court, clinking glasses and making everyone laugh. At the end of the night, one of our hosts came up to me and said: 'Jo Malone – you are married to an amazing, talented man!'

How true, I thought. Gary, standing right behind him, shrugged his shoulders and shook his head, as if to say, *'I don't even know what is happening.'* We both managed to hold our laughter until we got into the car, but I think it's fair to say that Gary loves Japan even more than I do.

The external trappings of success are all well and good – you'll never hear me moan about being able to lie flat in a bed on a transatlantic flight – but none of it changes you on the inside. For any entrepreneur, it is important to remember who you are, in the same way that you mustn't lose sight of your brand values. If you are true to yourself, and if your feet are on the ground in the first place, you can't be fooled or sucked in by the privileges, as nice as they might be.

The switch in lifestyle wasn't always easy to grow accustomed to, either. Once, when I was the guest of a client in the Far East, staying in the grounds of a royal palace, I had my own guest cottage, surrounded by the most spectacular gardens. On arrival, I was greeted by a man who I assumed was the bellboy, there to collect my luggage, but he didn't leave – it turned out he was my personal butler for the week. He couldn't have been nicer and he probably hadn't had a house guest who was so willing to muck in alongside him. I just didn't feel comfortable with him doing *everything*. It was bad enough that he stood the whole time; butlers never sit when on duty, I was told. Anyway, at the end of my first day, I bid him goodnight and went to bed. I woke around 4 a.m., feeling thirsty, so I went into the kitchen – and this kindest of gentlemen was still standing there, with a pleasing smile on his face.

'Wh-wh-what are you still doing here? Why haven't you gone home?!'

'You didn't dismiss me, ma'am.'

I was absolutely mortified, not only because the poor man was still 'on duty' but by the very notion that I had to 'dismiss' him. Unless you're in the armed services, how do you *dismiss* anyone?

'Is there anything I can do for you, ma'am?'

'Yes, you can go home and get some sleep. I'm so, so sorry!'

I didn't let him work another evening for the rest of my stay.

From the start of the millennium life became very different. The bank balance changed and the zeroes increased, but the part of the past carved into the psyche – the psyche that remembers struggle and worry – wouldn't be so easy to unknot. I thanked God more times than I can remember for how fortunate we were, but that wouldn't stop me checking my daily balance to make sure it was all there, that it wouldn't be taken away, that it wouldn't be squandered by some unknown force. The need to be responsible without being frugal would be constant. I had seen my parents be frivolous with hard-earned money and it was not a pattern I had any intention of repeating.

Ultimately, all wealth brings is the power of choice: where to sit on the plane, what holidays to experience, what fashionable clothes to buy. But it doesn't make you a better person, and it doesn't guarantee happiness. And the most important realisation for me? I'd be doing facials and fragrances even if the riches weren't there. I was one of those people who pursued a vocation and followed my passion, and that had manifested money. There are so many 'think and get rich' books out there, attempting to show entrepreneurs the way towards wealth. But, based on my experience and that of other successful people I have come across, the best advice seems to be: 'Follow your heart.' If you wake up each morning with a drive rooted in the passion of what you do, rather than a passion for the money you can make, I'd say you're on a wise path.

One bonus of our change in fortunes was the ability to help out family, whether that meant buying one relative a house or, as I did with my parents, paying off their debts. By now, Mum was living in Norfolk with Tracey, and Dad remained in Barnehurst on his own. We might hardly have had any contact in previous years, but that didn't mean I didn't care. I wanted them to be happy. Love doesn't cease just because contact stops. Our only other big expenditure was the purchase of a new home. We remained in London but moved to a beautiful, light-filled apartment. We moved because we needed more space, not only for ourselves but for our baby son – in the spring of 2000, at the age of thirty-six, I found out that I was pregnant.

I half-suspected I was expecting after being overcome with nausea within seconds of walking into the shop. The mere whiff of a candle or a fragrance made me want to throw up, and it kept happening, even with food – I couldn't keep anything down. I wish I could say that it was a mere bout of morning sickness but I had inherited the condition that Mum suffered from – hyperemesis gravidarum.

From the fifth week of the first trimester, right through to the delivery date, I was in and out of hospital. It felt like I was vomiting on the hour, every day, for eight months. Anyone who has had this condition will understand what I went through during this horrendous time: everyone else will just have to imagine having the worst hangover and food poisoning for more than two hundred days straight. I spent most of those eight months on my back because every time I stood up, I threw up. As if my poor body wasn't going through enough, I decided to cause further confusion by living on a junk diet of Mars bars, pizza and diluted cola. But instead of gaining weight, I dropped from eight and a half stone to seven stone two as I entered my third trimester. And throughout those torrid months, I was still trying to get used to the idea of becoming a mum.

As a career woman who had dedicated every waking hour to the growth and development of the business and fragrances, I had never yearned for motherhood. I can't remember ever experiencing a single pang, so I felt nervous for numerous reasons: I not only worried about my capability but also the impact on the business, my creativity, my focus. I worried about how much would change at a time when life was on such an even keel. I struggled to see where we had the room to fit in a baby. But how the head rationalises our *fear* isn't necessarily in alignment with our destiny and our capability to be parents. Our son Josh would be the single biggest achievement and blessing of our lives, even if I wouldn't realise it straightaway.

The nearer we approached my delivery date in early 2001, the more I felt scared that I wouldn't be the mum that my boy would need me to be. In all the pregnancy 'bibles', they don't tell you enough about how crazy-making the hormones can be, and how they infiltrate the mind and, sometimes, make you question who you are. They don't warn you that doubts become fears become truths become borderline insanity. Within this hormonal cocktail of irrationality, I managed to convince myself that I'd be an inadequate parent doomed to fail. Yes, Gary and I could now provide financial security, but would I be able to provide emotional stability? It is scary when, after the thrill of finding out you're pregnant, you then quickly start to dread the very thing that excited you. I felt unable to distinguish between a true thought and an insane one.

By the time I went into labour in hospital, I wanted the sickness and maddening thoughts to be over. I was physically, mentally and emotionally drained, and didn't know where I was going to find the strength to give birth. My amazing obstetrician took my hand and said, 'Together, we will do this, and you are going to give birth to a healthy, perfectly fine son.'

After twelve hours of labour, she was right – Josh Willcox was born.

And I felt nothing but emptiness.

I was spent, with nothing left to give, even when they placed him in my arms. I could see Gary's face drop as he registered my indifference, so he leaned in, scooped up Josh and did my job for me. I stared at father and son bonding instantly and thought, 'I cannot deal with this.' I turned my head away from all the expectation, wanting everyone to leave the room. Someone asked if there was anything I needed. I said, 'Yes – scrambled egg and sausage.' The moment Josh was born, the sickness ended instantly, replaced by a ravenous hunger. Scrambled eggs and sausage was all I could think about.

Later that night, attached to a drip and alone in my room, I stared at the ceiling and mapped the days ahead. I had everything worked out: I was going to go home, pack a bag, buy a ticket anywhere, divorce Gary, and go live in a city where no one would find me. I didn't want to run, I wanted to sprint. And the frightening thing? I felt completely sane while entertaining such thoughts. *I cannot be a good mother. I cannot love this child. Gary and Josh will be better off without me. Look at how they looked at each other. They don't need me . . .*

The craziness only stopped when I drifted off to sleep.

The next morning, I still felt the same.

A nurse came to see me. 'Morning, Jo! Ready to see your son?'

'No, thanks.'

She didn't react; she didn't judge. 'Okay. Would you like a cup of tea?'

'That would be great. I'd love a cup of tea.'

Five minutes later, she returned with a cuppa in one hand and, with the other, she wheeled in a Perspex, portable crib containing Josh, leaving it up against my bed.

'No, wait,' I said, 'I don't—'

Before I could say a thing, she was dashing out of the room. 'A call has come in. I'll be right back to collect him!'

The door clicked shut and I tried to ignore the presence of the day-old life beside me, but then Josh murmured. I looked to my right and there, swaddled in a white blanket, surrounded by Perspex, this tiny body wriggled and screwed up his face, all tired and sleepy. The most beautiful thing I had ever seen. I didn't know if I was capable of finding the love that such perfection deserved, but my instincts overrode my thoughts and I leaned in and picked up this almost weightless soul ... and smelled him for the first time. The most wonderful scent in the world, and the one smell that I cannot describe: the blanket, the top of his head, his cheeks, his neck. In that instant, the insanity ended and reality took hold of me. I held him to my chest and breathed him in, and I cannot begin to describe the love that engulfed me, pure waves of love, one after the other. And I wept.

I looked up to find Gary peering through the window of the door, tears streaming down his face. The nurse was alongside him, smiling – she knew exactly what she'd been doing, leaving Josh with me.

Come in, I gestured. *God, come in, I'm so sorry. I'm sorry.*

Gary rushed over and huddled into a group hug, which Josh managed to sleep through. The nurse stood at the foot of the bed. 'You can't hold him all day, you know!' she said.

'You watch me!' I said. 'I'm never going to let him go!'

Josh was worth every second of the sickness during pregnancy, and I would go through it again tomorrow, tenfold, because he is the dream son; a gift that I cannot imagine being without. As for those hormone-induced thoughts, I know my experience is not uncommon. Some women feel the joy at birth, some take a day or so, and, for some, it happens even later. But when that feeling, that attachment, that bond does click in, it feels no less intense or life-changing. Josh will forever be my greatest creation.

Within six months of being born, he joined us on the road as we opened shops across America. As I carried out personal appearances and signed bottles of fragrance, he was on my hip, stealing the show, never leaving my side.

We weren't just a family, we were now a family in business – and he would ride with us every step of the way.

TWENTY

Somebody once asked me to sum up the happy balance when motherhood meets entrepreneurship. 'Roots and wings,' I replied. 'I love the roots of family – they need to be strong, nurtured and treasured – but I also like having the wings to fly as a businesswoman and be creative.'

The arrival of Josh rooted me like nothing else. No longer could I give the business one hundred per cent of my time and attention, and no longer did I wish to. In those early days of parenthood, I read many articles about how women bosses and entrepreneurs need to 'juggle' if they are to succeed and be all things to all people: the company, the employees, the spouse, the partner, the children, the friends. I've never subscribed to that kind of thinking because I don't believe it's about 'juggling'. Only robots can be all things to all people.

Building a business had actually prepared me for motherhood more than I imagined: the long hours and fatigue, the ability to think on my feet, the disciplined time management, the need to become super-efficient, and the reality that when things go wrong, there is no room to sit and cry; you just handle it. I didn't feel the impact on the business or my creativity that I had once worried about. What actually happened was that a parallel lane opened up alongside the day job, often running at a similar pace! All I had to do was keep switching between the two.

That's why, for me, it's never been about juggling but more about a disciplined dividing of time that ensures you stay in the moment, and focused, within each lane. From day one, I accepted that there would be hours when I needed to knuckle down and concentrate on business, and there'd be more times when I needed to be 'Mum'. When making a fragrance, my focus has to be total, thought by thought, drop by drop. When with Josh, my focus is equally fierce, absorbed in every small detail and moment he provides. But I didn't try to cover both roles at the same time. When you're an untrained juggler, distractions happen and things tend to slip and go awry.

I also accepted that there was no such thing as perfection in motherhood. You simply find a way that works for you and your family, whatever the circumstances. When you've grown up in an imperfect family, the pressure to compensate can be strong, but all I ever set out to do was give my best. Motherhood isn't a product or a shop display that has to be flawless.

What matters to children is that they see your face at sports day, at parents' evenings, and at the dinner table. As Josh grew up, I didn't want to be the mum who was lost in my phone, missing moments and memories. I didn't want to be the mum who couldn't cancel meetings when he was sick, because none of us are as indispensable, or as busy, as perhaps we like to think we are, even when a company is expanding on an international level. When Josh is my age and looking back, he won't remember the smart shoes or the smartphones we bought him; he will, I hope, recall how often we were there for him, how hard we loved, and how much we nurtured, included and listened to him.

Not by any means would I find the demands of motherhood

easy, and there would be many times when I'd drop the ball. Like
the occasion when he had started school and I read an email on
the fly – a request from his headteacher asking that pupils attend
class wearing the colours of the Spanish flag. What I failed to see
was that this request was for another year. Josh's year actually had
an assembly with a local dignitary. And so there is now a photo
in our album of all the children dressed in their blazers while my
son is standing there, sticking out like a sore thumb, sporting the
colours of Spain.

I could probably tell a hundred and one stories of how stretched
things sometimes became, but I think the time that best illustrates
the challenge in those early years was the twenty-four-hour
period in Chicago in April 2002, when Josh was one and a bit
and I had a lunch date with Oprah Winfrey.

We were commencing a six-city, two-week tour of America that
had involved personal appearances and press interviews in San
Francisco, Los Angeles, Dallas, and Houston. Our first forty-
eight-hour stop was Chicago, where we had lined up a two-hour
meet-and-greet at Saks Fifth Avenue before heading on to a
British high tea for thirty select guests at the NAHA restaurant.

Josh was ready for a sleep by the time we boarded our plane
to 'the windy city', so I dressed him in pyjamas, which I always
dabbed with a dash of cologne because he learned to associate the
scent with going to sleep; he'd be out like a light. I don't know if
the use of my fragrances in this way is a handy tip, but it certainly
worked for us! The other bonus about Josh was that he never
screamed – until this flight, which was how I knew something
was wrong.

His temperature spiked and I stripped him down but he kept
burning up, wailing and vomiting. After landing in the evening,
we jumped straight in a cab to Chicago's children's hospital,

where we stayed up through the night as doctors ran tests, concerned that it might be meningitis. In the end, it was nothing but a scare – Josh had suffered a reaction to an inoculation he'd had the morning we left London. By the time we reached our hotel, it was already the next day, about 10 a.m. I looked at my bedraggled self in the mirror: dried vomit on my shoulder, dried vomit in my hair, eyes reddened through tears, and with bags under my eyes that looked sadder than a basset hound. Gary and I were effectively sleepwalking after ten fraught hours at the hospital. I then looked at my dairy: lunch with Oprah in two hours.

'Cancel it,' I told our American PR Cathy O'Brien on the phone. 'I'm not leaving Josh.'

Cathy went everywhere with us and she was a new mum, too, who brought her daughter on these mini-tours. She understood what I was going through. But, with her professional hat on, she also knew how rare lunches with Oprah were.

'Errr, Jo – you can't cancel Oprah.'

'Yes, I can.'

Since first going on her show, I had appeared for a second time, which was how this invitation to lunch at her home had come about. But I had no doubt that someone with Oprah's heart and compassion would understand the circumstances.

'You won't be able to rearrange for months; if ever,' said Cathy.

'And I won't be able to live with myself if anything happens to Josh and I'm at lunch with Oprah,' I said. 'That is why I'm not going.'

As I dug in my heels, Josh was toddling around the room, as happy as can be, one eye on his Lego, one eye on the television, and hands tucking into a plate of pancakes. There was a general chirpiness to him that might as well have said, 'Why look so worried?' His blood tests had come back clear and the doctors said he'd be fine, but I still wanted to wrap him in cotton wool and stay.

Gary stepped in. 'Look at him, he's fine. You go.'

Gary and Cathy persuaded me to release my fearful grip and jump in the shower in an attempt to make myself look at least half-presentable for the queen of American television. But that was definitely the first time I experienced what it was to be torn between maternal instinct and what the business required. It didn't help that I also felt as energised as a zombie.

'Just get through these next two hours,' I told myself; that's all you have to do. Oprah was even more amazing at lunch in her home than I thought she had been when we met on set. She wasn't 'on'; she could relax into her off-camera, private self and I found her to be disarmingly authentic and gracious. But I'll be honest, I was so dead on my feet that I struggled to be fully present. I am probably the only person in the world who has ever had lunch with Oprah and felt that they needed matchsticks to keep their eyelids open.

'Are you going to have wine?' she asked.

Oh my God, no. I'll be out for the count if I have wine!

'No, thank you,' I said. 'I'll stick with water.'

We had a lovely hour together, though I wish I could do it again properly.

Afterwards, I met Cathy in the car, where I could have lain down and crashed on the back seat. My first call was to Gary, to check on Josh. 'Is he all right? . . . Okay, great . . . I'm on my way back now.'

I looked at Cathy. She was shaking her head and biting her lip in that way that people do before they tell you something you don't want to hear.

'Jo,' she said, 'you have a tea at the British Consulate where you have to give a presentation. There are one hundred and fifty guests already waiting for you.'

If you were among those guests that afternoon, I apologise now. I don't know where I was, what I said or how incoherent

I sounded, but I was transitioning into motherhood. I hope you can understand.

If anyone knows the deft balance required between motherhood and the day job, it is women in journalism, whether they work in print or broadcasting. That profession is as relentless and demanding as entrepreneurship, with even more erratic hours. So each time I sat down to give a media interview, there was this mutual empathy – sometimes expressed, sometimes not – for what it took to build a career *and* be a mother.

One of my first interviews post-pregnancy was with a magazine journalist from America and we arranged to meet at The Lanesborough in London's Hyde Park Corner. I was shadowed by my new public relations assistant, Charlotte McCarthy, who had joined the team following the Lauder deal, bringing second-to-none PR expertise. She would become a mainstay in my life, and the shadow I couldn't be without. I think Josh could probably say the same, because she was brilliant with him, and he absolutely adored her, like a big sister.

We also have a great symbiosis, so we readily understand where each other is coming from. Charlotte doesn't feel the need to babysit me through interviews, which was why, as the journalist and I sat down, she took Josh and kept him occupied in the background. Twenty minutes later, I suddenly heard an out-of-tune BOM-POM-BOM-POM-BOM on the piano, and I swivelled around to find Josh in full Mozart mode, bashing away on the ivories, looking at me with a big grin on his face. The journalist thought it was hilarious and, before we knew it, Josh was the star of the Library Bar.

Moreover, this journalist actually acknowledged how hard it must be to balance motherhood with business. I can't remember if that was what she printed but she voiced the observation, woman to woman, appreciating what it took to be a mum in a modern-day world. Not every journalist would demonstrate that understanding, but I do think it's vital that we, as women, understand and acknowledge what each one of us goes through, whether we are a CEO, a shopkeeper, a nine-to-fiver, or a single mum trying to make ends meet. If we are to be truly empowered as a gender, then surely we need to support one another, rather than judge, or criticise, or project our way of doing things on to others. In today's social media world, where snap judgements seem common, that hope may seem unrealistic, but the more we imagine walking in the shoes of others, the kinder I think we can become.

Around June 2003, we devised a concept for a magalogue – a cross between a magazine and a catalogue. Magalogues were an emerging trend back then and *The World of Jo Malone* was to be a content-driven format focused on lifestyle that would place product in situ within themed photo shoots, from 'at home with Jo' to 'Christmas with Jo'.

I flew to New York to do a series of shoots with the incredibly talented photographer Chris Baker over the course of several days. He obsessed about every single detail almost as much as I did, and he was a joy to work with, as was the stylist, Daphna, who made me look the best I've ever looked on camera. Together, and through many wardrobe and set changes, they pulled off a photo shoot that did justice to the brand. But I was relieved when those long days were over because this was the first time I had been apart from Josh, who had stayed home with Gary. That's something else that takes you by surprise as a new mum – the gravitational pull that defies distance and renders you homesick. When we had spoken on the phone the previous day, I don't think he quite understood why my voice was there but I wasn't.

The next morning, on the day of departure, I rose at 8 a.m. and hit the shower to fully wake up. I stood under that blast of hot water for an age, eyes closed, head down, letting the steam fill the room. I imagined how the 'magalogue' would turn out. I thought about the long flight and how all I intended to do was read and sleep. And then, just as I was thinking about stepping out of the shower, a curveball came from nowhere to disrupt my perfect life.

TWENTY-ONE

Within days of being home, I underwent an examination with our family GP, Dr Guy O'Keeffe. 'We need to get this looked at, Jo,' he said. The tone of his voice was one of caution not alarm, but the inevitable thought still arose.

'It's not cancer, though? Is it?' I asked.

Cue a seasoned doctor's subtle deflection. 'Let's find out what it is first,' he said. 'It could be a cyst. It could be anything.'

The haste with which he acted, though, referring me that same afternoon for a scan at the Lister Hospital in Chelsea, perhaps told me something, even if my denial sought to push it away. 'Will this procedure hurt? Take long?' I asked. 'Because we've a dinner to attend and it starts at eight.'

In my head, I was already at the Serpentine Gallery's annual party. Gary and I had rushed home from the shop to change hurriedly: he, into a dinner jacket; me, into a shocking-pink dress shirt and black Armani dinner suit. That's how we had arrived at the doctor's surgery, squeezing in the 5 p.m. appointment before heading to a soirée that attracts names from fashion, art, architecture and music. In my pocket, I had a pair of diamond drop earrings to be worn later.

Even as he and I headed to the hospital, I kept telling myself that the lump was likely a cyst that would have to be drained. *It's a cyst. That's all it is – a cyst.*

In the waiting room at the Lister, I picked the earrings from my pocket and started rolling them between my thumb and fingers. Gary sat beside me, looking pensive. Neither of us really said much.

When my name was called, I headed to the imaging room and stood in front of a machine that looked like it belonged on a factory floor. Throughout the mammogram, I didn't take my eyes off the nurse, scrutinising her for the slightest reaction as the image flashed up on the screen. And that's when I spotted it – a subtle flicker of recognition registering on her face.

'I'll only be a minute,' she said, before disappearing out of the room.

Within a minute or so, she returned, explaining that they needed to do a second scan. As I was taken into another room for an ultrasound, my mind still clung to the possibility of a cyst, even throughout the procedure, even when a doctor came to see me.

'So, can you drain it?' I asked him.

'Drain what?'

'The cyst.'

'No, Jo, this is not a cyst,' he said, his voice grave, his face sorry.

'I've got cancer, haven't I?'

'It's a strong possibility, yes.'

I stepped into the corridor in a daze, and yet, in that daze, my sense of smell seemed more acute than ever: the all-pervading medicinal air; the strong coffee that someone nearby must have been drinking; the soap on the nurse's hands as she led me to the waiting room where Gary remained oblivious. From behind me, I heard hurried footsteps clipping off the travertine floor. I turned to see Dr Guy rushing towards me – they had called him, presumably before the ultrasound, and he hugged me like a relative, not a doctor.

He took me to see Gary, who knew as soon as he saw my face. I rested my head on his chest. 'We're going to deal with this together,' he said, putting his arms around me. But it's amazing how even your husband's arms don't feel safe when you've just been told you have cancer. It feels like every form of safety has been ripped away; that it's just you and cancer, stripped bare. And yet, as I stood there, I felt strangely calm within the eye of this storm. Or maybe I was mistaking the numbness for calm.

Within the hour, I was sitting opposite a surgeon in his office on another floor, feeling frightened and, perhaps, a little defensive. I think it's only natural to feel defensive when cancer's got you cornered. This would be typical of my erratic emotions in the coming days. One minute, I'd be scared; the next, numb; the next, prickly. But not once – not on that first day or at any other time – did I ever think, 'Why me?' I was as undeserving as the next person. To ask 'Why me?' would be to wish that it was someone else, and that didn't seem fair. Life doesn't always deal the good fortune cards.

The surgeon pinned up the image on a light box and there it was: a sinister-looking, shadowy mass with jagged edges. Within a week, following a needle biopsy, I would receive the confirmation that it was 'an aggressive type of breast cancer'.

On that first day, when all I had to go on was the scan, I went home, climbed upstairs and sat on the foot of our bed. Poor Gary didn't know what to do or say but he remained stoical. Josh, who was still up, came toddling in, wearing his pyjamas. He was too young to understand but he knew enough to realise I was upset. He sat on my lap, facing me, arms slung around my neck, and, as he looked into my eyes, he kept cocking his head to the side. 'Mummy, what's matter?'

How do you answer that?! Mummy's not well? Mummy's poorly? How do you wrap cancer in cotton wool and make it sound softer? I chose not to lie, so I said nothing and gave him the tightest hug, more for my benefit than his.

'Come on, Joshie, time for bed,' said Gary, as he carried him out.

I started pacing the room, thinking. *Okay, you have cancer – it's a curve ball you weren't expecting. Happens in business all the time. Think. Don't feel sorry for yourself. Think. Josh needs you to think. What are you going to do?*

In the time it took for my husband and son to share a bed-time story, I felt this energy and strength fill me up, which Gary noticed the moment he came in. I reached for the phone by our bed and started dialling. 'I'm calling Evelyn [Lauder].'

In the three years since we had joined Lauder, she had been so kind and helpful, someone who made it clear that her door was always open. But it wasn't only our easy rapport that prompted my call. Evelyn had founded the Breast Cancer Research Foundation in 1993 and was in the vanguard of the fight to find a cure. When it comes to the one-person-you-need-to-call-first, she was the obvious friend.

Genie, her lovely assistant in New York, answered and she knew me well enough to hear my news so I cut straight to the point. 'Genie, I've been diagnosed with breast cancer. I need to speak with Evelyn.'

'Hold on, I'll find her,' she said. 'It may take a little longer than usual to connect you but bear with me. Don't go anywhere.'

I waited about two minutes but I would have waited two hours. When I was first put through, all I heard was a fierce blowing into the mouthpiece, as if Evelyn was standing in a wind tunnel. I wasn't far wrong. A passionate hiker, she was halfway into climbing a peak and speaking to me from the middle of some nowhere. And I'll never forget her first wind-buffeted words.

'Jo?! Jo! We're going to help you, honey!'

She was the first person to whom I voiced my deepest fear, fully aware that Gary was listening. 'It's cancer, Evelyn. It's cancer. I think I'm going to die. I don't know what to do . . .'

That was what 'cancer' meant to me – death.

'You're not going to die, Jo. We're going to get you through this. You've got to stay strong. Remember, you make lemonade from lemons!'

If anything summed up that woman's spirit, there you have it.

'I'm going to call Larry Norton,' she added.

'Who's Larry Norton?'

'The man who's going to do everything to save your life!'

When someone whose opinion you respect says one man in particular is going to be your saviour, you go find that person, even if he lives in Timbuktu. When people ask why I didn't use our tremendous health service in the UK, that's the reason. I felt that I had only one shot at this, and Evelyn was emphatic in her referral when we spoke the next day – Larry was, she said, America's most eminent breast cancer expert.

Thankfully, Dr Larry Norton wasn't in Timbuktu. He was in Manhattan, working as the physician-in-chief for Breast Cancer Programs at the renowned Memorial Sloan Kettering Cancer Center – the clinic where Evelyn had once led a fundraising drive to establish a state-of-the-art diagnostic centre, the facility that would later bear her name. Within days of my needle biopsy and further tests in London, Gary, Josh and I flew to New York.

As my medical records winged their way to the clinic, we checked in at The Mark Hotel on the corner of 77th and Madison Avenue. I felt apprehensive about what the next few days had in store. Based on conversations with the consultant back home, undergoing a lumpectomy was inevitable, but I worried endlessly about the cancer spreading. Through the course of that evening, I drank bottled water like it was going out of fashion, downing litre after litre in the warped belief that I could flush the cancer away and cleanse my body. By now, I had already devoured books on nutrition and diet, and I came to the conclusion that the only non-acidic, non-toxic things I could eat were nuts and bananas. My appointment with the professionals couldn't come fast enough.

The next morning, as the sun pounded down outside, I felt incredibly self-conscious. I felt unclean, almost ashamed of a body where cancer was now resident, so I picked out the largest clothes I had – a billowing shirt and baggy pants – trying to hide what couldn't be seen.

The first doctor I met at the Sloan Kettering was Dr Alexandra Heerdt, a petite lady with shoulder-length hair and a comforting smile. She explained the procedure for, first, the lumpectomy that would remove the tumour, and, second, the biopsy of the sentinel node – the first lymph node to which cancer cells are most likely to spread. There was no prognosis or mention of treatment. Nobody was going to say anything until the results were on her desk from the joint procedure that would be carried out the following morning.

She carried out the biopsy under general anaesthetic and I remained in hospital overnight. By the time I returned to the hotel, I felt surprisingly well, apart from some soreness in my right armpit. As Josh cuddled into me on the bed and fell asleep, Gary was on the phone, dealing with some business in London – a semblance of normality. It was day two of our trip, the tumour had gone, the surgery was over and we would soon be allowed home, once the results were in.

My follow-up was scheduled for a Tuesday at 2 p.m., seven days later. On Monday, Dr Heerdt's secretary called our room, asking if we could make it 5 p.m. instead.

'That's not good,' I said to Gary.

'Jo, she's a busy woman. Something must have come up.'

My heart started pounding. 'She's moved us to the end of the day for a reason,' I said. And as much as Gary spent the rest of the evening trying to calm my worries, every bone in my body told me otherwise.

The next day, when we walked into Dr Heerdt's office, I wasn't in the mood for pleasantries. 'It's bad news, isn't it?' I said as soon as she greeted us.

She didn't say 'Yes' but she didn't need to; the solemnity in her demeanour spoke volumes. 'Let's please sit down and I'm going to talk you through the results,' she said. We sat around her desk on chairs with wooden armrests. Gary sat forward, on his seat's edge, not taking his eyes off the doctor, his face etched with worry. He reached out and took my hand.

Dr Heerdt got straight to the point, explaining that the lumpectomy showed that I had ductal carcinoma in situ (DCIS), and that some of my lymph nodes were 'positive'. And that's when she told me that my best option was a mastectomy.

Gary slumped forward on to his knees, head in hands, and sobbed. He just crumpled. Our worst fear had just been voiced. Whereas I didn't move, couldn't move. Not within myself and not towards him. I felt completely numb. It took all my strength to keep my eyes on Dr Heerdt.

'Is there any other way?' I asked.

She shook her head. 'I'm sorry, Jo.'

Gary pulled himself up and sat back in the chair, shaking his head. For once, this man who had words of wisdom for any given situation had nothing to offer. Probably because there was nothing to say. All he could do was hold my hand.

'Okay, when do we do this?' I asked.

'Within the week,' said Dr Heerdt.

Cancer creeps up surreptitiously, unnoticed. Who knows how long it quietly develops and grows? But then it jumps out of nowhere and mugs you from within. Ten days after arriving in New York, I had to get used to the idea of losing a part of my body. From this point on, the whole approach took on a system-atic, clinical feel, almost like a business strategy meeting. I was handed pale orange cards that further explained the surgery and the aftercare, answering every conceivable question long before my mind could think of them. It's not only head-spinning; it's a mental bombardment that comes at a time when you are strug-gling to get your bearings.

The next day, we went to see plastic surgeon Dr Joseph Disa, a charming, ridiculously good-looking man who, once my sense of humour had returned, I would later nickname 'Dishy Disa'. He talked reconstructive surgery options but he could see I was struggling.

'You'll get your life back, Jo,' he said, trying to reassure me, but I just bawled. All I seemed to have done for twenty-four hours was cry, unable to keep it together. I cried so much that it induced a headache, and I felt fed up with the sadness. So, as Dr Disa explained my options regarding reconstructive surgery, I decided that this subject matter would become my focus – some-thing to hold on to beyond the mastectomy, beyond treatment. An action plan always helps restore my balance. He gave me a lot to think about, too: take tissue from my back for an immediate, post-op solution? Have implants inserted at a later date? If so, what type – saline or silicone? Or do nothing? But the answers to those questions would have to wait because I first had to consider my course of treatment – and that's when I finally met Dr Larry Norton, a slightly built, bespectacled, straight-talking man whose kind face belied a warrior spirit.

As I would discover, he understands cancer like a general

understands war. The *New York Times* once said that he offered 'a bracing, pugnacious hope' to his patients, and that became evident in our first meeting when he wanted to know what I was made of; probably because I had started our meeting by saying that I didn't want chemotherapy and he'd have to find another way. I didn't want to do it and I didn't want to lose my hair, I insisted.

He listened, understood my reticence but, with characteristic compassion, told me that I really didn't have a choice. 'Look,' he said, gently, 'there are two kinds of people who walk in here: one that says, "Don't hurt me," and the other that says, "Give me back my life." Which one are you?'

He made me face the reality there and then. 'I want to live,' I said.

'Right, so from this day forward, you have got to trust me.'

And, boy, did I trust him. He had this air about him that suggested expertise, and I wanted to hold on to the tails of his white coat because that expertise told me that *he* was in control, not cancer. Surrendering to events outside my control has never been one of my strong points, but I happily placed my trust in Larry, in Evelyn's opinion of him, and in God.

'Do whatever you need to do,' I said.

'Good. We'll work out a plan and I promise that we'll fight this together,' he said.

When it came to chemotherapy, Larry was as precise as a perfumer, measuring the dosage to exact drops. He had pioneered 'dose–dense drug delivery', where the treatment is administered at an optimised level specific to the patient and unique to each cancer. It felt like I was listening to a mathematician not a doctor as he explained how he would calculate and keep refining the frequency and dosage, balancing the treatment with my body's equilibrium. This way, he said, I wouldn't receive high doses up front.

When my tumour was removed, the sentinel node biopsy found

that cancer was present in some lymph nodes, meaning cancerous cells may have migrated but they didn't know how many – maybe one, maybe several – so the treatment was designed to mop them up. Chemotherapy that Larry described as 'a belt and braces insurance policy'.

An insurance policy had never sounded so terrible.

It actually scared me more than the thought of a mastectomy. The first image that came to mind was Ali MacGraw in *Love Story*. The second thing I thought about was the wheelchair-bound young man I had seen earlier, dressed in a surgical smock, no hair, all skin and bone, with a face the colour of grey paint. I remember looking at him and thinking, 'Please, God, don't ever let that be me – he looks like he really has cancer.'

Months later, that *would be* me.

Larry warned me that my hair would fall out by the second dose 'but not forever'. That's what they do at Sloan Kettering – they deliver the hard truth with goals and hope attached. Yes, you'll go through a rough time, but you'll get your life back. Yes, you'll be sick, but we've pills for that. Yes, you'll be bald but hair grows again. 'What ifs' don't exist, only positive 'Yes buts'. That's because the mental approach is so important; something that I would not immediately find easy.

But being around the positivity of the Sloan Kettering ethos was one reason why I decided it would be best to spend the four months of treatment in New York; plus, with a chemotherapy-weakened immune system, the risk of infection would be too great on continual flights back and forth. It proved a wise decision, because I would come to depend on Larry's guidance to such an extent that I didn't want to be away from him. He would become more than a doctor; he would become a dear friend, who I love and respect, and I think it's safe to say that I won't be his only patient to declare that.

I flew to London with Gary and Josh that evening and, in a flurry of activity over forty-eight hours, we made arrangements for our home to be looked after, for the business to be set on the correct path, and for Vicky and Lorna to oversee the day-to-day running of the shop. Leonard, Evelyn and everyone else at the company were beyond supportive, even setting up an office for Gary in the GM Building. Nothing was too much trouble.

I essentially compartmentalised my life to focus on the one job at hand. In the same way doctors sought to isolate my cancer, I sought to isolate myself. I wanted none of this episode to infect my life in London and Sloane Street, so Manhattan would be the box where I'd confine my illness. I would approach these sixteen weeks in the same way I approached everything else: fully immersed, one hundred per cent focused.

Once we returned to Manhattan, on the weekend before my Monday mastectomy, we rented a seventh-floor, two-bedroom apartment in The Sutton, a condominium on 56th Street between First and Second, about twelve blocks from Sloan Kettering. We were a mere taxi ride or a long stroll away, and, for the foreseeable future, my world wouldn't go beyond that ten-minute radius. Manhattan was reduced to twelve blocks in length and width as far as I was concerned. My doctor, my notes, my treatment, my family were all within reach, along with a chemist, a café, and a local food emporium. I had everything I needed.

At night, from the balcony we could see the Chrysler Building lit up. The apartment itself wasn't much to look at: grey carpets, tiny white kitchen, lemon yellow bathroom, and dark wood furniture throughout, but I wasn't complaining. It was a base, not a home. That said, I hated the smell of the bed linen, so the first thing I did was buy new sheets, pillow cases and a blue-and-white patchwork quilt that I sprayed with Grapefruit fragrance. The apartment had to smell like home at least.

On the wall opposite the front door, there was a large, full-length mirror and, as time went on, it would offer a reflection that I refused to look at. But on the morning of the surgery, as Gary finished getting Josh ready, I stood there and stared at myself. I was wearing a red, oversized Abercrombie & Fitch zipped-up sweatshirt with blue jeans. It's a surreal thing to look at yourself, contemplating the imminent removal of a part of your anatomy. No matter how hard I tried, I couldn't imagine the 'before' and the 'after' that would later confront me.

At that moment, Josh came tottering up to me, proudly showing off a piece of Lego that he had managed to construct – that was his achievement, and that was my perspective. To one very important person I wasn't a cancer patient; I was a mum, come what may. We left him with the nanny and he carried on playing contentedly. For as long as he was happy building and dismantling Lego, oblivious to what was going on, Gary and I were okay with that.

At the bottom of the elevator, our resident porter opened the door. I would come to know this dark-suited gentleman as Paul, a gentle giant of a man who, come rain or shine, would greet us with a smile. I swear that this wonderful human being was an angel posted to the main entrance to be a constant source of assistance in the coming months.

Once outside, Gary wanted to hail a taxi. I asked if we could walk – 'a walk will do me good', I said. I was probably the only person in Manhattan that morning who wasn't in any kind of rush. As we walked, a taxi driver berated another motorist, blaring his horn. I must have noticed the same thing happen a thousand times in New York and London but only now did it seem so petty. We passed a man sweeping the streets, literally whistling while he worked. I had definitely not noticed anyone doing that before in New York or London, and all I wanted to do was trade places.

As we neared the hospital, I felt like I was going to throw up. Fear, I discovered, operates in much the same way as creativity: it grips you, takes over, and consumes your every thought. But it wasn't the fear of losing my breast; it was the fear of what lay ahead – the chemo, the treatment, the not knowing where this path led. What if it didn't end with a mastectomy? What if this cancer proved bigger than me?

The clinic's doorman must have noticed the trepidation in my face. Why else, instead of holding open the door, would he take my hand and lead me inside?

At the registration desk, they placed a pink medical band around my wrist – 'Joanne Willcox'. We then took the elevator to the surgery floor, where I changed into an orange-coloured gown and white surgical stockings. I went through to a room where about twenty other women – some with partners, some not – were waiting, sitting in the same gowns and socks, prepped for their lumpectomy, biopsy or mastectomy. No one said a word. The oldest must have been a woman in the far corner, who looked in her seventies. I had to have been the youngest, and it seemed as though I was the only one trembling like a leaf. Gary took my hand but I only transferred the shakes to his wrist and forearm.

And then my name was called.

'I'll be here when you wake up,' Gary said.

They don't wheel you into the theatre at Sloan Kettering; you walk in, fully conscious. As I pushed through the double doors, I recognised the anaesthetist from the biopsy – his name was Charlie. Dr Heerdt was standing behind him, surgical mask on. To their right was the duvet-like bedding where I would lie, beside metal trays laid out neatly with surgical instruments.

As I lay down, staring at the overhead lights, I felt embarrassed that I was shaking so much. Charlie reassured me that everything was going to be okay, but he needed me to relax so that he could get a line in. You'll soon be asleep, he said.

'Charlie? Can you hold my hand a second?'

He stopped what he was doing. 'Of course, Jo.'

I gripped his hand and asked Dr Heerdt if it was okay if I said a prayer.

'You go ahead,' she said.

Holding Charlie's hand, I prayed out loud for God to bring me through. And yet, even after praying, I still couldn't help one last-minute plea to Dr Heerdt.

'Is there any other way?' I asked. 'A different kind—'

'There isn't,' she said, placing her hand on my wrist. 'We have to do this.'

Charlie got his line in, told me to relax and count to ten.

I kept staring at the light. I think I made it to five.

TWENTY-TWO

I heard the beep–beep–beep of a monitor as Dr Heerdt leaned in to say the operation had gone well. I opened my drowsy eyes and became aware of a cocoon-like blanket around me, puffed up and filled with warm air. Another female voice asked what the pain felt like on a scale of one to ten, but I felt nothing. 'One,' I said. 'Where's Gary?'

His hand closed around mine. 'Right here, darling. I'm here.'

And I must have nodded off again.

When I next woke up, I had been moved to a room that appeared instantly dull. I turned my head on the pillow, left then right, looking around – not a single window. I glanced down at my chest and saw a thick mound of cotton wadding and bandage, and suddenly understood the first sensation that I felt: a rigid, zipped-up tightness, as if my own skin was a jacket two sizes too small. I noted the numbness in my right arm and right side of my back. I felt the crispness of the sheets beneath my hands, my mouth as dry as dust . . . and the despondency. The despondency seemed to override any other feeling – a stark sense of emptiness that I had never before experienced, one that made me wish I were still in an anaesthetic-induced oblivion. In sleep, I wouldn't have to face the reason I was lying there, or the bleak thoughts that consciousness activated.

How will I ever be the same woman after this? How can I feel feminine again? Will anything feel the same? Will people look at me and know? That's what cancer does – it infiltrates the mind and whispers its negativity, and it does so when you are at your weakest, filling you with a defeatist belief that makes you wonder if you've got the energy for the uphill road ahead.

Ever since Larry's first pep talk, all I had ever asked myself was, 'How can I fight?' and 'How can I get my life back?' But now I didn't feel like I had an ounce of fight within me; it was as though my hope had been surgically removed as well. Pessimism isn't me, but that was cancer again, taking my half-full glass and pouring its contents down the sink, leaving it not just half-empty but completely empty. Part of me wanted to feel fear again, because at least fear motivates a fight or flight. With emptiness, there's nowhere to go. I didn't even seem able to muster the slightest reaction; only self-defeating thoughts existed, and they kept stacking up to make the emptiness feel heavy.

If only someone could have pulled me out of this pit, transported me into the future and shown me how much better life would be. But I couldn't see beyond the next hour let alone the next few weeks.

Gary remained by my side, a nurse came in to check my vitals, and Dr Disa stopped by to see how I was doing, but my monosyllabic responses – out of character for such a chatterbox – probably said everything. I had never suffered from depression but I imagine that this was the closest I came. Admittedly, two factors didn't help: one was the morphine that put me in a somewhat altered state; the other was the windowless room that created a boxed-in feeling that did nothing for my ruminating.

The next forty-eight hours not only felt like forty-eight days

but they would be the lowest of my life, even lower than when
chemotherapy would do its worst. I wouldn't have climbed out
of bed had the nurses not insisted I attend physiotherapy to work
my right arm. Every person who came into the room, including
my own husband, appeared to be standing on the periphery,
with distant voices. I had no interest in what anyone had to say,
however gentle and compassionate. I was not only down, I was
angry, too.

In my addled mind, I mistakenly believed that no one understood what I was going through. Weeks earlier, I had a thriving
company, financial security, a loving family, and a happy future,
and I felt angry that my peaceful world had been disrupted. I
wanted to believe again in the illusion that I was in control of
my own life. I wanted everything restored to how it was, framed
within the context of my comfort zone. The truth about the
impermanence of life – the impossibility of things ever staying
the same for anyone, cancer or no cancer – couldn't find a way
through.

Meanwhile, in the corridor outside, Dr Disa and Gary were
sharing their concerns about my low mood, agreeing that it would
be best to move me to a higher floor, and a room with a window.
Gary knew me well enough to know that a light-filled space was
vital to my sense of well-being.

The next morning, I was transferred on a trolley bed to a
room with a view and a totally different feel. It felt like I was
emerging from a tunnel as the shafts of sunlight bathed my face.
Once comfortable, propped up against a nest of pillows, I could
see the sky, the buildings of Rockefeller University, and the East
River that cut between Manhattan and the sliver of Roosevelt
Island. I could see life, not just four walls, and my gloom started
to lift. I can't say that angry, negative thoughts would stay away
entirely – the journey through chemotherapy would continue to

be challenging – but I was pleased to be rid of the post-surgery moroseness that had me scared for a while.

I found strength hour by hour, day by day, in trying to empower myself in the smallest ways. Knowing my mind's propensity to dwell, and because I didn't wish for any kind of depressive episode to return, I set out to understand every little detail of what was happening around me. I asked the nurses to explain my vitals, my blood pressure reading, and the medical chart on the clipboard posted to the bottom of my bed. 'Why are you taking those bloods ...' and 'What's that you're doing now?' or 'Why's that necessary?' I wanted to preoccupy myself with knowledge because even the most rudimentary understanding of minor medical protocols made me feel more in control.

I'd also make lists of things I needed to accomplish, less a 'things to do' list than a 'things to think' list. I've made lists since being young, whether it was chores to do, food to buy, or product needed, so I figured that a feel-good list would aid my recupera-tion *and* mood. 'Think twice today of something that makes you happy,' I wrote. 'Imagine two places in the world you'd like to go on holiday when fully recovered.'

And this list-making would continue through chemotherapy, with goals laid out for the week: 'Go to Banana Republic and buy two wrapover dresses' or 'Go to Barney's and have its sausage pasta with green peas' or 'Take Josh for a bagel'.

If the task/goal was written in thick pen, it had to be done that day; if it was written in thin pen, it had to be accomplished within the week. It seemed strange to be making lists that weren't business-oriented but it kept my mind focused and made me feel a ton better. One task written in thin pen was: 'Look at the scar.'

I didn't actually confront my reflection in the bathroom mirror until the final day in hospital, when a nurse stood alongside me for moral support. Suffice it to say that once the shock had subsided and the tears had dried, I realised that the scar was less frightening than my imagination had pictured. Thanks to the meticulous work of Dr Disa, it looked like someone had used a red felt-tip pen to draw a line across one side of my chest.

Another sight, and sensation, I needed to get used to was the tissue expander that had been inserted as a temporary replacement for my right breast. This rubber device, designed to stretch the skin and pectoral muscle, would make room for the permanent silicone implant I had chosen to have. Over twelve weeks, and in a completely painless process, it is gradually filled with saline via an injectable port, expanding like a water balloon, though it was hard to imagine any growth amid the bruising and tightness that first week.

For me, the self-consciousness was greater than any shock. I had prepared myself for reconstructive surgery but hadn't figured how much restorative work my self-esteem would require. I couldn't imagine wearing a swimsuit again, or any kind of slinky outfit, or shopping at Victoria's Secret. With my sense of femininity so bound to my own body image, my confidence was hit hard.

But in the coming weeks, numerous people would demonstrate that a normal life can follow a mastectomy, and I received tremendous insight from the medical staff. The biggest source of strength came from a woman called Stacey, a friend of my American PR Cathy O'Brien. Stacey, who had previously survived breast cancer, was a walking example of how good a woman can look following reconstructive surgery. It became clear just by talking with her, over coffee or on the phone, why she had survived and why she was glowing – she had such a tenacious positivity. Thanks to the flashforward provided by her personal story, she made the unknown known while also empathising with my fears, tears, and insecurities. She had been there and she kept urging me to keep the faith that I'd feel confident again in the long term. Stacey was one of those rocks on whom I came to depend, and a big reason why I got my hope back. The return of hope was timely because my chemotherapy would start within five weeks. And no matter what inspirational stories you collect from others, no one else can walk the road but you.

But I wouldn't be walking that road alone. Gary would be alongside me for every step and stumble, to urge me on and pick me up. What I went through, he went through, too. He might not have physically taken the chemotherapy in his arm every day, and yet he did. He wouldn't literally lose his hair, and yet he did. His unfaltering love would be the one rope I'd hold on to and, on the occasions when I'd feel too weak to maintain my grip, he'd carry me. I pinned my rediscovered hope to my husband and son – the two reasons I was determined to overcome this rotten disease.

At Bible school, I remember it being said that all anyone needs is faith, hope and love, 'but the greatest of these is love'. I beg to differ. At this time, the greatest force for me was hope. The love of my boys was constant and my faith in the doctors was rock-solid. But hope promised me that there would be a tomorrow, and my tomorrow with Gary and Josh was the one horizon I kept my eyes on, however distant it sometimes felt.

I bought a calendar for the period August–December 2003. Over those sixteen weeks, I would receive the chemo every ten days in different cycles, and I wanted to chalk off those days one by one. An 'X', written in black marker, would chart my countdown to Christmas. I don't think I had ever focused on a Christmas so fiercely since being a child.

The rhythm of chemotherapy – how it works and how your body responds – took some adjusting to, but I soon learned to know the three-day pockets when my body was at its strong-est, which allowed Gary the time to head back to London, do some work and return for the day my chemo started again. The poor guy bounced between time zones for the last quarter of 2003 because, with so much continuing to happen with the business, he wanted to ensure everything kept ticking along. Somehow, he managed to be the business partner, the dad, the husband, the mum, and the carer all at the same time. And despite his regular transatlantic commute, he'd be at my side for every dose of chemotherapy and each important hospital appointment.

One bonus about being in New York was that we had friends to rely on. Steven Horn had moved to Manhattan for a new job with Swiss Army, and he would come over to cook dinner and play with Josh, even when Gary was 'home'. 'Uncle Steven' would become a big part of our temporary American life, as would our dear friend Susan McCone, who knew me better than most, and would offer constant succour over coffee and lunch. With her fashion designer days behind her, she had been ordained that year as an Episcopal priest and her soothing wisdom pulled me through many a dark hour.

But not once – not with Gary, Steven, Susan or anyone for that matter – did I talk business or fragrances. I didn't even think about making product, although that hadn't been my intention. I was due to tweak and finesse a collection of basil-scented candles while in New York, but the chemo put paid to those plans. As soon as the test candle arrived, I felt violently sick. I couldn't even open the bag without retching. In fact, I began to heave at many smells, even the plastic of the shower curtain, which we had to remove, and there was certainly no more spraying of Grapefruit on duvets and linen. My nose was rendered useless. All I could smell and taste was metal – a common side effect of the treatment.

Going through chemotherapy was the grimmest experience I had suffered. Edna, the Russian nurse who administered my every

dose, would tell colourful stories and jokes in an attempt to dis-
tract me from the procedure, but it turned my stomach watching
the toxic red juice leave the syringe to travel through my veins
intravenously. For a long time, I couldn't look at cranberry juice
without feeling nauseous. And then there was the daily require-
ment of self-injecting the medication that artificially elevated my
infection-fighting white cell count – an imperative to combat the
depletion that the treatment causes. For someone like me, who
had previously hated needles, this was a tough ask.

'There's *no way* I can inject myself. I'll pass out!' I told Karen,
the sparky nurse charged with teaching me the technique. But
when she explained that the alternative was to come in for daily
injections at the clinic, I decided that my discomfort was preferable to that constant back and forth.

Karen was my Florence Nightingale, on hand to deal with any
ailment or side effect: the mouth ulcers, blurred vision, memory
loss, and faintness. And under her patient guidance, I soon mastered how to grin and bear the self-injections, pushing the needle
into the fatty tissue of my leg. But knowing how to do it didn't
mean I found it any more enjoyable, and so I set myself an incen-
tive – I couldn't watch an episode of *Sex and the City* until I had
carried out each nightly jab.

Oddly enough, that programme was the only thing I could
watch. By day three of my chemo, it felt as if every muscle and
bone in my body was made of lead, and I couldn't concentrate
on reading a book or watching TV without my head banging.
Except, that is, for *Sex and the City*. The half-hour bursts of Carrie,
Samantha, Miranda and Charlotte had unknown chemo-defying
qualities, and their humour was often a great tonic, even when I
felt too tired to laugh.

Chemotherapy has a cumulative effect and brings on a gradual
decline in energy, from 'tired' to 'exhausted' to 'feeling like I've

been hit by a ten-ton truck'. Even nipping to the food emporium on the corner – no more than one hundred metres away – felt like a gruelling hike. Eventually, I relied on deliveries but, even then, I occasionally underestimated my own weakness.

On one such day, with Gary away, I went down to meet the deliveryman in the lobby. I bent down to pick up the bags and Paul, our resident doorman, could see that I was flagging. 'Let me take those for you, Miss Jo,' he said. But he didn't only take my food upstairs, he placed each item in the fridge and cupboards. It wasn't the only time he'd come to my aid.

In week ten, when the chemo really had me in its grip, I caught a taxi home from the hospital. 'You're here, ma'am!' said the cabbie, impatiently hurrying me along. As I pushed the door open, the distance from the pavement to the main entrance seemed like a mile. The driver was going to be of no help, so I swivelled around in my seat to put my legs outside and, at that moment, Paul's hulk of a figure leaned in and lifted up my rag doll of a body. He didn't say a word – he simply carried me inside, into the lift, into the apartment and lay me on the bed. When people talk about the spirit of New Yorkers, I always, always think of Paul.

I think of a lady called Mary, too.

In the gaps between chemo, and if I felt well enough, physiotherapy was every Thursday, and this buxom lady, who enthused about her Pentecostal faith, brought the gym alive with her Gospel songs and fine voice. By the sounds of it, *By the Rivers of Babylon* and *How Great Thou Art* were her favourites.

'Do you sing all the time, Mary?'

'Singing is my medicine!' she said.

'So, what kind of cancer are you being treated for?'

'Oh, honey, I've had cancer since 1962!' She was undergoing chemo for the umpteenth time and was still fighting, still singing, and still remaining upbeat. When I said earlier that I got my hope back, what I didn't say was that it kept being fortified by the people I came across, like Paul, with his humanity, and Mary, with her never-surrender spirit.

There was a café opposite the hospital. After a workout, I'd bob across for a sandwich or a snack. 'You want anything, Mary?'

'Cwa-fee,' she said, while riding the exercise bike, pedalling at a leisurely pace. 'A cwaf-ee and a donut!'

God, I loved that woman.

When my spirits were low, I'd walk into Larry's office with a barrage of queries, moans and groans, which both he and Karen soaked up with infinite patience. More than once, I'd vent my frustrations, unable to maintain stretches of positivity, no matter how hard I tried. Angry thoughts didn't totally go away and, as the chemotherapy took its toll, I used to resist its advancement and unfairly blame Larry for putting me through the mincer and then expecting me to emerge intact.

'You keep saying I'm the same person,' I'd say. 'But how does anyone emerge from *this* as the same person?!'

'Well, you are the same person,' he'd reply. 'But I think it might help if you go see someone and talk these issues through.'

'Ohhhh, a shrink! Of course! That's the answer to everything in America, isn't it?'

What a pain in the backside I must have been to this man trying to save my life and make me understand the nature of cancer. I was awful at times. I admit it. But Larry, unruffled and unfazed by emotional reactions that he had seen a thousand times before, simply scheduled an appointment with Dr Mary Massie, the psychiatrist who 'specialises in the psychological treatment of women with breast cancer'.

I told him that I'd begrudgingly see Mary for 'counselling' not 'psychiatry'. Such semantics mattered to me at the time, though

I'm not sure it did anything to diminish my bolshie resistance. On the way to a Sloan Kettering satellite office, my defences were up. *I know exactly what I'm thinking! I know exactly who I am! I have cancer. I'm not messed up in the head!*

Mary, slim, studious, in her fifties, with round, black-rimmed spectacles and shoulder-length fair hair, greeted me warmly at the door with her gravelly New York twang.

'Well, Mary,' I said, sitting down on the sofa and folding my arms, 'you've got exactly ten minutes to give me three ways I can get my life back, otherwise I'm out of here.'

She raised her eyebrows, looked at her wristwatch and sat down opposite me. 'Okay. Ten minutes.'

'And you'll have to turn that radiator off – it's too hot. I'm burning up,' I said.

'Can I suggest you move away from the radiator then?' she replied. 'I can't turn down the heating just for this session – it's a joint heating system.'

My pretence at control was soon dismantled. 'Right, yes, of course,' I said, shimmying to the other side of the sofa. She began to dismantle my resistance, too, explaining how women in my position often feel overwhelmed with emotions. 'You arrive here with the same fears as every woman diagnosed with a life-threatening illness. Will I survive? If I get through this, how long will I live?'

I softened as I listened but the process still felt futile. 'But what's the point? I mean, I'm going to die before you. Look at me, disappearing. Look at you, all lovely and healthy!'

'How on earth do you work out that you're going to die before me?'

'Well, I've got cancer.'

'And you're being *treated* for cancer.'

'Right, but—'

'Jo, as healthy as I sit here today, I could go outside and be hit by a car and die. You could walk out of here and live for another fifty years. Your illness doesn't have to be viewed as a permanent thing.'

Mary Massie had me onboard in less than ten minutes. She understood the psychological devastation and the power of the word 'cancer'. Indeed, as she explained, there was a time when doctors could never say it, preferring to use 'lumps', 'bumps' and 'masses'. 'But we can talk about it now,' she said. 'And we don't have to allow cancer to affect the mind.'

As to my question – how do I get my life back? – I wouldn't get the immediate answer that I had demanded. But, over many weeks, she would help me keep matters in perspective, even on the occasions when I derailed slightly. I came to rely on Mary because, with each session, she helped me find the way out of a dense forest into a clearing where my thoughts felt less over-whelming. I must have seen her two times a week as we discussed my need for control and my anxiety about the unknown. We had conversations about God, about verses in the Bible, about spirit-uality. I would scream, shout, despair, cry, and sit with my head in my hands. Mary encouraged the raw emotion, wanting me to keep nothing suppressed.

'Do you know why I think you'll survive this process, Jo?' she said one day. 'Because you come in here and you're truthful with your emotions. You're not afraid to rant and rave. That's not anger, that's your fight. Don't lose your fight, Jo.'

In the end, I couldn't wait for our sessions to begin, for the optimism and sense of stability that her insights brought. I couldn't have been happier to be sitting in the *psychiatrist's* room. Larry was pleased, too, I think – it meant he no longer had to face my bombardment of questions.

*

In the middle ground between my cancer and my survival, in a bedroom that was fast becoming a colourful den of Lego, sat Josh, then nearly three, always playing, smiling, and being loving. Ironically, as I went through my darkest time, he would have only happy memories of those months in Manhattan: sledging in the snow in Central Park, throwing jagged pieces of ice into the frozen lakes, pizza at Serafina's on 61st Street, and, of course, the hours spent at FAO Schwarz toy store, on the ground floor of the GM Building where Estée Lauder was based. Josh wasn't interested in the jellybean counters, or the array of cuddly animals, or the famous floor piano. No, he darted off to find the Lego department, eyeing the castle that we'd buy him for Christmas two years later. What's interesting is that these weren't just any old memories; these would be his first conscious memories of life.

The only cancer-associated memory he'd retain was the day I asked him to shave my head, but even that was couched as 'giving Mummy a buzz cut'. I had started to shed so we wanted to involve him so as to dilute the shock of seeing me bald. We never hid the cancer from him. We said its name and told him why we were in New York, even if we did keep him away from the hospital. In being upfront and honest, whether he understood or not, we intended to remove the fear.

A hairdresser came to the apartment for the haircut and, when we arrived at the moment of the shearing, she offered Josh the electric shaver as I sat in a chair in the living room, with a towel around my shoulders. He lapped it up, giggling as my blonde locks fell to the floor and Gary looked on. But then he noticed that I had fallen quiet, and I didn't think fast enough to wipe the tears from my eyes. Josh stepped forward, looked at me, and fell quiet, too, thinking I was upset about my new style.

'Don't worry, Mummy,' he said, 'it will soon grow back.'

Once done, the hairdresser grabbed the mirror to present my

new back and sides. 'It suits her, doesn't it, Joshie?!' said Gary. 'Our own G.I. Jane! Isn't she?!' Josh started cheering, without really knowing what he was cheering; so I cheered with him, celebrating my new Demi Moore look.

Two or three weeks later, there was a wonderful moment in a playground near the hospital. The nanny had taken Josh to the swings while I had a routine scan and blood tests. Afterwards, I went to join them and, as I approached the gardens, I noticed him in the distance, playing with another boy on the roundabout while the nanny talked to a couple sitting on a bench. As I got closer, it became obvious that Josh's new friend was a cancer patient; he was gaunt and had no hair.

I walked over to the nanny and that's when I noticed the father was crying.

'Are you that boy's mother?' he said, standing to greet me.

'I am. What's he done?'

He laughed. 'Have you any idea how magical your son is? My boy comes here every day and none of the kids will play with him because they're too scared. But your son came right over, took his hand and off they went to play.'

I looked over and the little boy was laughing and squealing as Josh pushed the roundabout. He earned some extra Lego that day, and if anything positive came out of this time, it was the fact that he wouldn't grow up being frightened of people who looked different.

Roughly three weeks after receiving the buzz cut, I was relaxing at the apartment one evening. Gary was catching up on some work, Josh was in bed, and Steven Horn was round, cooking spaghetti bolognese. We were idly chatting about the movie we'd recently seen at the cinema, *Love Actually*, when I happened to scratch an itch on my scalp . . . and all these bristles dropped like dandruff. Not thinking anyone had noticed, I slipped off to the bathroom, rubbed my head with both hands and more bristles fell into the sink, like they do when a man has an electric shave. Eventually, my eyebrows and eyelashes would go and there wouldn't be a single hair left on my body but, in that moment, as I stared in the mirror and realised that even the G.I. Jane moniker no longer fit, it was a horrifying sight. I seemed to be fading away – in hair, in weight, in presence. I looked like an emaciated, wizened, androgynous being.

Meanwhile, Gary, who had quietly observed my rush to the bathroom, had prepared Steven – time for the men to steel themselves. None of my closest friends were ever frightened of my cancer, but that's not to say they found it any easier to witness.

When I emerged from the bathroom, Gary hugged me and asked if I was okay, not wanting to make a big fuss. I headed to the kitchen for a glass of water. Steven was standing at the stove, his back to me, stirring the spaghetti. He heard me approach but didn't turn around, keeping his head down. 'Another ten minutes and dinner will be ready,' he said.

'Steven? You okay?' I asked.

But he kept stirring the pan, as if I wasn't there.

'Steven, it's okay – you can look at me.'

He turned around and the tears were streaming down his face. 'Jo, I'm sorry. I just can't bear seeing you go through this.'

The next morning, aware that I had refused a wig because it was too itchy and made me look like a mannequin, he unexpectedly turned up at the apartment with a gift: a *Sex and the City* baseball cap. Until that moment, I don't think I realised how much the people around you share the pain and distress, yet it is so often suppressed because they don't feel they have the right to voice it. While cancer hasn't invaded their bodies, it certainly grazes them. And no one's grazes were bigger than Gary's.

He had actually vowed to himself not to cry in front of me because he didn't want me worrying. But as stoical as he was, I knew that he, too, was going through his own emotions. I knew it for sure one Sunday because Josh told me.

They had both been to the park together and, that evening, I was the one who tucked Josh into bed.

'What did you and Daddy do today?' I asked him.

'Daddy, cried – he cried a lot.'

While the tears were inevitable, Gary kept us laughing equally as much, and that's what I preferred to focus on. My cancer didn't dim his humour and he'd search for the silver linings and be a constant source of amusement, sometimes unintentionally so. Like the day he returned from a haircut at Bumble and bumble., my favourite salon.

Knowing it was my favourite, he brought me back a little treat, tucked inside a brown paper bag. I picked out the familiar plastic bottle, took one look at it, looked at him and asked, 'What's this?'

He looked puzzled, as though it was a trick question. 'Your favourite shampoo.'

I stood there, non-eyebrows raised, saying nothing.

Then the penny dropped. 'OHHHHHHHHH!'

What I loved about this gift was the fact that Gary still viewed me as the person he loved, unchanged; not a woman who was fighting cancer. We both roared with laughter and, you know what, sometimes the cliché is true – laughter really is the best medicine. Humour, like pain, is subjective but I needed moments of light relief to make an otherwise miserable experience feel bearable. And we didn't toss away that bottle of shampoo – we kept it in the bathroom, looking forward to the day when I'd be able to use it again.

*

A strange thing happens when you lose your hair and walk down the street in a city like New York – you feel conspicuous and invisible all at once. But even with my *Sex and the City* headgear, there was no hiding the sickly palour and the hairless nape of the neck that told everyone I was bald beneath the cap. I sensed the sympathetic glances from passers-by but also noticed those who didn't wish to make eye contact. Some days, I found it hard to look at myself.

I had a portable make-up mirror in the bathroom, with a magnifying side that allowed me to scrutinise every detail of my face, not for wrinkles or signs of ageing but for the drawn cheeks, scrawny neck and sunken eyes that I'd trace with my fingers just to feel that they were still mine. 'You look awful,' I'd say to myself. And I did. Which was why the bathroom, and those moments at the start and end of each day, became the place for *my* quiet crying. From the end of November, as my physical decline continued, I prayed a lot, too, saying silent prayers in my head, whether at the church down the road, or lying in bed. I didn't ask God for much. I simply asked for the strength to get through because the weaker I felt, the more I wondered about making it.

I maintained the medical rituals, rubbing Cetaphil moisturising cream into my scalp to stop it becoming flaky; gurgling with Biotène mouthwash to prevent mouth ulcers; and downing the anti-sickness pills to stop me from vomiting. But there was nothing I could do about the memory lapses. Let me tell you, 'baby brain' in pregnancy cannot hold a candle to 'chemo brain' – I'd walk down the street and forget where I was. As for imagination, forget it – my mind was too tired to wander anywhere. What with the daily injections and chronic fatigue, it felt like I was spending most days either sleeping or dealing with side effects. But I kept marking down those 'X's on the calendar, through Halloween, through Thanksgiving, and into the final month of treatment – December.

That's when the snow came and I developed the most awful neuropathy – a condition that causes a maddening itch within the hands and feet, but it's an itch within the veins that can't be scratched. Think of the worst case of chilblains and times it by a hundred.

There must have been two inches of snow on the ground when Steven took us to choose a Christmas tree in Union Square. On the way back, after ordering our tree for delivery, the itching was so unbearable that we stopped at a Starbucks for respite. While Gary bought a round of hot chocolates, I sat at a table, removed my shoes and socks, and scratched the soles of my feet more furiously than a dog with fleas.

'Oh, my Gaaad, that is *dis*-gusting!' said a woman sitting nearby.

Steven almost flew at her. 'Hey, lady, have you any idea what—'

But I stopped him. 'Let's go,' I said.

I didn't want the aggro or the sympathy. I just wanted the itching to stop.

We flagged a taxi, but, as my feet continued to burn up, I asked the cabbie to drop us four blocks from home. In the street, using Gary for balance, I again took off my shoes and socks, then padded through the snow barefoot – it was all I could do to extinguish the fire in my nerve endings. I don't think I have ever been so happy not to feel my feet due to the numbing cold.

The one person I turned to throughout this itching torture was a gentle soul called Dr Lily Zhang, the acupuncturist whose expertise was used by Sloan Kettering to alleviate side effects. I had seen her every fortnight since being in New York. When she inserted those needles into me for the first time, I felt my body fill with energy. I started to understand why the Chinese swear by this traditional medicine. I swore by Dr Lily, as well as the apple-spice tea she served in her Zen-like office with its bamboo shutters and a trickling waterfall in the waiting room. I felt so safe in that space as I lay with ice-cold towels draped over my hands and feet while she worked her magic, bringing me relief.

One night, I had a temperature so high that there was talk of me being admitted into hospital, but the doctors were wary about the risk of infection so I stayed home and Dr Lily came to me. My body was obviously fighting something, because I was dripping with sweat and aching all over. 'We do some things, then you relax,' she said.

She inserted her needles then sat at the foot of my bed, reading a book. That woman brought my temperature back to normal in less than two hours – she was a miracle worker. Once her job was done, she packed away her tools and off she went. I've never met anyone in alternative medicine who can compare to her and, bit by bit, she pulled me through the chemotherapy, the final dose of which was on Tuesday 23 December 2003 – an occasion I was determined to mark in style.

I had been anticipating this date for sixteen weeks, and knew exactly what I was going to do: I was going to have the last word. I was going to take back from cancer what it had taken from me in the summer of 2003.

On the morning of my final dose, I applied make-up for the first time in weeks, wore my black Armani suit, and slotted two diamond earrings in my pocket – a repeat of the outfit I should have worn to the Serpentine Gallery party before my diagnosis ruined the evening. Symbolically, this was my way of picking up where I had left off.

I arrived at the clinic overdressed to the nines, aware that every other chemo patient would be wearing the usual comfortable clothes: tracksuits, sweats, t-shirts. Edna, the Russian nurse who administered my every dose, didn't bat an eyelid as I strode in, head held high, looking glamorous – she understood what the day meant and she wasn't going to make a big fuss. No one made a fuss at Sloan Kettering. Be who you want to be. Do whatever you need to do in order to get through. That's the philosophy.

I'd be sick over Christmas but I didn't care because this was the final lap. I took my seat in one of the 'chemo cubicles', rolled up my suit sleeve, relaxed into the chair, rested my head, and closed my eyes. And as I felt that cold juice coursing through my veins one last time, I smiled.

I managed to get through Christmas morning for Josh before we headed to Steven's for the turkey and trimmings, although I fell asleep for most of that afternoon and evening. I didn't expect a memorable festive time, but he and his friends did their best to recreate the magic.

The spirit of Christmas past will forever contain elements of the magic that Mum and Dad created for me as a kid. Conversely, there had been many Christmases since when we hadn't spoken at all. During our stay in New York, my parents called me a handful of times, maybe once every two months. I remember Dad crying in one call, saying he wished I wasn't so far away. And yet we had been so far away for so long, even when we were in the same country.

My mother-in-law, Maureen, was amazing at this time, and she flew out to spend a week supporting me and looking after Josh. Gary's Dad, David, shaved his head the moment my hair fell out in a show of bald-headed solidarity. 'And I won't grow it back until yours has grown back,' he promised. I honestly don't know how I would have got through those months without the special people in my life.

Among them were women in New York like Evelyn Lauder, Rose Marie Bravo and *Town & Country* editor-in-chief Pamela Fiori, who turned up unannounced on my fortieth birthday in November, armed with balloons, cake and sorely needed cheer. 'Honey, we weren't going to allow you to celebrate alone!' said Evelyn.

London friends sent care packages filled with British tea bags and M&S treats. They wrote letters sharing their news, attaching photographs of different events attended and occasions cele-brated – their way, in those pre-Facebook days, of keeping me updated and involved.

I would also lie in bed, close my eyes and imagine dinner and laughter with my circle of friends. I'd go there in my mind, re-living past events and favourite memories. I'd visit our home, too, and 'walk' from room to room, wanting to feel its comfort and familiarity from three thousand miles away. But on Boxing Day that year, I didn't need to imagine my London life. Because two London friends came to me.

Gary had been saying how he had bought tickets to the circus and wanted me to get dressed. All I wanted to do was lounge around in my dressing gown, but I made the effort for Josh. Around noon, as we prepared to leave, Gary made himself scarce, and that was when the doorbell rang. Expecting it to be a delivery, I answered the door . . . and my friends Joel Cadbury and Ollie Vigors were standing there, having jumped on a plane that morn-ing from Heathrow. Suddenly aware that I was without baseball cap, I picked up a book from a side table in the hallway and used it to cover up my baldness. 'Don't look at me! Don't look at me!'

Joel rolled his eyes. 'Do you think we care about that?!' he said, hugging me.

Their visit made my Christmas, and Gary had secretly made up stockings so that everyone had a present to open before we went to lunch at the Mandarin Oriental. For a second, I could have kidded myself that everything was back to normal. Indeed, in the knowledge that I had completed my final cycle of chemo, 'normal' was just around the corner – 2004 couldn't arrive quickly enough.

*

When I next saw Larry, in the first week of January, the only thought on my mind was 'the switch' – the swapping of the tissue expander for my permanent implant. Get that done, and I could go home. I arrived for my appointment full of relief that this day had finally come.

'Okay,' I said, with a sigh. 'We made it – the end!'

Only it wasn't the end. I could tell by the look on Larry's face.

'What's wrong?' I asked.

'I don't think we're quite finished, Jo.'

'What do you mean? You said sixteen weeks. Sixteen weeks of chemotherapy and I'd be done. That's what you said, Larry. I've done everything you asked. I can't do this again . . .'

I could feel myself shaking as I spoke; part dread, part anger. But Larry, as gentle and compassionate as ever, explained that not all treatments run to plan. 'I know it doesn't seem fair but it's important we get this right. I'm sorry, but the chemotherapy has to continue.'

The prescription of potentially another sixteen weeks threw me completely. My approach to life is to know the plan, the timetable, and the direction, and to stick to it – to know where the finishing post lies. Now, after crossing that line, and dressing up to celebrate the victory, I was being told to return to the start and rerun the marathon.

Larry could see my dejection. 'I asked you to trust me at the beginning,' he said, 'and if this wasn't necessary, I wouldn't be putting you through it.'

Fall. Get up. Dust yourself down. Get on with it. Turn the page. That's what I told myself. Later that day, I bought a second calendar and marked out another sixteen weeks, to be chalked off with an 'X', day by day, from January to April 2004. Instead of Christmas, I now set my heart on the change in seasons, from winter to spring.

That same week, I received a photograph in the post from Ruth Kennedy: a framed holiday snap of her, me and our friend Jane Moore, the author and journalist, in a restaurant in Venice. And across the top of that picture, Ruth had written: 'One day, you will wake up and feel on top of the world.' I pinned it to the top of my second chemo calendar – a daily reminder of another finish line that I had to cross.

Even though I wouldn't repeat the exact same cycle – the chemo would now be administered in smaller doses much closer together – the second round hit me harder than the first, mainly due to the continued cumulative effect. It also meant that I couldn't have the implant fitted, meaning another four months wearing the uncomfortable tissue expander, which, come Christmas, couldn't expand any more.

Physically, my body felt against the wall. Mentally, I really didn't know how much more I could give. My chemotherapy-scrambled mind couldn't think straight, became easily confused, and my memory lapses seemed greater than ever before. The spirit within me wanted to fight but sometimes I wondered if I had the strength. Some nights, it felt like I was on the edge and cancer was winning.

It certainly felt that way in the early sleepless hours of one morning, sometime around March 2004.

Gary was fast asleep beside me at the end of a particularly rough day. I felt as poorly as I had ever felt. My temperature was high, the sweats and aching wouldn't stop, and there was a great rash across my torso that resembled a burn. I didn't even have the energy to roll over on to my side. As I lay there, still tasting the ulcer-preventing mouthwash that I'd swilled before bed, I heard and focused on Gary's breaths: his lungs full of life; mine, feeble and wheezy. In the dark, I reached over with my right hand and placed it on his chest to feel the rhythm of him sleeping soundly. I closed my eyes and kept my hand there for a while – each of his breaths anchoring me.

I was too scared to sleep, because I had convinced myself that I wouldn't wake again. What scared me was the sense of calmness that surrounded the fear, and that calm sent my mind racing. *Was I calm because I was accepting it? Is this how death happens? You reach the nadir of suffering and then the body meekly surrenders as you sleep?* Whether in my mind or body, death seemed close enough to frighten me.

I lifted up the duvet and looked at my skinny frame – there was nothing really there; nothing I truly recognised as me. I pulled the duvet up to my chin, and, even though Gary was beside me, I felt panic – a panic that I had probably generated with my own downward-spiralling thoughts but a panic nonetheless. And I felt a compulsion to see Josh, regardless of how weak I was.

I slipped out of bed on to my knees and I crawled across the carpet, on to the landing, into his room, towards his single bed, where I placed my hands on the safety bar and kneeled there, looking down on him, in his pyjamas, on his back. I now listened to his breathing – slight and full of innocence. I hated what cancer was doing to me, and I hated the idea that it could take me away from my son. I spoke to God there, though it was more a plea than a prayer. 'Please, God,' I whispered, 'I don't want to die. Let me see my son grow up. I don't care what I have to go through, but let me see him grow up.'

I kept watching Josh because just being with him brought calm. I gave it a good ten or fifteen minutes before crawling back to bed and, as my head sank into the pillow, I felt instantly at ease, no longer scared of the dark. Gary was still fast asleep. I tucked my hand into his and closed my eyes.

I had a dream that night, one that I remember as vividly today as I did the following morning: *I'm sitting in a swing chair in a garden on a summery day. I feel utter peace. I'm holding a glass of white wine. I glance at my hand and notice brown spots – the aged skin of an elderly woman. I look up. In the distance, I see Josh as a grown young man, with his arms around a girl, and they are giggling out loud. And that's the only sound I hear and then I sense someone telling me, 'This is the day I'll call you back . . .'*

It may have just been a dream but it gave me one more thing to hold on to – and, psychologically, it would mark a turning point.

TWENTY-THREE

I sensed my 'fight' returning while having lunch one day in a small Italian trattoria eight blocks from the apartment. It offered the tastiest home-made pasta but, more than anything, it rarely got busy and the tables were nicely spaced apart – important factors when, due to my vulnerable immune system, I had to be wary of other people's germs. That's a point worth noting: a cancer patient is the one who's at risk of catching something, not the other way around.

There was only me and one or two others in the restaurant on this particular day – Gary was flying back from London that evening – and I was tucking into a bowl of spaghetti when I noticed an old lady walk in, swamped by a big fur coat, and accompanied by a young man who turned out to be her grandson. The waiter showed them to the table next to where I was seated. There must have been three feet between us but, as I took a sip from my glass of water, the woman was eyeing me warily. I had grown used to frowns and stares, so I ignored her. Yet even though she said nothing, her discomfort remained loud.

When the waiter returned to take her order, she spoke to him from behind a cupped hand. Then she gathered her handbag, stood and moved with her grandson to the other side of the room, making me feel contagious, unclean, like I had the plague.

How dare you do that to me!

I didn't take my eyes off her as she relaxed at her new table, seemingly comfortable now that she had removed herself from potential harm. I placed my fork and spoon in the bowl, dabbed my mouth with a napkin, stood and walked over. She looked aghast at the sight of this fast-approaching disease, dressed in an Abercrombie & Fitch sweatshirt, white Gap jeans and a baseball gap.

'Excuse me,' I said, polite but firm. 'Can I just say how hurtful that was. Can I also point out to you that I have *breast cancer*. You can't catch *cancer* by sitting on the table across from me. You can't catch *cancer* even if we were to hold hands.'

She blanked me, nonchalantly avoiding eye contact, but I had made my point and she heard me. I returned to my table and ordered coffee, feeling a little proud of myself for standing up for myself and for everyone else whose humanity is ignored because of an illness. A minute or so later, the young man came over. 'I'm so sorry,' he said. 'My grandmother – she's from a different generation.'

'No need for you to apologise,' I said. 'I thought it was rude, so I had to say something.'

He and I went on to have a pleasant chat about my treatment and my time in New York. The lady, too old to give a damn, never came across or said anything, turning her head as I paid my bill and headed out. Sadly, this wasn't an isolated incident.

That same week, I had gone shopping at a famous apparel store, in search of a cashmere sweater for winter. I felt lousy and probably looked terrible, but even cancer patients need retail therapy now and again. I was browsing a circular table, picking up one sweater after another when a stroppy shop assistant hurried over. 'Can I help you?'

'No, thank you. I'm only looking.'

'Well, if you're only looking, please don't touch the sweaters.'

'I beg your pardon?'

'Just don't touch the sweaters, honey.'

Translated – you have no hair, you're ill, and you're infecting our clothes.

I looked at her; she looked at me – a battle of wills. And so, like a child wrecking someone's sandcastles on the beach, I used both of my hands to fan, ruffle and scatter the entire collection of sweaters, leaving them in disarray. I turned on my heels and left the young lady to pick her chin up off the floor.

I hadn't felt so empowered for months – back to being the disruptor, my old self. And as I walked down the street, I heard Mary Massie in my head. 'Don't lose your fight, Jo. Don't lose your fight.'

Mary continued to be a source of strength. I took my vivid dream into one session and explained how close to the edge I had felt that night. What bothered me, I told her, was that my every waking thought was consumed with my illness. All I seemed to do was bounce between the apartment and hospital, and the link between 'A' and 'B' was cancer. Every task I did revolved around cancer. Even New York felt like an all-immersive experience of cancer. It was in me and around me, and I wanted it to stop. 'I get up every day and it's all I think about. I go to bed at night and it's all I think about. It's even in my dreams.'

'Explain to me why you think about it so much,' she said.

'Because I'm fighting it, and it's hard to forget what you're fighting.'

'Jo, the more we think about something, the more we expect it, the more it's there. A day will come in the not-too-distant future when you'll think, "Oh, I haven't thought about it in the last hour", and then, "Oh, I haven't thought about it all afternoon." But we get there by not attaching to the thought of cancer. You make it sound as if the thoughts are in control of you when they're not.'

She made me see that the less I ruminated, the more room I would have to think about life in general; the less intense my focus on the disease, the more I'd be able to appreciate the bigger picture. We spoke about my creative process and how I choose to focus on fragrance; likewise, she said, you can choose *not to* focus on something. How ironic that I, this woman who needs to feel in control, couldn't control her own thoughts.

With practice, and fortified by those moments in the Italian trattoria and the apparel store, I found more room to focus on the horizon, rather than just the spot where I stood. As Mary said, it was the doctors' responsibility to focus on dealing with the cancer; it was my responsibility to keep the mind focused. I was done with feeling lousy, with crying, with being constantly fatigued. I wanted to fight for the future portrayed in that dream. I hadn't felt so determined in months. And, as things would turn out, the arrival of this renewed defiance was well timed for the next challenge that lay around the corner.

A month or two into my treatment, I contracted shingles, which was a worrying new side effect because it wouldn't take much for a virus like that to turn into a critical condition. For my own good, I was hospitalised and placed in isolation – a bubble within my New York bubble. I didn't care that I felt cut off from every-one else. Those four walls felt like my safe room, protecting me within a pocket of air that only I could breathe. Doctors, nurses and caterers, even Gary, had to gown up each time they came in to see me. Two weeks in a bubble is a long time, let me tell you. But there was an unforeseen benefit to having this virus – Larry halted the chemotherapy.

He said the virus was a sign that my body had taken as much as it could. 'It's over, Jo. You're finished,' he said – the words I never thought I'd hear. More than six months after my mastectomy, I could now look forward to 'the switch' and finally go home. All I had to do was have a final scan to make sure everything was okay.

Days later, I underwent the scan without an ounce of apprehension. I couldn't remember the last time my mind had been worry-free. I joked with the nurses. I told them how excited I was to return to London. Afterwards, I sat in the waiting room, awaiting the formality of the results. And then Dr Heerdt walked in, sat down beside me and gently explained that they had detected something suspicious in the other breast.

As much as this news was a sucker punch that winded me, I wasn't frightened. I wasn't frightened because the instant she told me, I knew exactly what I was going to do. This time, I would be the one calling the shots, not cancer, not the doctors. In fact, I had never felt stronger as Dr Heerdt showed me the scan, pointing out speckles of calcium deposits that concerned her. Such deposits can sometimes be an early indicator of cancer, and sometimes they can be nothing. 'But we'll have to keep an eye on them,' she said.

I didn't even ask another question. 'I've had enough, Dr Heerdt,' I said. 'I'm not living with that kind of worry. Take it off. Book me in for another mastectomy.'

She, and Larry, implored me not to be so rash, to sleep on it, to go speak with Mary Massie. But I was emphatic. I wasn't going to live with a one per cent chance of cancer returning. 'I don't care what anyone says, I am *never* going to go through this again.'

I knew what this decision meant: more surgery, more pain, another scar, and another damn tissue expander to join its ever-lingering companion on the other side. But a few weeks of discomfort was preferable to years spent worrying. Knowing the nature of my mind, that's exactly what I would have done, forever checking for lumps and going through the anxiety of cancer possibly returning. I didn't want that sword hanging over me, which was why it didn't even feel like a big decision. In the scheme of life, and with my heightened appreciation for that life because of everything I had gone through, a preventive, prophylactic mastectomy was no price to pay. In fact, it would be one of the best decisions I would ever make. And that was the point – it was *my decision. My choice. I* was eliminating risk, claiming *my* survival and doing it on *my* terms.

After going through the motions of mandatory counselling, I strode into the operating theatre a week later, feeling like a completely different person the second time around. No tears. No prayers. No fear. And when I woke up, there were no bleak thoughts. I went into surgery and lost not only my left breast but also cancer's hold over me.

I opened my eyes to find Gary sitting by my side. 'How do you feel?' he asked.

'Great,' I said. 'Empowered.'

We went on to have the kind of conversation we hadn't had for a while: one that didn't revolve around cancer or treatment but around hopes and dreams, and going home and taking holidays. 'I want to go and sit on a beach, paddle in the sea, play with Josh and not worry about a thing,' I said. Neither of us could remember the last time we had felt sand between our toes.

When you marry young and take your vows, you say the words 'in sickness and in health' without really imagining that you'll have to live them out, but Gary had honoured that promise to the letter. He was still by my side and, mercifully, I was still by his.

'Any regrets?' he asked, checking in on my decision to have a second mastectomy.

'No, I won't regret this,' I said. And I never have. Not once.

Three weeks after surgery, Dr Disa issued the green light for a holiday in Antigua. After almost a year in the concrete jungle of Manhattan, and after the monotony of chemotherapy and hospitals, the prospect of white beaches and Caribbean tranquillity couldn't have sounded dreamier. Even though I was still bearing my matching tissue expanders, I packed my beachwear and new Eres swimsuit, which is ideal for any woman who has had a mastectomy; to this day, I wear it and no one would guess that I've had surgery.

I wanted a true, sun-soaked, get-away-from-it-all escape involving nothing but relaxation and, to make it extra special, we arranged for our friends Joel and Divia, Ollie and Darcy, and Steven to fly in. We booked a place belonging to my friend Gordon Campbell Gray – the Carlisle Bay Hotel on the south side of the island. Think white beaches, palm trees, bright green-hued waters, and a rainforest for a backdrop – the most perfect, idyllic escape.

I knew Gordon, a big-hearted Glaswegian, would look after us but, on arrival, he didn't look quite as relaxed as normal. He pulled me to one side, wringing his hands. 'I don't want you to worry. I've got this handled,' he said, 'but when I booked you in, I hadn't realised that we have a big press launch going on.'

'What kind of press launch?'

He winced. 'A beauty press launch – the world and his wife are here.'

Oh, the irony. Over the previous months, Charlotte had fielded and declined requests from magazine editors and feature writers for an 'exclusive' interview with me about my cancer. One Fleet Street journalist even tried a classic manipulation technique, warning that, 'If Jo won't give us an interview, we'll stand outside the hospital and take a picture anyway.' They never did get that picture. In fact, no one did. And yet there I was, on an island, in the same hotel as every beauty/fashion journalist and editor from Britain. You've got to laugh at life's comedic timing.

My hair was probably half an inch thick by now but I was still thin, with skin desperately in need of sun and an expander-enhanced bosom that could have rivalled Dolly Parton. But what could I do? I certainly wasn't prepared to hide away – I'd done enough of that in New York. So I decided to enjoy my holiday come what may, well aware that this crossing-over of worlds was unavoidable, and that word would soon get out. In the end, I had nothing to worry about because not one of those editors or journalists approached me or called my room. I spent time on the beach and paddled in the ocean, but no one published a photo, and not a single sentence was written anywhere. As one of them would say afterwards, everyone respected what I had come through and didn't wish to intrude. I don't think I'll ever be able to express my gratitude for such collective decency and kindness that placed me ahead of any story they could file.

I was able to kick back and enjoy a holiday in which I started to feel normal again. As a group, we lazed and read books, hired a boat and drank rum punch, sat underneath the stars and enjoyed candlelit dinners on the beach. Ollie and Darcy got engaged, and Steven bought Josh his first bicycle, leading to much excited giggling as he learned to ride on the beach path. We had a mar-vellous, memorable time in a paradise location that told me the good times were back. It would take me a while before I fully felt like my old self, but this was a happy start. All I had to do now was return to New York so that Dr Disa could finally carry out 'the switch' and provide me with my 'new look'.

*

There is a funny story attached to that final operation because Gary had been told that surgery would take no longer than sixty to ninety minutes. Two and a half hours in, having read every available magazine in the waiting room, he started to worry that there had been another complication. By the time Dr Disa emerged, Gary was in a bit of a state. 'What's the problem? Why the delay?!'

Dr Disa laughed. 'Gary, you and I both know your wife. We spent forever in there making sure the implants were evenly matched and *absolutely perfect,* otherwise she'd have us back here within the week, doing them again!'

Bless Joseph Disa – he knew me so well.

I couldn't travel for seven days post-op so, as Gary and I started preparing our return to London, we went shopping and I had only one destination in mind: Prada, to buy a treat I had long been eyeing up as my reward when everything was over – a tan brown leather handbag with orange lining. As I walked down the street, with short, cropped hair, and dressed in a leather jacket, knee length black dress, and biker boots, no one stared or frowned; no one seemed wary of me any more. Recovering from cancer is a lesson in rebuilding self-confidence, and the smallest gestures or comments from others seem to carry extra significance. So when I walked into Prada and the male shop assistant came over and said, 'Oh my God, lady! I *love* your look!' he had no idea the boost he gave me that day. I was only buying a handbag, and it was probably a standard compliment that he issued to others, but those words made me feel feminine again. A stranger – someone who had no idea about my story – had acknowledged me as a woman, not a survivor of cancer, and it felt bloody wonderful.

Back at the apartment, Gary and I decided to celebrate my new-found confidence by sending out a general email that announced not only our imminent homecoming, but some surprise news that not everyone knew about. Typical of our humour, we wrote a message to our friends that simply said: *'Gary and Jo will soon be returning home, and they are pleased to announce the birth of two bouncing girls!'*

We were, of course, referring to my new boobs but some people who hadn't heard from us for a while initially thought we were having twins. One friend even sent matching babygrows! The humorous and confused messages we received kept us laughing for the rest of the week. I think people are frightened to laugh when a friend comes through cancer, but, for me, it was the first indication that everything was returning to normal. Second only to the words, 'Oh my God, lady! I *love* your look', laughter is probably the best sound in the world.

My *Sex and the City* baseball cap was the one memento I'd retain from my time in New York. The rest – my trainers, bed sheets, patchwork duvet, and every top, sweater, tracksuit and pair of jeans – were bundled into a pile and thrown out, because to me each garment still smelled of that sterile hospital air and chemo-therapy. This was my small purging of belongings that no longer served any purpose as we packed up our Manhattan life.

We would, of course, return to New York on business but it was nevertheless sad to leave behind the friends who had offered such loving support. None more so than people like our doorman Paul, for whom I perhaps reserved my biggest hug. 'I'll never forget what you did for me,' I told him as he waved us off one last time.

'Just doing my job, Miss Jo,' he said, but we both knew that he did far more than just his job. I do hope that he is reading this somewhere and realises what a unique human being he is, and how much I regard him as a hero.

I said my goodbyes to the wonderful doctors and nurses at the Sloan Kettering, giving everyone a Jo Malone London gift bag.

As Evelyn Lauder had predicted, these were the people, led by Larry Norton, who had saved my life, and I went round each department, expressing my eternal gratitude. It felt strange saying farewell to those people who had picked me up and put me back together again, and yet they couldn't be happier to see me walk away – after all, that's the very outcome they are always shooting for. And that's why I chose Coldplay's *Fix You* as one of my Desert Island Discs on BBC Radio 4 in 2015, dedicating it to Larry and every doctor and nurse who stands and fights cancer. Larry and I would remain dear friends because when someone as special as him walks into your life, you make sure you stay in touch. We didn't know it yet but we would share a special occasion together in London – four years in the future – that would truly allow me to demonstrate my gratitude.

My re-entry into London, in May 2004, felt like a reunion with an old friend who, in my lowest moments, I hadn't been sure I'd see again. After disembarking from the plane at London Heathrow, the first thing I did was bend down and kiss the floor on entering the airport. It wasn't quite the green, green grass of home but it was English terra firma nonetheless.

The only work-based task I faced when I got home was the prospect of doing an interview about my cancer. The requests intensified once word got out that I was back, and if I didn't address it straightaway, it would linger like a cloud. Charlotte had covered my back up until that point, but we both knew that the best approach to any difficult subject matter was to take control and lead from the front foot. Personally, it also felt important that I share my story in the hope that other breast cancer patients would know that there can be a positive outcome. The more we shine a light into the darkest, scariest of places, the more acceptable it seems and the less alone we have to be.

The only people I trusted to do justice to my story and handle it sensitively were Sue Peart, the editor of *You* magazine, and journalist Fiona McCarthy. We had done interviews in the past and, for me, their integrity is second to none.

A day or so after the interview was published, I was shopping at Marks & Spencer, buying every kind of meal – you would have thought an M&S prohibition was imminent the way I filled my basket. I must have been standing in the queue less than a minute when the lady in front, who was having her shopping bagged, turned around and said, 'Excuse me, you're Jo Malone, aren't you?'

'Yes. That's me.'

'Oh,' she said, 'I read the article in *You* magazine. Can I ask you something?'

'Of course you can,' I said, smiling.

'Do you still have nipples?'

I promise you, I'm standing in a busy M&S, with three or four people behind me, and enough chicken Kiev to feed an army, and that's what she asked me. I felt gobsmacked that anyone could ask such an invasive question, within earshot of so many others. The cashier, mouth agape, waited for my reaction but I was too shocked to say anything. I'm rarely left speechless but I couldn't find the words.

As the woman's query was greeted by silence – mine and everyone else's around me – I think the awkwardness dawned. 'Well, it was a lovely interview. Nice meeting you. Good luck!'

London: how I missed its weird, wonderful, unpredictable, brazen, unapologetic but well-intended ways. It felt great to be home.

One event that I had been really looking forward to was the 6th Annual White Tie & Tiara Ball to benefit the Elton John AIDS

Foundation. At Elton's invitation, I had served on the event's committee since 2000. Two years later, I had made a limited edition White Tie & Tiara fragrance to be given as a gift for each guest before one thousand bottles went on public sale, with a share of the proceeds going to the foundation.

This event, held in the grounds of his home in Old Windsor, brings so many friends together, and the 2004 ball would be the first time that I'd been able to see everyone gathered under one marquee roof since returning from New York. I now had a healthy head of short hair and an equally healthy weight, so it felt good to be stepping out in my glad rags for a night out with a group of special people that included Jane Moore and Gary Farrow, Alan and Caroline Levy, Ruth Kennedy and Bruce Dundas, and Joel and Divia Cadbury.

Midway through the night, I was at our table chatting with Gary when we heard a lot of whooping and cheering behind us – Elton had taken his place at the piano on stage to start playing some hits, which was a guaranteed way to get the party started. Three numbers in, I heard the opening bars of a recognisable song and I saw Ruth rushing over to pull me on to the dance floor. 'You're not missing this one!'

I'm Still Standing was being played and, with my girlfriends standing around me, we started jumping and dancing and belting out the chorus as one, like it was our anthem and my song.

'*Don't you know I'm still standing better than I ever did / Looking like a true survivor, feeling like a little kid / I'm still standing after all this time / Picking up the pieces of my life without you on my mind . . .*'

I turned to Gary, standing by my side, clapping along, looking as happy as I felt. And then we all started punching the air for the chorus. *'I'M STILL STANDING! YEAH! YEAH! YEAH!'*

It was the day that Ruth had promised would arrive when she wrote her message on the photo she'd sent me in New York. 'One day, you will wake up and feel on top of the world.'

In this precious life, those are the kind of memories and marks that people leave behind, far more visible to me than any tissue scar. When I look at the faded red line that runs across my chest, I don't see a reminder of cancer; I see a reminder of a wound from a war that was won with the help of friends. Moreover, it doesn't define me – it only signifies eight months and three chapters in my life story. Mary Massie taught me that. She taught me all about putting cancer into perspective.

PART THREE

Reinvention

TWENTY-FOUR

Having got my life back, my first instinct was to reawaken the businesswoman and start making product again – the sure-fire way to reconnect the part of me that had been dormant for almost a year. Ordinarily, my inclination would have been to hit the ground running but Mary Massie had already pulled on those reins.

Before I left New York, she told me: 'It may feel as though you are walking a tightrope without a safety net so go easy on yourself.' She went on to explain that many cancer survivors feel a little fragile and unsure of themselves for the first year – the body and mind don't so easily forget the rigours of treatment. So when my old dynamic self didn't immediately snap back into place, at least I understood the reason.

In my mind, it also explained why I didn't feel an immediate 'click' on being back at work; why my sense of smell made a stuttering return, and why my creativity was more a pilot light-sized flame rather than its usual blaze. My nose had been subdued by the effects of chemotherapy and, like throwing wet wood on a fire, it wouldn't ignite straightaway.

Knowing that I had no choice but to be patient, I eased my way in, working in Sloane Street, attending meetings, and working on plans for a new shop in New York. At home, I began tinkering around with different notes to rework my nose, allowing it to ramble until it felt ready to create again.

It would take a year for the next fragrance to come to me – Pomegranate Noir.

I wrestled to create that fragrance – the creativity arrived piecemeal rather than flowing, and I still didn't feel the 'click' of everything falling into place. So when I nailed that scent, I definitely felt a sense of accomplishment because part of me had privately wondered if chemotherapy had caused some kind of irreparable damage. What I couldn't have known was that it would be the last fragrance I'd make for Jo Malone London.

Gary and I flew back to New York for the grand opening of our new flagship store in the US on the Upper East Side on Madison Avenue. It felt good to be back in Manhattan for purely business purposes, and I was determined to shine on my first 'official' stepping-out post-cancer.

For that reason, I wore my 'lucky' DKNY black leather jacket, which always made me feel kick-ass confident. I'd often pick out those outfits or shoes that made me feel good about myself. In the initial months of resuming an active life, confidence-boosting fashions become suits of armour to cover up a sense of vulnerability that was hard to shake.

'Ready?' asked Gary, holding out his arm to link with mine as we left the hotel.

I took a breath. 'Ready,' I said, even though I felt an unusual trepidation that I didn't voice and couldn't explain. Something niggled me even before we arrived for the spectacular launch.

Throughout the evening, as the glitterati and media turned out in force, a mix of strangers and familiar faces wished me well and offered congratulations on another elegant store.

'Thank you,' I said to one person.

'That's kind of you,' I said to another.

'Yes, it is exciting, isn't it?' I said, lying to everyone.

Because the truth was that I didn't feel the usual excitement. At one point, I looked around and saw my name everywhere – on the signs, the gift bags and the product – and felt weirdly detached, as if this was somebody else's life. A complete disconnect. Something had shifted so dramatically that it caught even me by surprise.

It's difficult to pinpoint how or why my feelings changed, but there is no doubt that coming through cancer changed my perspective. I think a period of re-evaluation follows any life-changing experience, especially one in which you have to confront your own mortality, and I began to rethink and reframe a lot of things. Indeed, I had a spring-clean of anything and everything that didn't make me feel good. I cleared out my closet, discarding old clothes. I sifted through friendships, putting aside the ones that only brought gossip, negativity or self-centredness. I reviewed my priorities and contemplated what I wanted to do with the rest of my life. And as I stood in that shop on Madison Avenue, the future didn't seem so clear any more.

In my absence, the business had understandably carried on without me and continued to grow, but something felt strangely different. This disconnect – the feeling that my heart wasn't in it any more – perturbed me, though I didn't breathe a word to Gary, not wishing to give voice to the doubt, just in case it made the doubt grow louder.

At first, I tried dismissing it as a mood or a phase, but, with each passing week, I increasingly viewed my one-time passion as nothing more than a business, and it had never been that to me before; it *could never* be that to me. I will forever be a person who is one hundred per cent or nothing and, though I couldn't quite understand why, I felt incredibly half-hearted about everything.

I even started to wonder if this was because my sense of smell wasn't firing in the same way, as if all this doubt was blocking my creativity. Estée Lauder had been wonderful to me, and wonderful for the brand, but the dynamics had changed somehow during my time away. Whether that change was within me or a part of the business, I didn't know.

I also found myself pondering the preciousness of time. When undergoing chemotherapy, time drags and time gets lost. Every minute can feel like an hour, especially with itching hands and feet. But then, in contrast, days blur and merge into one. I'd wake up on a Friday and suddenly it was Sunday.

Sitting in London, having come through the other side, my appreciation of time had changed, and the only tick-tock I could hear was that of my time with Josh. He was now four and a half, about to start school, and I contemplated how fast the next fourteen years would fly by, and then I worried how many of those years I would get to share with him – I no longer viewed life as a guarantee that could be taken for granted.

Together with Gary, I wanted to be there every morning that Josh left for school, for every school pick-up, for every sport's day, and for every Friday night dinner-as-a-family – the ritual that remains sacrosanct to this day. I wanted to invest my time in *him*, nothing else. The fact that my heart felt sad but not heavy at the thought of leaving the business told me everything. And the emotion I felt at the opening in Madison Avenue was still speaking to me, saying the same thing: 'You don't belong here any more. It's time to move on.'

I knew I couldn't hide this feeling of unrest from Gary for too long and, sure enough, one evening he noticed that I seemed subdued and asked what was wrong. I had been reluctant to say anything because our business had been his dream as well as mine. Once I aired my doubts, the genie would be out of the bottle, so to speak, and I didn't know what the ramifications would be. Little did I realise that he, too, was feeling disenchanted. But, like me, he had been keeping his own counsel, not wanting to upset the apple cart so soon after getting our lives back on track.

The moment we uncorked our innermost feelings and talked them through, the more we agreed that the dynamics of the business had changed; it felt less 'ours' and more corporate all of a sudden. Maybe Gary, like me, viewed life through a new lens now; maybe cancer had taken the edge off things for him, too. Even as we turned our feelings inside out, we couldn't really pin down one fundamental cause for this shift, but the bottom line was that we didn't feel the same, and neither of us was one hundred per cent happy any more. We asked ourselves one question: 'Is this the dream we still want?' The joint answer was no. Once a confessional chat reaches that kind of admission, there really isn't much more to know.

When we first struck the acquisition deal with Lauder in 1999, I think he and I thought it was forever. I know Leonard did, too. So when I telephoned him to say that we felt it was time to move on, I don't think he saw it coming. He didn't want us to leave – we did talk about alternative options to keep us involved somehow – but he knew what I'd been through and respected our reasoning. 'As long as you have thought this through and you are sure?' he said.

'We've thought it through. It's the right thing to do, Leonard,' I said.

I put the phone down and I can't say that I felt complete conviction in those words, but the decision had been made and I was determined to stick to my guns. It was time for a change, I told myself. I won't regret this. 'I won't regret this,' I kept thinking.

They would turn out to be famous last thoughts.

I had made the right decision for the business *and* for Estée Lauder but, for me, purely creatively speaking, as someone whose purpose in life is to make fragrance, it would turn out to be the worst decision I could have made. But that realisation would come later, with the benefit of hindsight, once there was more distance between me and my recovery. For now, two sets of lawyers would reconvene to activate a clause that had always existed as part of the original buyout – the clause that permitted my exit.

As in 1999, the first thing I did was ensure that the existing staff was kept on. My decision should have no bearing on their liveli-hoods, and Lauder respected that. With that guarantee secured, I gathered the team in our offices at the Old Imperial Laundry and broke the news. That was a tough day. We had shared the same pride in the brand. We had flown the flag from Walton Street to America and to the rest of the world. One employee begged me to stay. 'Change your mind, Jo. Find a way. This company is you,' she said. I felt the business pull on me. I felt every fragrance tug on my coat-tails. But I kept moving towards the exit door, believing I was doing the right thing.

My lawyer Jeremy came over to the apartment to run through the proposed exit terms, but he specifically wished to discuss one aspect – the 'lock out' clause that insisted that I couldn't compete, or even work, in the industry for five years. 'You have to under-stand what this means,' he said. 'You are literally locked out for a long period of time. No making fragrances. No involvement or association with any cosmetics or beauty business.'

In 2006, the year 2011 seemed an age away. Josh would be ten. I couldn't even look that far ahead. 'That clause is irrelevant to me,' I said. 'I won't be building another business. I won't be creating fragrance ever again.'

Had anyone asked me to place every penny I had on the square that said 'Won't be making fragrances again', I would have shoved all my chips on to that promise.

I only ever had one moment of hesitation, and that was when Leonard came to London for a farewell dinner at Harry's Bar, joined by John Larkin, the finance director, and Sally Sussman, the global head of communications. Leonard said some kind words about our achievement in building a brand that had gone global and, I won't lie, as he spoke, painting a verbal montage of the previous few years, a little voice within me did ask, 'Are you making the biggest mistake of your life here?' But I dismissed it as a natural hesitation that sentimentality creates. Isn't that the trickery of nostalgia, misleading us into believing that we can still have things as they used to be? Anyway, it was too late. The contracts were drawn up, the press announcement had been prepared, and all we had to do was add our signatures to the paperwork.

The formalities went ahead and, on 1 February 2006, the news was announced. 'JO MALONE BOWS OUT OF HER OWN BRAND' said *Women's Wear Daily* in an article that noted the 'personal challenges' I had recently faced. But even the magazine's journalist, Pete Born, wondered about my decision. 'It is difficult to imagine Malone leaving the business. It is in her blood,' he wrote. From what I have since learned, I think many in the industry felt the same way.

I didn't find it easy to tear myself away, which was why I offered no comment to the media beyond a letter of resignation that was widely circulated to the press, and it seems right that I choose to rely on those words now to sum up my accurate feelings at the time: *'After much soul-searching, I believe that this is a good time to make this decision as the brand is in a secure position and I have many other dreams and passions I would like to fulfil. Every moment of building this special business — from the first day we opened our doors through to today, and all the wonderful moments in between, has been a magnificent journey.'*

On our last day in the Sloane Street shop, after thanking and saying goodbye to so many loyal customers, I counted down to closing time by walking through a few memories and honouring some hard-to-surrender retail rituals. The place where I lingered longest was the treatment room. I took a few moments in there, folding towels and stacking away some sheets as I remembered all the clients who had walked through that door after first trotting up the stairs to our flat in Chelsea. I then headed to the shop floor where I rearranged some gift bags beneath the till before restocking the shelves with fragrances one last time, making sure everything was perfectly in place for the next morning. I remembered how Gary and I had stood in Walton Street and watched the awning go up – the first time I'd seen my name above the door. It seemed odd to be leaving that name behind now and yet it also felt good to know that the heartbeat of the brand would keep ticking.

We turned out the lights and, a little under twenty years since launching the business with a portable treatment table and product carried in two holdalls, Gary and I walked away from Jo Malone London and everything we had created. But, as I would soon discover, walking away was one thing – letting go would prove harder to do.

TWENTY-FIVE

On the first day of the rest of my life, I rose as usual at 6.30 a.m., made a cup of coffee for Gary and me, and helped Josh get dressed, all the while pondering a gloriously free day, week, month, year. I didn't have a shop to open, a fragrance to make, a meeting to attend, a flight to catch, or a problem to solve. Nothing. And 'nothing' felt strange. I can't say that I had given much thought to this day so, when it arrived, I didn't really know what to do with myself; it was perhaps the one occasion when I hadn't written a things-to-do list, probably because there didn't feel a pressing need to do anything. After walking Josh to school, a five-minute stroll from home, I stood and watched him go into class, and thought, 'Now what?'

Out of habit, I took the phone from my pocket – it had never been so silent. Back at the apartment, I flicked open my diary and all I saw was white space and empty hours. White space and silence – that's how I remember this time.

I stood in the kitchen, made another cup of coffee and, as the kettle boiled, my eyes spotted the letter on the fridge, from Josh's teacher, announcing a 'cake day' that same week. I doubt there has been a time, previously or since, when the words 'cake day' had stirred such excitement. Before I knew it, I was wrist-deep in flour, caster sugar, butter and eggs, feeling a little proud of myself. I hadn't made a proper cake since being a teenager and baking one each year for Mum's birthday.

Previously, I had bought some M&S muffins and stuck Smarties on the top for my contribution for Josh's school, but now I had the opportunity to channel my inner Mary Berry, bake a whole cake and be the star mum.

I carried on in this vein for the remaining four days of that week, going on food shops, running errands, and baking a tray of chocolate brownies as a treat for Josh. But I soon realised that all I was doing was clock-watching until 3.30 p.m., when it became time to pick him up again – and this was how it would be for months on end. Now, I acknowledge that for some people this kind of day is heaven but, for me, it wasn't – a fact that was dawning a little too late.

I took a breath. *Give it time.*

Time – that thing I had said I wanted.

Not once did I doubt my decision to spend more time with Josh; my evenings and weekends with him would be endless fun, filled with precious memories that I wouldn't swap for anything. My difficulty was not knowing what to do with myself in those vast chunks of time outside of 'motherhood', between 9 a.m. and 3.30 p.m. I hadn't expected to feel so redundant. I hadn't expected 'freedom' to feel so confining.

'You're bound to be restless,' said Gary. 'Relax. Let's enjoy this time!'

He'd keep saying that and the more he said it, the more elusive being able to 'relax' became.

I'd hoover the house, polish the shelves and every piece of cutlery, reorganise the fridge and rearrange my wardrobe, finessing its colour co-ordination. I'd complete all the chores and errands by 10.30 a.m., leaving the apartment looking immaculate. I made the husband in *Sleeping with the Enemy* look messy.

Gary took up the guitar, and he'd practise morning, noon and night, but that only served to expose the fact that I had found nothing to engage me. We got a dog, Teri, and I swear she became the most-walked dog in the whole of London; by the end of our two-hour-long 'walkies' each day, I swear she was pulling *me* home. I indulged in some retail therapy. I filled my weekday diary with lunches with friends. I started running with Gary and we'd go for leisurely breakfasts afterwards, reading our newspapers in life's slow lane. I loved doing all those things but these 'treats' now became daily occurrences. If it is Christmas every day, Christmas is bound to lose its appeal.

One month, I seemed to spend the entire time making ice cream, trying to see if my sense of taste was as effective as my sense of smell. The end result was a freezer filled with everything from Limoncello to orange blossom to beetroot ice cream; you name it, I tried making it. But inspiration didn't bite. No matter how much I tried to keep myself occupied, I couldn't shift a fidgetiness and frustration that felt more pronounced week on week.

Back then, I didn't understand my inability to relax; in fact, it infuriated me that I couldn't enjoy a well-deserved period of downtime like Gary could. There I was, in a privileged position, spending quality time with my family, with sufficient money in the bank, and yet the void felt cavernous. I wouldn't blame anyone for thinking: 'You had a nice house in a nice area, and cash in the bank – you didn't even know you were born.' Trust me, I had that same chastising thought a million times. Yet thoughts and reality checks didn't give me purpose. I needed to work, to create, to build something – that's what I had been born to do. A musician wakes up and wants to make music. An artist wants to paint. I wanted to make fragrance, but I had taken myself out of the game. What a fool.

I can now see that I didn't know *how* to stop. As a child, I learned to associate work and busyness with survival, whether that meant staying on top of the chores, or making face creams when Mum fell ill. As a teenager and young woman, I worked all hours God sent in order to stay afloat, first for Mum and then for myself. From then on, Gary and I had only ever built and kept building to secure our future together. Even dealing with cancer was a pursuit of survival. Every day, I'd had to fight for the right to live. I think that's why the sense of redundancy was so instant. My psyche had only ever known life chasing goals, so when I suddenly stopped, my entire being wondered what the hell was going on.

The words of my lawyer Jeremy – 'Are you sure you know what this means?' – would return to haunt me more times than I can remember during the five years of my 'lock out'. I had extended my wrists and put up no resistance to the golden handcuffs. I had been naive to think I would never want to create again, and I kicked myself for not paying closer attention to that one clause. I foolishly believed that I could turn off creativity, contrary to everything I had known in the past. But I realised too late that you can't switch off your very expression in life. Day in, day out, I could find nothing that would hold my attention and make me feel the same way as fragrance.

Cancer hadn't changed me as much as I thought.

Within weeks, as if to compound matters, my sense of smell returned stronger than ever, conjuring inspirations and notes that now had nowhere to go. The period of 2006 to 2011 felt like being lost in a wilderness, without bearings, without compass. I was a city girl who thought that camping without the proper equipment would be a good idea. And I came to my senses at the bottom of a cliff face, looking up, wondering how I'd fallen, and how on earth I'd ever be able to clamber back to the top.

*

One Saturday, while out shopping, I wandered into Harrods and was inevitably drawn to its beauty floor, aware that while my old brand had an in-store presence, it wasn't housed in either the white hall (cosmetics) or black hall (fragrances) either side of the Egyptian escalators. I only visited places where there was no risk of our paths crossing – I wasn't emotionally ready for that meeting yet. It proved hard enough walking around amid other brands and fragrances.

I can't remember at which counter I stopped, but I picked up a face cream, undid the lid, breathed in its fragrance, felt its texture, and found myself welling up. I walked to another counter, and then another, asking myself the same questions that always came to mind when perusing any cosmetics floor: *What would I add to that cream? What twist would I give that fragrance? What note is missing there?* But those questions no longer felt like seeds of ideas; they felt like a barrage of torment, taunting me. I was in the kind of environment where I belonged but I could only participate as a consumer – and the regret slapped me across the face. I turned around and, with a quickening step, I hurried out into the street, cursing myself for ever stepping foot in there.

Creators – those whose heart and soul are invested in their product – will know the connection that stirred me that day, mainly because it reminded me that I had barred myself from doing the one thing I loved. The longer time dragged on, the harder that creative deprivation would feel.

My response to that visceral reaction was to do something pro-active to try to shake off the feeling. I arrived home to find Josh running up and down the hallway playing with the dog. Gary was in the sitting room, strumming his guitar, learning a piece of music. I grabbed a pen and paper and sat at our long, oblong kitchen table at the back of the apartment, determined to get a job, because sitting around doing nothing was sending me stir-crazy.

That sense of desperation might explain the weird thoughts that led me to write down potential new careers: hairdresser – I had always imagined that if I couldn't do fragrances, I'd learn to do hair, so maybe now was the time? Marketing – I knew about branding; someone was bound to value that. Working for M&S – I loved its food, so maybe this was a way to remain in retail? Building a vineyard – I loved wine, why not? Running and redesigning a hotel – on my travels, I had seen many great establishments and this could be a way of keeping my hand in the luxury industry.

I stared at that piece of paper and sighed.

I even went to the trouble of drafting a curriculum vitae, but that exercise proved even more disillusioning, because all roads led back to my former brand. Hobbies: building a business. Achievements: building a business. Experience: building a business. The rest of it didn't read that well: quit school, no qualifications, and three brief stints as a shop assistant when a teenager.

I walked into the sitting room and interrupted Gary's guitar session. He took one look at my face and stopped strumming. 'My CV is pathetic!' I said. 'Outside of beauty and cosmetics, I think I'm unemployable.'

Gary didn't understand my self-imposed pressure – he thought I was being needlessly hard on myself – and I felt for him because as much as he tried to find the positive, he could see the regret forming within me. We had both made the decision together and jumped together, but for the first time in our lives we were reacting in very different ways. Our enforced gardening leave was Gary's bliss but my kind of hell. As a result, I cannot have been easy to live with, rattling aimlessly around our apartment.

Because I didn't want him to bear the brunt of it all, I met up with Joel Cadbury for lunch and poured it all out: how demotivated I felt, how I had abandoned all that I had valued, and how my recovery from cancer may have fogged my clarity. And then I told him about my CV.

Joel shook his head, disbelievingly. 'What are you doing, Jo?! I don't understand. You don't need to work for someone else. You're an entrepreneur!'

He shared with me a wonderful story about his mother, the late Jennifer d'Abo, who had passed away three years earlier and was 'one of Britain's best-known entrepreneurs', as the *Daily Telegraph* described her. If you've ever used a colour Post-it note, then you've been touched by this formidable woman's vision because it was she who turned around the fortunes of the Ryman chain of stationery shops among countless other achievements, and introduced the multi-coloured, self-adhesive, mini-notepads to the market. Joel told me that she never had a curriculum vitae in her life, and whenever she was asked to present one, she would reach into her handbag, pick out a conjoined, solid silver 'C' and 'V', and place them on the table of whatever male-dominated boardroom she was in. 'And that, gentlemen, is the nearest you'll get to a CV from me,' she'd say. In other words, 'If my record doesn't speak for itself, then what are we doing?'

A week or so later, after talking me down from the walls I had been climbing, Joel came round to the apartment with a gift, and he placed into my hands his mum's solid silver letters. 'Let these be a reminder – you don't need a CV either,' he said.

The one blessing of this enforced hiatus was that Gary and I could watch Josh grow from a cheeky, tender, irrepressible boy into a mature, wise-beyond-his-years, big-hearted ten-year-old. I may have struggled with the hours when he wasn't home but not the hours that he enriched when we were all home together. I'm proud that we provided him with a loving, happy, secure childhood, and I'm sure that our tightness as a family today is rooted in the cohesiveness that we had the room to nurture as he grew up.

If anything, our closeness brought into sharp focus my distance from Mum, Dad and Tracey. That gulf was glaringly obvious in how little I'd heard from them when fighting cancer. But my time away from the business provided an opportunity for reflection, and I felt the need to find peace between us, even if I didn't harbour any expectations about becoming the best of friends.

Sadly, after several attempts at reconciliation – lunch at our apartment, day trips to the countryside, and several lengthy phone calls – it became obvious that nothing was going to change. I see no purpose in revisiting the details; suffice it to say that in the years we hadn't nurtured ourselves as a family, it was clear there had been a dissolution of everything we once shared. For me, the love remained, but I realised that I was trying to rekindle something based on memories and ideals and how I wanted things to be, rather than how they were. Sometimes, love cannot fix everything, although it did enable me to forgive and move on. I forgave myself for not trying harder in the past. I forgave them for being equally as ambivalent. And so I decided that the only thing I could do, for my own good, was place my early years into a box inside my head, to be preserved as childhood memories that couldn't be distorted, forever remembering them as the people who had meant the world to me.

It became clear that severance was also required with my over-attachment to the former business. I struggled with being on the sidelines, and I couldn't help but keep looking over my shoulder. Gary knew how rudderless I felt, but he also believed that I wasn't helping myself. 'Darling, you can't move on until you let go,' he kept saying.

I knew he was right but it's not easy to let go of the monkey bars until you feel confident that there is another bar to leap towards and hold on to – and I didn't have anything else to hold on to. I did not regret, and still don't, the sale to Estée Lauder but I did underestimate the power of my connection to the brand. It had been my best friend, my teacher, my passion, and my one source of creativity. It was so much more than 'just a business'. And yet, as it turns out, I needed to lose it before truly grasping what it represented.

Whether you are Jo Malone, Jil Sander, Anya Hindmarch, or Coco Chanel, you become inescapably defined by what you have created, like it or not. Indeed, I think I had defined myself by it, so much so that I struggled with the public split between name and person. Anyone who has ever owned an eponymous brand will understand this inherent dichotomy in distinguishing between the public persona and the private person. Indeed, it is a psychological test that most people will grapple with at some time in their lives, when stripped of a title, a role, a status or a career with which they identify themselves. Who are we when made redundant, or when we retire? Who are we when we stand aside from something for which we have become known?

I suppose that's why I felt lost at the age of forty-two. I had to stand aside from my own name, because that was the deal we had signed. I had to pretend that I didn't feel the emotional connection between me and the fragrances I created. But I didn't truly understand how difficult I was finding the separation until one afternoon, sitting in the back of a black cab, stuck in traffic, directly outside the Sloane Street shop.

Up until that particular day, I had somehow managed to go a good year without spotting my name above the door, or seeing anyone walking in the street with a gift bag. This was part good luck and part deliberate avoidance. I would drive different routes to avoid our old shop. Of course, some associations were unavoidable: official invitations would be sent out, saying 'Jo Malone invites you to . . .' and people would come up to me and say, 'I can't wait to see you at next week's event!' I'd have to make it clear that it wasn't me; that I was no longer involved. Honestly, at times it felt like I was caught up in my own warped version of the movie *Trading Places*, standing on the outside looking in.

Which is exactly the scene that unfolded when the black cab took a turn down Sloane Street and stopped outside No.150.

I kept my eyes dead ahead, not wanting to look left, willing the cars in front to start moving. But, as the cab continued to idle, the pull proved too strong, and I turned to face the shop, which looked as elegant as ever. In my mind, the window reflected back to me the past: shopfitters asleep on the shelves, the wooden trestle table for our impromptu 'market', the laughter from the opening party, and me, busy inside, reorganising the shelves. And as those bittersweet memories flooded in, making me want to smile and cry at the same time, all I could hear was Gary saying, 'You can't move on until you let go' over and over.

As the cab drove away, I felt this immense wrench, far more intense than my last day in the shop, and I found this 'closure' – if closure was what it was – befuddling. Am I still the creator? Or am I now the consumer? I actually felt like neither. So the better question was, as Gary suggested that night, 'Who am I going to be now?' The answer to that question would take its time, but I resolved there and then not to connect emotionally with the product any more.

I also decided that it wouldn't serve me to work my nose for the foreseeable future – I would normally test it two or three hours a day, keeping it tuned, if you like. I'd cut a lemon in half and focus on the notes that came to mind. I'd pass a restaurant, smell the aromas and run with it. But no more. In my field, there is nothing more frustrating than being stuck in a creativity cul-de-sac and having nowhere to go. So I made the conscious choice to tune out, shutting out notes like I'd shut out negative thoughts. And with that decision, I placed my Jo Malone London years into another box inside my head, to be preserved as memories that couldn't be distorted, forever remembering the business as it was when it meant the world to me.

When an official-looking cream envelope, addressed to '*Mrs Joanne Willcox*', arrived in the post, I was instantly suspicious. When I ripped it open and unfolded the Downing Street headed paper, I rolled my eyes. And when I read the typewritten words explaining how Her Majesty the Queen was honouring me with an MBE, I laughed out loud. Someone was clearly playing an elaborate joke, which, among my circle of friends, was more than possible. *Why on earth would I be receiving an MBE from the Queen? And now, of all times, when I had left the business?* It seemed too implausible to be true.

It was only on closer inspection, and after running it by Gary, that I realised it was the real thing. I was being made a 'Member of the Most Excellent Order of the British Empire for services to the beauty industry'.

It took some believing that I was being honoured by my country for doing something I loved. It was as though life was telling me to focus not on what I had lost but on what Gary and I had achieved. And even though the award was in my name, it was actually our honour to share – the ultimate recognition of a dedication that I had perhaps lost sight of in recent months.

I was sworn to secrecy until the 'gongs' were announced in late December 2007, although I obviously shared the news with Gary and Josh. And there was one other special person I had to tell in confidence: Larry Norton. You are allowed to take three guests to the ceremony, so I would take my husband, my son, and the man who saved my life.

I waited until the afternoon to call New York, allowing for the five-hour time difference. Larry is one of the busiest men I know so I wasn't sure if he'd be able to make space in his diary, but the way I couched the invitation made it hard for him to resist.

'Larry, do you think you can spare a week in London next July?'

'Why, what's happening?'

'I have a date at Buckingham Palace. I'd love you to join me . . .'

The last time I had visited the palace had been twenty years earlier when the Queen's home was one of my house-to-house calls, at a time when I was unsure if the business would ever grow beyond two dozen clients. And now I was returning to receive an MBE, presented by HRH Prince Charles, at a time when the brand was flying high around the world, without me.

An added bonus of the day was that Kylie Minogue was being honoured at the same time. She and I had grown close after being introduced by a mutual friend in 2005 when she was diagnosed with, and then survived, breast cancer. But because we had both been sworn to secrecy, we hadn't known about each other's 'gong' until the list had been published in the newspapers. She was receiving an OBE for services to the music industry – recognition of the more than sixty million records she had sold worldwide. It was going to be a poignant day for both of us and, for me, having her there only added to the sense of occasion.

For the investiture, I had bought a dark navy Louise Kennedy lace dress, and a rather dramatic, bright pink Philip Treacy hat, complete with a long pink feather. Shaune, my hairdresser, came to the apartment to fix the hat to my head before I dashed out – in a t-shirt and jeans – to pick up Larry from his hotel. I couldn't have been happier that he, too, would share such a special day. When I had been at my lowest ebb in New York, the idea that we would be attending Buckingham Palace together, to witness me receive an MBE, would have been dismissed as a chemotherapy-induced hallucination.

When I arrived outside the hotel and saw him standing there, I was so excited that I parked up, jumped out and gave him the biggest hug. 'Welcome to London!' I said. I was so excited to see him that, as I hurriedly got back in the car, I forgot all about the antenna-like feather protruding from my hat. I slammed the door shut, chatting away to Larry, and my head was slightly yanked to the right – pulled by my trapped feather. In fact, it was more than trapped. To my horror, as I reopened the door, it fell to the ground, snapped in two.

There was nothing I could do. We were racing the clock as it was, and so I would have to make do with a featherless hat and hope that no one noticed the stunted, broken stem that I couldn't remove.

I thought I had got away with my fashion faux pas until we arrived at the palace and approached the main door, where a cheeky member of the Royal Household raised one eyebrow and said, 'Nice hat, Miss Malone.' Trained eyes missed not a detail, and Josh couldn't stop laughing.

As the boys took their seats in the Ballroom, I lined up in the Throne Room, which is where I first saw Kylie, along with the crowd of other recipients. I definitely felt the nerves that the sense of occasion brought on, and it helped having a friend there, going through the same surreal experience. Ordinarily, I suppose most visitors would be in awe of the ornate majesty of the room, but I was in awe of a group of British soldiers who were all being decorated for their service and courage. That was a sobering comparison as I took my place among them, thinking, 'These men and women have served their country and done heroic things . . . and all I've done is make bath oils.'

Everyone's excited chatter died down as the investiture began. It feels like you are waiting in the wings, about to walk on the grandest stage, and no amount of preparation can ready you for the sound of your name being called. As I walked into the formal hush of the Ballroom, I glanced to my right and saw Gary sitting beside Larry, and then Josh, his eyes out on stalks, craning his neck. And then I was standing before HRH Prince Charles.

'I've been so looking forward to meeting you,' he said, as he leaned forward and pinned the beautiful medal, with a rose-pink ribbon, to my chest. I cannot remember another thing he said because I was concentrating so hard on not bursting into tears. I don't think I've ever felt such a deep sense of patriotism and pride.

Outside, in the shingled courtyard, I posed for the standard press pictures, though my attention was distracted by the sight of my now thoroughly bored seven-year-old son bending down, picking up stones and putting them in his pocket.

'Put them back, Josh! What do you think you're doing?!'

'Collecting some of the Queen's pebbles!'

He was fascinated by the fact we were at the Queen's house. I took him with me to the ladies before we were due to head off to a celebration lunch at Harry's Bar with Larry. When we came out, Josh was aghast at how old-fashioned the toilets were.

'Mummy,' he whispered, 'there was no chain in there!'

I laughed. 'Yes, I know, darling, you have to use the pump.'

'You'd think the Queen could afford a chain, wouldn't you?!'

That night, my friends threw a party at the Admiral Codrington, a little pub not far from Walton Street. There must have been about sixty of us in a private room at the back, including Aunty Dot and Uncle Gordon. But we didn't only toast my MBE, we toasted Kylie's OBE, too – I invited her along to make it a double celebration. We were two breast cancer survivors who had come through the other side to be recognised for our life's work, so it seemed fitting that we should raise our glasses together, surrounded by the most amazing group of people, who I will forever regard as my chosen family.

TWENTY-SIX

As wonderful as the MBE was, it didn't stop me feeling in a state of limbo. I chalked off days in my mind the same way I had counted 'X's on the calendar in New York, somehow managing to stumble through the first half of my lock-out period. Gary compared me to a caged tiger prowling our home, which I couldn't refute – it seemed like an eternity since I had been meaningfully creative (outside of jam- and ice-cream making).

Because of this drought, and because I needed to find *something* to do, I went in search of ideas and inspiration, wandering food halls and markets until I was blue in the face, surrounding myself with merchants, trying to feel connected to creativity. 'What about that – could I do that?' I asked myself, flitting from stall to stall. I'd see a florist and wonder about turning back the clock. I'd see kitchenware and imagine my own version of Crate & Barrel. I'd see sheets and towels and entertain vague notions of my own lifestyle brand. And yet as lovely as these thoughts were, why go from the master of one to a jack of all trades?

But this exploration of the markets didn't turn out to be a

waste of time because, in seeing the array of products on offer, and in talking to different traders, I appreciated the extent of the undiscovered entrepreneurial talent that existed, with savvy retail brains and impressive brands, but perhaps without the connections or road map to take the next step up. One Saturday, while visiting Camden Market, the idea came to me that if I couldn't do what I loved for the foreseeable future, then maybe I should help others develop their brands. I remembered how an agent had recommended us to Bergdorf Goodman, so how great would it be, I thought, if I could be the bridge for someone else? That random idea might well have come to nothing had I not later mentioned it to television agent Jacquie Drewe at Curtis Brown. We had been introduced a few years earlier and, over coffee, she coincidentally aired the possibility of me doing a TV show. 'Funny you should say that,' I said. 'I had an idea only the other day: imagine being able to take an entrepreneur from a market stall to a deal of a lifetime?'

And that is how the BBC series *High Street Dreams* came into being.

Within the week, Jacquie had hooked me up with a production company called Twofour. Within the fortnight, we had an outline of the format. Within the month, we were sitting in front of programmers at the BBC who effectively commissioned us there and then. Jacquie Drewe is my kind of straight-talking, make-it-happen woman.

Initially, I had no interest in being a host. I thought I could be a sort of consultant producer who would make occasional, advice-led appearances. I had no interest in being a television personality. 'But they don't want a personality,' said Jacquie. 'They want you as the on-camera expert because that's what will give the programme gravitas.'

One or two screen tests later, plus a few more of Jacquie's

confidence boosts along the way, I entered the world of television as a debut presenter with no real idea about how it worked but excited about using my experience in a non-commercial capacity.

I made only one request as part of my first TV deal – I wanted my former communications director Charlotte McCarthy to be part of the team. In the fragrance industry, she had been my right-hand woman and I knew that in order to find my voice in TV, it was important to have her by my side. Charlotte had stayed on at Jo Malone London and she, like me, had missed working as a duo, so this represented a fantastic opportunity to join forces again. Once she was onboard as a producer/publicity manager, I felt happier about entering a totally alien but exciting environment.

Was this a diversion I would have ordinarily taken had my choices not been so limited? Probably not. But I'm a doer, not someone who can sit around killing time. And when Jacquie Drewe first floated the idea, I came back to those three choices I had faced when torn between staying with Mum's business or going solo: change your mindset, change your situation, or accept it. This time, I chose to change my situation, intrigued to see if a new landscape would lead to other things. I didn't necessarily know where this road would lead, but I knew it would lead somewhere and lift me out of a period of stagnation.

It felt good to have something to sink my teeth into, and 'something' was better than nothing. Besides, I had long felt that not enough was being done to encourage or equip young entrepreneurs with the necessary information and know-how, so here was my chance to provide whatever insight I could, not only to the contestants but to viewers with small businesses – the same reasoning that would motivate my own column in the *Evening Standard* a few years later.

In a small way, this series was also about me finding my voice again. Only this time, an idea in my head wouldn't become a fragrance but a four-episode show on primetime BBC1 on Monday nights, up against *Big Brother* on C4 and the *Wormwood Scrubs* documentary on ITV.

Together with a team of researchers and my co-host, the property developer Nick Leslau, we scoured Britain looking for contestants. We travelled north, east, south and west during the second half of 2009, visiting food shows, fairs and markets to find people with great product, a fascinating story, and fire in their bellies; entrepreneurs who had the self-belief that can walk through walls and never give up.

We came across hundreds of contenders but, in the end, we had to whittle down an exhaustive list of applicants to eight contestants, covering the markets of fashion, homeware, children's products, and food and drink. We would film between January and March 2010, on the road and at a purpose-built set in Maidstone, but the format wasn't about anyone competing or winning investment; it was about mentorship, helping them to develop their brands in preparation for each of them to pitch to a high street retailer. I'll never forget the first day – and I'm not sure producer Alison Kirkham will either – because a last-minute tizzy left me fearing a repeat of my fluffed Heinz TV ad. At concept stage, and during screen tests, I experienced no jitters about being on camera. But when I walked on set into a hive of activity, buzzing with crew, I suddenly felt like the non-swimmer I am, jumping into the deep end. And just as I realised how deep the waters were, one of the directors thrust a script in my hand. No one had mentioned anything about a script. 'Just look through it,' he said. 'We will go over it tomorrow.'

No one knows I'm dyslexic. What am I doing here?! Who was I kidding?!

I felt like a fraud who was going to be rumbled.

With filming due to start the next day, I returned to my hotel that evening and experienced a full-blown panic attack. Or maybe it's what they call 'stage fright'? Having never been on stage, I wouldn't know, but I'd never known anxiety on this scale. It felt like my throat was constricting and I was running out of breath; that fight or flight surge – and I wanted to run. The other thing that panic tends to do is amplify self-doubt, making failure appear guaranteed. All I saw was me drowning in front of a nation of viewers.

I've gotta get out of this . . . I've gotta get out of this.

The only way I found calm was to calculate on my phone how much I was going to have to pay the crew, production company and the BBC for cancelling the project. Yes, that's what I was going to do – I was going to quit. Far rather pay a heavy cost in sterling than the price of humiliation.

The next morning, after a fitful night's sleep, I collared Alison on set and asked to have a word. Alison is one of those cool, calm and collected producers, though I feared what I was about to say was going to test her unflappability.

'Look, I know this is a bad time to tell you, but I've made a terrible mistake. You've got the wrong person. I'm not sure I can do this. I'm really sorry.'

Understandably, she looked totally dumbfounded. 'What do you mean?'

'I can't do it,' I said, pulling the script from my handbag. 'This – it's not me.'

With that, she took the script from my hand, ripped it in half, and handed it back. 'That's for everyone else, Jo. We want you to be unscripted. Just be yourself! Is there anything else?'

Even though 'just be yourself' isn't the easiest mode to find when a TV camera becomes your shadow, my anxiety subsided when I realised I could speak off the cuff. 'Okay, that's great,' I said, blowing my cheeks. 'I'll give it a go!'

Insecurities: I'm not sure they ever leave us, whatever success we achieve – mine certainly haven't – but I think many of us can shrink in the face of an overwhelming situation, without stopping to consider what our capabilities might be if we push through the fear. Sometimes, we'll succeed; sometimes, we'll fail. But I hate to think how close I came to ducking out of that opportunity, especially when I went on to thoroughly enjoy the experience. Talking into a camera and being on set felt like the most natural thing in the world, in the end, even though it would be a short-lived foray into TV land. Sadly, the series wouldn't get recommissioned because, as good as our ratings were, they weren't a match for the viewing figures that *Wormwood Scrubs* pulled in. I'm not sure I'll ever understand why that was so, but there was much I had to learn about television.

I learned the hard way that every programme depends on the necessary ingredient of 'jeopardy' – the high stakes and conflict that hook the viewer. I'm not sure I fully understood that concept until one episode when a woman contestant became visibly upset about some aspect of her business, and the director stopped filming – or, at least, I thought he had.

I removed my lapel mic and disappeared with this woman into a private room, wanting to console her. When I re-emerged, I didn't understand why people were frowning, until it was explained that 'by removing your mic, you denied us that drama'.

I didn't find it easy thinking like a producer, viewing every interaction, on or off camera, as potential material. I wasn't necessarily cut out for television in that regard, but the wonderful part of the experience was getting creative again, advising on branding, packaging and marketing, immersing myself in all matters retail.

ONE DAY YOU WILL WAKE UP & FEEL ON TOP OF THE WORLD!
xxxx

Getting stronger – back to real life, my first party after finishing chemo.

My two dear friends, Jane Moore (left) and Ruth Kennedy, together in Venice. This was the photo I pinned on my 'chemo calendar' . . . and I'd look at it every day.

A very proud day – receiving my MBE at Buckingham Palace, with Gary, Josh and Dr Larry Norton, the doctor who saved my life.

Charlotte and me outside No.10, where I was about to give a keynote speech.

Strolling down the beach at Parrot Cay – the place where Pomelo, my first
Jo Loves fragrance, came to life.

Great Friends

My dear friend Isy Ettedgui (left), who helped me create the iconic packaging for
Jo Malone London; Joel Cadbury (right), who's always been there for me; and Charlotte
McCarthy (below) on the morning we announced Jo Loves to the world . . .
from the kitchen table.

Launching Jo Loves with a pop-up at Selfridges – from our initial red and black branding, to working flat out through the night, to stocking the shelves with product.

Life comes full circle and takes me right back to the beginning:
from Justin de Blank at No.42 Elizabeth Street to Jo Loves –
my forty-ninth birthday present.

The beautiful fragrance brasserie, as seen from the front of the shop, looking through to the Candle Cocktail Bar at the back.

Kathy Phillips joined me in making a candle. Kathy is a dear friend as well as the first journalist to write a story about how we built our first brand from a tiny kitchen.

In The Candle Shot Studio with Jacquie Tovey, making lots of candles for the Christmas orders.

Showing Gary and Naomi Harford the beauty of Grasse and my beloved Mougins.

In the heart of Mougins – rediscovering a love affair with creativity again . . . and trusting the artist in me. I love this picture because it's captured by my son, Josh.

The Perfumer's Organ – an array of notes from which 'a nose' selects the scents that make up a fragrance.

Dubai 2016 – the great honour of being received into the World Retail Congress Hall of Fame, followed by a private audience with His Highness Sheikh Mohammed Bin Rashid Al Maktoum, UAE Vice President, Prime Minister and Ruler of Dubai, and his ministers. A truly wonderful moment.

Over the three-month period of filming, I met some amazing people and some of the entrepreneurs we featured were a joy to work with, like teachers Jo and Kay, who founded the 'flibberty' with its children's playtime den kits, and Claire, who designed her own luxury pieces as the Special Jewellery Company.

But no one better defined the get-up-and-go entrepreneurial spirit more than Roland and Miranda Ballard, with their company, Muddy Boots. Unafraid of risks and graft, they had left behind two media careers to produce quality, ethically farmed Aberdeen Angus beef, and we took them from a farmers' market to Waitrose supermarket, which now stocks their burgers in more than one hundred stores. Since then, they have gone from strength to strength, and they epitomise the kind of small-business success story I love to see.

The power and value of entrepreneurs, whether it's your shopkeeper on the street corner or the owner of a local factory, truly hit home during the filming of *High Street Dreams*, and I often said that Britain needs thousands of small businesses to drive 'a Dunkirk economy'. When this country was called to rescue all those people from France in 1940, the bigger boats couldn't get close to shore. It was the little boats, which set out from Ramsgate to rescue 70,000, that ended up bringing 300,000 home. And that's what we'll always need to keep this country on its feet: small businesses flying the British flag all over the world.

While the daring to be an entrepreneur is incomparable to the courage of those seven hundred private boat owners and fisherman, I truly believe that the people in small vessels are as important to reviving our economy as the generals at the helm of the corporate ships.

What I couldn't know when I signed up to do the programme was that in trying to help others achieve their dreams, this series would lead to me rolling up my sleeves again and returning to the high street, prompted by an unexpected trip down memory lane.

It was snowing, and even my brown winter coat struggled to keep out the chill as I stood in the middle of a terraced street in Mile End, East London. On such a grey morning, a camera crew, bright lights, and a blonde-haired woman wearing TV make-up tend to attract attention, and two hooded teenagers on bikes hovered in my peripheral vision as I awaited my cue for a scene-setting 'long shot' – walk up the road and knock on the door of our featured family.

'What ya doin' just standing there?!' one of them asked, laughing to his friend.

I pretended not to hear. The director had already advised me not to engage them.

But this kid was annoyingly persistent. 'Oi! I asked ya what ya doin?!'

I flashed him a look, put on my most authoritative voice and said, 'Operation Bumblebee.'

I don't think I've seen two kids skedaddle so fast, pedalling furiously up the road.

'Annnnnd action!' the director shouted.

I walked halfway up the street and turned down the path leading to the front door of Hardev Singh Sahota, a grandfather who had first started making hot chilli sauce in his kitchen in the 1980s. Together with his eldest son, Kuldip, he had been selling *Mr Singh's Sauce* at trade shows, and we were preparing their pitch to Asda. I was sceptical at first as to whether this venture could take off but they bowled me over with their family spirit – the mum, two other sons and daughters-in-law all mucked in – and their passion for the product, which was mixed in a shed at the far end of their backyard.

I donned hairnet, white coat and Wellington boots to join father and son on that production line, and the space was so small that the cameraman had to sit on one of the shelves, with his head smushed against the ceiling. We also had to contend with the overpowering smell of chillies, to the point where it made my eyes and nose water. It wasn't the most comfortable of set-ups and yet the compactness instantly reminded me of the tiny kitchen where Gary and I had first started. And then, as I filled the glass bottles with sauce and screwed on the lids one by one, the jolting flash-backs came thick and fast. The white lab coat. Making product. Filling bottles. The confined space. Helping build a brand – the whole experience was transporting.

Bottle it, label it, package it, PR it, sell it, make it fly. Remember how that feels?

The director was issuing instructions from the doorway, the cameraman was asking me to step aside for a better angle, and I was trying my hardest to stay focused and be present, but the past kept speaking to me.

This is what makes you happy. This is what you can do again.

As soon as we finished filming, I stepped outside to find Charlotte waiting in the yard and, before she could say anything, before she could even ask about the scene, I blurted it out: 'I've got to make fragrances. I've got to start again.'

'I was wondering when you were going to say that,' she said. Charlotte never did buy my often-stated assertion that I'd never go back into business.

Before I had even removed my coat and hairnet, I was imag-ining the launch of different shops across Britain and America, leaping way ahead of myself. In a matter of seconds, I had gone from filling bottles to building a global brand.

As ever, Gary would be there to keep my feet on the ground, wanting to make sure that I was not simply reacting to nostalgia, so we decided that if I still felt the same in a few months, then we would seriously explore the idea. With about eight months remaining of the lock-out period, we had time to consider it carefully, he said.

I decided to sit on my hands a little longer, but while many thoughts run through my mind and out the other side, this one would anchor itself and refuse to stay quiet, growing louder and louder – and everything I did after the show seemed to nudge me nearer to a reunion with fragrance.

When it came to mentoring, I didn't seek only to steer the small crop of talent on *High Street Dreams*; I also wanted to do my bit in helping to inspire the next generation of businessmen and women. As different schools and colleges invited me to give talks about brand-building and creativity, I viewed it as a tremendous opportunity because, if left to me, entrepreneurship would be folded into the national curriculum.

Young people are not only thinking quicker and smarter, they appear to be more savvy, innovation-minded and prepared to go it alone, building apps, launching YouTube channels, and pushing crowd-sourcing campaigns. We seem to be blessed with a new age of outside-the-box go-getters unafraid of risk, and we can only benefit if we better cultivate such vision and ambition at grass-roots level. Children's experience of entrepreneurship shouldn't only be limited to lemonade stalls outside the front gate or jumble sales in the garage.

Josh's school in central London was one of the first places where, alongside three other mothers, I experimented with 'entre-preneur lessons' in one class, focusing on the four 'P's: product and packaging (which is art and science), pricing (maths), and place-ment (English for marketing/storytelling). We discussed costs, profit margin, VAT, product quality, and the value of PR, before embarking on the task at hand: the design, creation and sale of a yo-yo, as manufactured by David Strang, an Australian toy maker whose expertise we used on *High Street Dreams* and whose charm went down a storm with the pupils.

The most remarkable thing happened as we selected two designs for the yo-yos that were sold among pupils and families at £6.95 each: not only did the children, aged between eight and nine, earn an overall profit of £300 for charity, but I noticed that it was the kids who struggled academically, or came from a more difficult background, who proved to be the most creative, the quickest thinkers, and the best at problem-solving. By their nature, entrepreneurs swim upstream – they can be different, quirky or loners – and they are often bored with theory and only interested in 'doing'. I can't think of one other subject other than entrepreneurship, where grades and socio-economic factors are rendered irrelevant – such lessons, if adopted nationwide, could be the greatest leveller and source of confidence for those who don't ordinarily shine the brightest. Stimulate interest at a young age, and we stand a better chance of stimulating the economy many years down the road.

I had a lot of requests to talk at school assemblies to inspire the children, but it was the teenage pupils at one school who ended up further inspiring *me*.

I was giving a talk about the construction of a perfume and, instead of passing around different vials for pupils to smell, I decided to turn it into an art lesson, taking out a paintbrush and different paints to show how I connect scents with colours when a fragrance comes to mind.

I stood there in front of an easel, presented a lime note around the class and I painted what came to their minds: lime green, green grass, and fields. I took a mango note and they saw yellows, sunshine, and crystal clear waters. When I presented those two notes together, as an accord, and asked the class to smell and *listen* for a sound, one girl shouted out, 'I hear a violin ... and a drum in the background!'

'Okay,' I said, 'now look down at your feet – what do you see?'

Another girl's hand shot up in the air. 'Sand and white pebbles.'

We painted this picture together, through smell – I told them this was 'Alice in Wonderlanding', peering through the looking glass of creativity. Children are so comfortable and spontaneous with their imaginations, and it stirred the embers of mine.

I deliberately hadn't worked or tested my nose in more than four years. I hadn't seen colours or heard sounds. I wasn't even sure if my sense of smell would ever be as sensitive or effective as it used to be, but standing in that classroom, seeing those young minds light up and react to fragrance, I saw in them the same magic that once brought me alive. Each experience I was having only confirmed the feeling I'd had while bottling the hot chilli sauce. As we entered the late autumn of 2010, it wasn't only an instinct or a curiosity that propelled me; it was a compulsion to return to what I did best.

For too long I had been sitting on the sidelines, denying the person I was before cancer skewed my perspective and fogged my clarity. I now realised that without being a fragrance designer, without building something, I'm not whole. I had fought cancer to live but, in terms of personal fulfilment and happiness, I hadn't been *living* to the max, engaged with my purpose, carving out a sacred space to be creative. The period away from fragrance had given me what I had wished for in 2006 and time is indeed precious, but, surely, that time only has value if spent being true to yourself, following your heart's desire?

I had so many realisations, including the sobering fact that I was forty-eight and didn't want to grow old feeling the regret of never trying again. Professionally, I wanted that soulful feeling back, the one I felt when playing with notes, not knowing what fragrance would emerge; or when doing a facial, or when walking through Grasse, or when I was on the shop floor. I wasn't looking to recapture the past. I was rediscovering who I am and, in doing so, reclaiming my future.

I instinctively felt that there were more fragrances within me, buried deep, waiting to be unlocked. And the mere thought of embarking on a new adventure with Gary – the prospect of building another global business – was a shot in the arm. There was also an element of wanting to prove to *myself* that I 'still had it' after five years away. Part of me had always wondered if I had just been the beneficiary of one lucky break or whether I was, at heart, a serial entrepreneur.

Can you do it again? Can you?

That was the question that kept niggling away at the back of my mind, pushing me along. I didn't immediately have the answer and I'm not entirely sure I felt one hundred per cent confident, but I was determined to give it a good shot.

TWENTY-SEVEN

Admittedly, when taken at face value, we didn't appear to be in the most promising of positions. No manufacturer, no perfume house, no fragrances lined up, and no idea about our brand image. Before, we had launched with a client list, product and a clear identity, growing organically and being swept along by momentum. Now, with five years of silence behind us, we were sitting around our kitchen table staring at a blank piece of paper, with nothing more than a fervent desire to launch a business. Had that kind of template for success come across my desk during *High Street Dreams*, my first question would have been, 'Where's your product?' followed by a swift rejection.

As if our odds weren't long enough, there was also a minefield of legal restraints to navigate surrounding the right to use my name.

The non-compete clause had locked me out of the industry for five years but the overall terms, as is commonly the case, meant that I couldn't freely use 'Jo Malone' without being subject to certain covenants and restrictions – my personal identity was inextricably entwined with the brand identity I no longer owned. That's the restrictive nature of any deal involving a namesake brand, but I don't think I had previously considered its enormity until seeking to trade again as a fragrance designer.

In 2006, I walked away with almost a blithe disregard for such matters, thinking I'd never launch another business in a million years. In 2011, I found myself confronted by my own lack of foresight, sitting down with the eminent intellectual property specialist James Mellor QC, receiving quite the education. Put simply, I would, for the rest of my life, have to watch how I used my name, and how I referred to myself in a commercial sense.

As much as I understood that I had signed away my rights, the stark reality nevertheless made me wince. It felt like I had permitted a monitoring tag to be tied to my ankle, one that would bleep should I ever use my name in the wrong context.

When you launch a business and start from nothing, it doesn't cross your mind that the name on your birth certificate will one day have value. When the life-changing dream happens and you sell the business, you can be blinkered by the deal or prevailing circumstances – standing in that Madison Avenue shop, seeing 'Jo Malone' everywhere, and not feeling any connection. But it is a truth of life that situations, feelings and perspectives change, and therein lies the salutary lesson for any entrepreneur: even though you don't think a certain way at the time, still make sure every eventuality is covered, however improbable, leaving the land ahead clear. How I went about selling a business in 1999 wouldn't be how I'd go about it today, that's for sure. Such are the lessons that shape us.

I'm not the first founder of a namesake brand to have not fully considered the long-term consequences; to have walked away from the mirror and wondered why my reflection – my identity – was still standing there. But once Gary and I better understood the legal parameters, we had no choice but to get on with it and start from scratch. Indeed, it was crucial that in *everything* we did, the consumer saw daylight between my new venture and *Jo*

Malone London. I had to stand apart and be different – a prospect I started to relish.

Stare at obstacles long enough and they will only appear bigger. See through and around them and they only diminish. The more I thought about carving out a new identity, the more it felt like an opportunity. It may have made things more complicated at first, but there has always been something thrilling about embarking on an unwritten chapter, not knowing where each turn of the page will take you. I looked at Gary and saw how reinvigorated he was, pumped up for the challenge, feeling the excitement again. Neither of us could wait to get started.

The irony was that I would effectively be competing against myself, but while that might have been the case in actuality, I could never view it that way personally. It is inconceivable to me that I could ever compete against my own creativity. How can there be proper rivalry if two brands share the same heartbeat, no matter how separate they have to be? Besides, the only rival for any entrepreneur should be the rival within – the person you are, pushing you to be better, week in, week out.

Either way, I couldn't afford for sentimentality to become another hurdle. If we were to succeed again, I had to stay focused, so I sat down with that blank page and asked myself the three fundamental questions that each of us should ask ourselves when standing at a crossroads, whether you're an entrepreneur with a kernel of an idea, or someone who has lost a job or gone through a divorce, looking for a new direction. Those questions are: *Who am I? How can I reinvent myself? Where do I begin?*

My answers helped bring me clarity. First: I may no longer own my old brand but I remained Jo Malone *the person*; that's who I am, a creator of fragrance. I had sold my name, not my instinct, my nose, my creativity, or the future. I had started with four plastic jugs and a saucepan at the very beginning. I could do it again. Second: I reinvent myself by tapping into the creativity that served me before. I was a different person now and that difference will be reflected in the product I make. Change. Keep evolving. Trust in the one thing you're good at. As to where I begin, that was easy: today, right now – you seize the moment and physically get to work. And I knew what we had to do – we had to get back to basics.

The first foundation that needed to be laid was the issue of our new name. I couldn't think about fragrance without knowing who we were, what we were about, and how we looked. I needed the fixed co-ordinates to find my bearings, otherwise I wouldn't have anything to connect to. I wish I could write here that it proved as easy as picking out baby names, but it would take *weeks* trying to figure out a brand that represented my ethos and style – and even then, we would make mistakes.

Our oblong kitchen table became our base. Gary, forever the prudent one, wasn't going to pay rent on office space until our idea was more concrete. Over endless hours and weeks, he and I sat there together with Charlotte, and the benefit of our trio was the combined expertise in finance and PR while I flitted in with my creative input. Gary and Charlotte sat in front of their laptops and I sat in front of my notepad – being computer illiterate, I prefer pen and paper – and we tried to think up a brand identity that bore no resemblance to the past. Yet there was no escaping the truth that every fragrance I would go on to make would inevitably be imbued with my character, my signature.

Dress me up in a clown's outfit and call me Coco, the DNA of my creativity won't alter. If Monet had been told to paint cartoons, his brushstrokes would have been unmistakable. If Adele suddenly decided to sing rock, you'd still know her voice. The true nature and ownership of any creation will always reside with the artist, no matter the wall it hangs from, the music system it plays on, or the bottle the fragrance sits in. We now had to dream up a brand that was unmistakably me and yet encompassed a wholly different style. If that sounds like a head-scrambling conundrum, then welcome to the inside of my head in 2011.

Meanwhile, Gary erected a flip chart in the corner of the room, sketching designs and projecting forecasts as we simultaneously unpacked boxes of sample bottles, lids and packaging – none of which we liked. We analysed colours, fonts and ribbons. We flicked through catalogue after catalogue and called round suppliers to see what ideas they could offer. All we seemed to do was go round in circles as the coffee mugs, the pizza boxes, and the late nights stacked up. It was madness. Absolute madness. As well as exasperating.

After a month of getting nowhere, I did wonder if we'd ever leave the starting blocks. We seemed to be doing nothing but spinning our wheels in the same spot, and that spot increasingly felt like square one. There was a lot of thinking, planning, theorising and speculating but zero progress.

At *Fortune*'s Most Powerful Women event in London two years later, I was interviewed in front of an audience with the magazine's assistant managing editor Leigh Gallagher and, as we looked back on this pivotal moment, she said, 'So, this is like, if Howard Schultz was throwing another coffee chain, or if Richard Branson was starting another airline, this should be easy . . . but you were right back at the kitchen table. You were very much a start-up. It's not a walk in the park.'

She made a pertinent point, because I think part of me had initially expected it to be a walk in the park. How could returning to something I loved be so difficult? As usual, my own expectations exerted the pressure. But having been denied access to the industry for so long, I was desperate to make up for lost time, which is why the mire of details and technicalities, framed by the legal parameters, felt so frustrating. I longed for the naiveté of those carefree days prior to Walton Street when we made up the rules as we went along, armed with boundless creativity, adhering only to intuition. Everything seemed so simple then. And we didn't know what the summit of the mountain felt like. Now, in our attempt to repeat that climb, we almost knew too much, and cared too much about not putting a foot wrong. Consequently, the whole process started to feel more engineered than organic.

One Friday afternoon, at the end of a particularly draining week, I felt thoroughly fed up. I sat on the back step and Charlotte, who felt the collective frustration, joined me. She could see my weariness, and I was done trying to conceal it.

'I knew it was going to be hard,' I said, 'but not this hard. I left a business that was flying high, with territories all over the world, and, here I am, unable to find a name, the right bottle or the correct packaging. What are we doing?'

'We're starting again, and this is what starting again feels like,' she said. Charlotte had worked with us at the top level and, like Gary, was more realistic about the step-by-step process. 'We're going to have to earn the right to come back,' she said. 'There is no picking up where we left off. We have to build this house again, from the foundations up.'

I didn't admit it at the time, but I think there was a layer of fear beneath my determination. I was scared of putting my head above the parapet. Scared of failing. Scared that lightning in a bottle couldn't strike twice. Perhaps I viewed the slow grind as an excuse to back away at a time when, let's face it, the vast majority of people didn't realise I had left the old brand anyway. I can't pretend that I was consistently gung-ho and charging ahead, but I believe fear is sometimes healthy. Because once I've exhausted the emotion of fear, I tend to come back fighting. Fear represents that inner voice that dares to say, 'You can't do this', and that breeds an even stronger resolve within me.

Ultimately, I was determined to find a way – the motto that should be seared into every entrepreneur's mindset. It shouldn't matter if doors are slammed shut in your face or the legal obstacles seem too high. Find a ladder. Or find a way to climb over the wall. Or dig a tunnel. Just find a way.

I had a stern word with myself that weekend – a pep talk not dissimilar to that time when house-to-house calls felt like a trudge. 'If you really want this, you've got to prove to life that you want it. Time to dig deep and put into practice all you've ever known, gal.'

By Monday morning, Charlotte didn't even need to ask where my head was; she knew as soon as she saw me scribbling away. The next day, she bought two mugs. One said, 'Keep Calm and Carry On'; the other, 'Now Panic and Freak Out'. You can guess which one was mine. We kept them side by side on the table – our daily reminder that with level heads, and maybe the odd freak-out, we'd nail the brand and start making progress. There remained only one other crucial component of the business that required my attention – the one essential tool that I hadn't used professionally for more than four years. My nose.

Ever since I first understood the abilities within my sense of smell, I never took them for granted or assumed they would be forever within reach. Indeed, there are accounts of perfumers who lose the power of smell because the olfactory nerves into the limbic system of the brain have, like a muscle, atrophied through lack of use. My obvious concern then was that if a few months of chemotherapy had once dampened the effectiveness of my nose, would a long passage of time have the same dousing effect? I had no field of reference in that regard. If an opera singer rests her voice for four years, does it come back as strong? If a footballer doesn't kick a ball for four seasons, can they ever return as sharp? The only way of finding out was to retrain my nose, day by day, note by note.

In accepting how slow this process could be, I had actually started testing my nose in the months before we began working on a brand, setting aside two-hour, daily blocks, as I used to do. I took out the vials of notes I had boxed away, along with my fragrance sticks, weighing scales and pipettes . . . and then I did too much, too soon, bowling in, as usual. I sniffed some strong musk and jasmine notes that overpowered my nose, to the point where I couldn't smell anything else for days, which sort of defeated the purpose. So, I had to go easier and take it more slowly, as you would if you were returning to the gym after a lengthy absence.

I'd slice a mango and wait to see a colour or hear a sound, or I'd take an old citronella note and ask myself what could make it sharper – a drop of camphor or eucalyptus? I'd sit for hours with fragrance sticks – one in my left hand, one in my right – wafting them beneath my nose, seeing what the combinations would trigger, if anything at all. We had rose bushes, rosemary and lavender on the back terrace, and I'd spend hours sitting there, with my eyes closed, trying to get those floral notes to lock together and paint a picture, but nothing special happened. Yes, one or two 'nice' accords came together but I wasn't interested in creating *nice*. I needed something memorable, so I kept plugging away, going for walks around the neighbourhood, stopping to smell the flowers in different garden squares, or breathing in the aromas as I passed cafés and restaurants. I'd also hum tunes in my head but none of those tunes translated into anything. Nothing came back to me naturally, as if fragrance itself couldn't reach me, as if there was a block in the frequency between us.

But as painfully slow as this time proved to be, I tried not to overthink it or get stressed – a mind cluttered with thoughts would only hinder creativity further. Indeed, when the telltale flicker happened – the breakthrough moment – it was when I was relaxed, sitting in the living room with Gary, not consciously working my nose.

He had his guitar out and I was reading a book when I picked up the musty smell of wet plaster, as if the interior walls were damp. I got up and started sniffing, wandering over to a corner in the living room, like a dog tracking a scent. Gary couldn't smell anything and thought it was my imagination. 'No, there's water in these walls,' I said, but, to touch, they were bone dry. I told management, suspecting a leak somewhere – they said, no, nothing was wrong. A few weeks later, leaking water behind the walls flooded the flat of the man downstairs. I think I knew then that my nose was kicking back into gear. Granted, detecting leaks and being as accurate as a barometer didn't guarantee the creation of another bestselling fragrance, but it was an encouraging sign nonetheless.

In the following weeks, similar encouraging flashes kept happening. I told Gary that I could smell rain; half an hour later, it poured down. Another day, I told him I could smell snow – same thing. 'Nothing wrong with your nose,' he said. 'It's like a dog with butter on its paws – it will always find its way home eventually!'

Once my nose started to 'work' again, everything else fell into place – the name and our first brand image soon followed and, again, a moment of spontaneity unlocked the inspiration. We had thought of so many name permutations that I was almost punch-drunk with suggestions, most of which I have obviously consigned to forgotten memory. We had sent ourselves crazy playing our own version of *Blankety Blank* with 'Willcox _____' and '_____ Scents' and 'Jo _____'.

At one point, Gary and I thought that we'd combine our names and call ourselves 'Gaz & Jo' but Charlotte soon shot that idea down in a ball of flames. 'Ab-so-lute-ly not! Makes you sound like Chaz and Dave!' she said. But that provides its own illustration about how much we were reaching and grasping for the answer. Someone even raised the idea of using an image of my face but I didn't see the point: few people know what I look like, and my original philosophy remained – only the fragrances should lead.

We were throwing around names one afternoon when Josh wandered in after school and observed the usual scene of three adults looking vexed, with heads in hands. He went to the fridge, got himself a drink, and listened in from the sidelines to our haphazard brainstorming, as I said, 'Like it, don't love it' or 'Hate it! Not me'.

That night, with Charlotte gone, and as we sat at the same table having dinner, Gary and I continued the name conversation when Josh suddenly piped up.

'Mum, you're always saying what you love and don't love, and fragrance is about what you love. So if everything is about what you love, why don't you call it Jo Loves . . .?'

I looked at Gary. Gary looked at me, and Josh looked at us both, as if to say, 'Why have you been making this so hard?'

'I love it,' I said. *'I love it!'*

That evening, Jo Loves was born, inspired by our son.

Within the week, the colours and packaging clicked into place, too: a blood-red background with a central black box, bearing the name in white letters. Bold. Striking. Stand out. And way too loud. The boldness of those colours would be something I would later come to regret but, regardless, the spirit of Jo Loves was alive and kicking, bursting with life.

Before taking another step forward, I decided that the right thing to do was to approach Estée Lauder and declare our hand, out of respect more than anything else. In my heart, Jo Malone London was my first child and I didn't want to do anything that would harm her in any way, shape or form, so we sat down with Lauder's head counsel and showed them everything we were doing. And, for the sake of clarity, we suggested adding a qualifying statement on the underside of each box that said, 'Jo Loves is not a subsidiary company or an associated business of Jo Malone Ltd.'

Gary had already started the process of legally registering the name of our trademark, and we officially joined the ranks of Britain's SMEs (Small Medium Enterprise). That's what the government today calls the small business owner but it sounds *so dull*, doing little to convey the dynamism of the people who make or build something, and contribute to our economy. Gary joked that the acronym summed me up perfectly – Stressed Menopausal Eccentric. Although I prefer my suggestion: Seriously Motivated Entrepreneur.

I certainly couldn't have been any more motivated to start again. Of course, no one other than the three of us sitting around the kitchen table had an inkling about my return, and we wanted to keep it that way. Red boxes, registered trademarks and good intentions wouldn't mean a thing unless I could create a whole new product range. Until then, all we had was an empty shell of a business, waiting for its soul to arrive.

I was well aware of the risks of re-emerging with a new brand. Unlike the first time around, there was now a reputation at stake; a height from which to fall. Comebacks in any field are only ever performed on self-made pedestals. It's you, no one else, putting yourself back out there and past glories only buy a limited period of goodwill. It didn't matter how successful I had been before, or what I had built. What I would go on to create as Jo Loves was all that mattered now.

I would be inviting the scrutiny, so I knew that I'd need a fragrance that would put me back on the map, which meant placing all my chips on red, and putting my faith in a sense of smell that was only just beginning to flicker back to life.

TWENTY-EIGHT

The boys were still dozing in bed. 'I'm off to clear my head. See you at breakfast,' I said to Gary, wrapping a white sarong around my swimsuit and slipping on my flip-flops before heading outside. We were on a two-week holiday to Parrot Cay, one of eight habitable islands on the archipelago nation of the Turks and Caicos, and beach walks had become my morning ritual.

At 7 a.m. the tropical heat was perfect, tempered by a cooling ocean breeze. I stepped off the tiny terrace at the front of the villa, cut through a gap in the hedge and turned on to the beach which, at that time of day, I had to myself – a sweeping expanse of the whitest, powder-soft sand I've ever known, in a setting far removed from the demands and pressures that come with preparing to launch a brand.

In that respect, this getaway couldn't have been better timed. Back home, I had tried and tried to lock in a fragrance but to no avail. As much as my sense of smell had returned, I couldn't build any exciting accords that promised something dynamic and original. I'd think about a lemongrass note but it would become nothing more than a lemongrass note; same with a grapefruit note, a mimosa note and a lime note. I remembered how Dad used to sit in front of his easel, staring at a blank canvas for hours, waiting for a painting to form in his mind. I hadn't truly appreciated that struggle, or patience, until now.

I'll go in search of inspiration anywhere – cafés, busy streets, or city parks – but, sometimes, I need to remove myself from distractions and find that mental blank canvas, so Parrot Cay was ideal. I've never meditated in my life but my beach walks were the nearest thing I could imagine to finding a meditative headspace. I'd practise deep inhale-exhale exercises, becoming conscious of each breath, trying to clear the mind and relax the body, allowing myself the space to reconnect with creativity. I don't find it easy to relax, especially when anxious about an inability to create. At night especially, I lay wide awake in bed, listening to the waves crashing over coral reef. It seemed that even the ocean was calm by day but more restless in the dark.

I knew exactly *the type* of fragrance I wanted to create – something unique, beyond trend, with qualities never before created, powerful without being overpowering, neither male nor female, neither soft nor strong – a scent that was in danger of almost contradicting itself and yet always self-assured. The kind of scent that when it walks by you in the street, you want to turn on your heels and follow it. I needed something excep tional, worthy of a comeback. With that outcome in mind, I was intent on creating an unbelievable citrus, staying true to my signature.

I had arrived in the Turks and Caicos with many loose ideas swimming around my head, but the one that had the most poten- tial concerned the pomelo note I had brought with me. This scent was already forming but it was more a lone drumbeat, awaiting the rest of the orchestra to create the symphony.

I had been fascinated by this tropical, melon-sized fruit ever since being introduced to its bittersweet taste in Thailand. But when I first started experimenting with its capabilities, I discovered that it's a watery, temperamental note; nothing I added gave it dynamism, charisma, or any sense of magic. The other inherent challenge was the fact that it's such a fleeting note; it smells amazing but evaporates in an instant, so it needed other notes to give it power, strength and hold it in place. Good for washing sheets and liquid hand soap maybe, but its fuller structure as a fragrance eluded me. It was such a frustrating time because I could smell its presence tantalisingly close but couldn't see or reach it.

Wherever I travel, even if it's for a weekend, I always pack my little fragrance kit: vials of notes, strips of fragrance-testing blotter paper, my teat-pipettes, and a notebook. In the same way some people will relax in the evening with music, I relax by fiddling around with different notes. In the villa at Parrot Cay, I'd sit at the table as the sun went down, smelling a single note to see if an image or memory came to mind. Even when I drew a blank, I still persevered, as all creatives must. Dad sat there with a blank canvas and brushes to hand. Writers face an empty screen and play with words until a paragraph strings together. Likewise, I still worked my nose, even when nothing stirred. Pursue creativity in its absence. Invite inspiration. Keep the door open. Eventually, creativity will manifest itself and whisper to you in the most unexpected forms. Which is what happened to me on that morning when I took my walk.

I had removed my flip-flops and was strolling alongside the blue, crystal-clear water. Aside from the sea breeze in my ears, there was not a sound. I glimpsed a slate-coloured object out of the corner of my eye in the shallows, a few yards away to my right. At first, I thought it was a giant pebble but then it quivered slightly – a stingray. I stood there, trying to get a closer look, and the ripples produced by my shuffling feet didn't even cause it to twitch. With my curiosity satisfied, I ambled on; it followed. I stopped; it stopped, hovering, with its long tail flat against the sand. I giggled, thinking how gentle and graceful this beautiful creature was. Remarkably, as I continued further along the beach, it mirrored my movements for the next twenty minutes or so, seemingly as intrigued by me as I was by it. Even when I reached the far end of the island and turned around, it turned back with me.

I don't think I've ever felt such oneness with nature, as if life was reminding me that whatever comes naturally will always be by my side; at least, that's how I interpreted the symbolism. This moment wasn't about a smell or a memory, and it conjured no notes. All I know is that I felt a surge of creative energy and, with it, a tremendous feeling of peace – an inner calm that I hadn't felt since 2003 or so, prior to my cancer diagnosis. And, as soon as that calm arrived, my walking companion disappeared, darting away into the ocean.

Gary and Josh were already sitting at the table on the terrace having breakfast by the time I returned to the villa, but first I lay on a sunbed, needing five minutes to digest what had happened, like someone waking and trying to remember a vivid dream.

My mind raced with the sights and smells that lined up in a chain link of images: the heaviness of the stingray yet how gracefully it floated; Josh's red bucket by my side, filled with sand dollars collected the previous day; the dazzling white of the beach; the clean white towels rolled up on the neighbouring loungers beneath the umbrellas – more stark white against blue; the salty air; the lemongrass broth being cooked nearby; the peppermint geraniums and herbaceous scents from the hedges behind me; the bottle of fizzy water Gary had half-drunk while I was on my walk, plus a glass with crushed ice melting reluctantly around a slice of lime; my manicured toes with red nail polish, tanned, sun-kissed. And when I headed back into the villa, I saw the crisp, ruffled bed linen on our unmade bed, and felt the coolness of the wooden parquet floor beneath my feet.

There and then, I consciously started to construct the concept for my comeback fragrance. This process wasn't necessarily about finding the scent – not yet; it was about painting a picture in my head and asking myself how I would interpret each of those moments and sights with a fragrance. And that clean, crisp, simple picture was a beachy, sun-kissed landscape, with a refreshing sharpness in the air, capturing that feeling on the last day of a memorable holiday when you want to gather all the moments together and relive them. I wrote everything down in my notebook before going to breakfast – every thought, theme and observation, not wishing to forget a single thing. Those very pages were what I would later show the perfumer in Paris as we brought to life the creation that would become my new No.1 fragrance: to be called, quite simply, Pomelo.

No sooner had we touched down on European soil again than I was jumping on the Eurostar to Paris. Months earlier, I had already decided not to renew my collaboration with the perfume houses and 'noses' with whom I had worked previously. If there was to be a clear distinction between old and new, then it made sense – and felt right – to find a team who had no knowledge of my methods. I was so wary of perceived similarities with the past that I didn't wish to repeat *anything*, regardless of how successful that team and formula may have been.

For the same overcautious reason, I somewhat naively expected my new ideas to be accepted on merit, and not simply because of who I am. So when it came to ringing round the different perfume houses in search of new collaborators, I thought I'd use my married name, announce myself as a fragrance designer and land a meeting. It goes without saying that discarding a known calling card for an unknown name was futile.

'I'm sorry but we're not taking on new clients' was the stock response and no one returned my calls either. I dialled-and-smiled for about five days in the forlorn hope that my enthusiasm would shine through, but I didn't receive a single receptive response.

Sod this, I thought.

I brought out my light from under the bushel, called back the first house on my list, went through the same spiel as before, and ended my call by adding '... and can you tell them that it's Jo Malone. I'd appreciate a call back when they can.'

My phone rang within the hour, a new door swung open, and a new relationship formed with a perfume house and different 'noses' whose identities are the secret ingredient to a winning formula. Suffice it to say that these genius collaborators would be as precious and important to me as my old industry relationships had been.

My opening words at my first meeting in Paris, in the months before Pomelo came to me, were something along the lines of: 'Look, I've not done this for five years so while I think I can still do it, I might need a little assistance.'

I felt like a little girl asking for help when I first sat around the table with my new team and admitted to that vulnerability. Initially, I think they saw my reputation walk in ahead of me, which was why I was quick to issue the reminder that the person seated before them was perhaps more tentative in her approach than first time around. I understood that I would need to refresh, relearn and be retaught a few things.

The team, from the CEO down, were amazing with me. 'We will work with you and offer whatever assistance you need until you feel comfortable in creating again,' they said.

I don't doubt that they, like me, privately asked themselves if I could repeat my success but they took that risk and, as I outlined my vision for Jo Loves, they were prepared to do whatever I wanted to do, and go in whatever direction I chose. When that kind of collaborative spirit kicks in, it creates a shared passion and a synergy that I believe only benefits the end product and both parties.

In working with new perfumers and re-exploring an ever-competitive industry, I came to realise how much the landscape had changed in my time away. When I first started out as a fragrance designer, I was regarded as unique, but the marketplace was now crowded with like-minded designers with their own niche brands. I was no longer out front, leading the way. I was in the pack, trying to find a new way through. What's more, consumer habits had changed, too: shoppers seemed more informed about fragrance, alive to the choices – buying a fragrance from one boutique and a scented candle from another. They sought out niche scents that were different and utilised alternative ingredients. And then there was the rise of social media and fragrance bloggers, who were now regarded as key influencers, transforming the way brands advertised, engaged with customers, and launched product.

Personally, I think competitive tension in any field is healthy – it prevents complacency and encourages originality. But before I could start thinking about raising my game, I first had to create more fragrances to complete my launch collection.

Originally, I intended to run with only one citrus, one floral, and one spicy fragrance but my love of orange blossom – the one note I would take to heaven – proved irresistible, so I ended up with a quartet. With my creative block released by Pomelo, the following three came to me effortlessly, with scents conjuring their own memories and inspirations: Gardenia; Green Orange & Coriander; and Orange Tulle.

The product line would be complete with the inclusion of two layered, scented candles, which in itself was a first. Instead of a single note, I wanted to structure a candle into three separate fragrance layers, and so I created: Lemongrass, Amber, Tiare Flower; and Frangipani, Wild Reseda, Tuberose.

It can take anything from three months to a year to move from concept to development to formulation to finished product, and the team of people I now had in place a stellar staff replete with industry expertise and experience – would know when I had approved a product because, under a new system, it would be signed off with a red dot, the date and my initials. 'Has Jo red-dotted it?' is a question that can often be heard around our offices these days. It can be a fragrance, a photo shoot, a press release, a box, a ribbon or a bottle top – that red dot is my green light.

But it was more of a red-letter day when the samples of those four fragrances and two candles were delivered to the first-floor office we now rented off Sloane Square. This temporary 'head-quarters' had a white-walled meeting area that we called 'the think room' – a space where we could brainstorm as well as meet beauty journalists, bloggers and buyers. We also had an adjoining showroom whose walls were lined with black shelving, which was where I 'displayed' those samples on a single shelf – the first time I had stacked product since closing the door on Sloane Street. To see my fragrances again, in finished bottles, standing side by side – one year on from being unable to knit together any kind of notes – was one personally proud moment.

Unscrewing the top and putting the bottle rim to my nose, breathing in each scent, made me grateful for that day I stood in a small shed in Mile End, imagining this flashforward. I had struggled with making fragrance more than I thought possible. I had been scared, and doubted myself, more times than I can remember, but the sense of elation now made every ounce of angst worthwhile. My new range didn't guarantee success but it was enough for me to know that my instinct had been right: this was unfinished business and I still had something to offer.

I compare this moment to looking down a telescope turned the wrong way, because that's the best way I can sum up how emotionally different it felt second time around. Before, when we opened in Sloane Street, it was like looking through the lens properly: everything felt large and magnified, looking outward into infinite possibilities. Now, looking through the wrong end, everything felt narrow, reduced and small – just four bottles and two candles on a shelf – and no one yet knew of our presence.

That's why November 2011 couldn't come fast enough – the date we had scheduled for the official launch of Jo Loves, eleven months after the lock-out period had ended. All that was left to do now, in the absence of word of mouth, and with the aim of generating some anticipation during the spring and summer, was to formally make the announcement that no one expected.

As far as the rest of the industry was concerned, I had dropped off the radar in 2006, and I'm sure some still believed that I would continue to pursue a career in television. Not once had I publicly hinted at making a return, not until sitting down with three journalists for interviews that would be published over the first two days of March 2011, announcing the launch of our new brand later in the year.

Gary, Charlotte and I crowded around one laptop screen on our kitchen table, waiting for the different articles to break the news, and the first that dropped was from Vogue.co.uk with an intro that read: *'Jo Malone is returning to the world of fragrance with a new company called Jo Loves, we can exclusively reveal today.'*

'No turning back now!' said Charlotte, who could probably feel my heart racing as I stood next to her.

Women's Wear Daily came next with the headline 'Jo Malone

Returns to What She Loves'. But my favourite line, probably because it made me sound more rock'n'roll than I actually am, came from Bryony Gordon in the *Daily Telegraph* the following day, twenty-four hours after everyone had had a chance to read the news: *'Malone has decided to start all over again ... It's like the cosmetic equivalent of Led Zeppelin reuniting. Fashion and beauty websites exploded with excitement when the announcement was made ...'*

Charlotte's mobile phone and email inbox almost went into meltdown for the rest of the week on the back of those articles, which we followed up with a media release sent out globally. Beauty editors and bloggers from London to New York to Sydney wanted interviews, and retailers from around the world wanted to talk about stocking the brand.

I felt that familiar frisson that comes with the nervous thrill of a launch and the great unknown of each fragrance's reception. But the one thing I made clear in each interview was the truth that I wasn't coming back to massage my ego or merge into the crowds. From the get-go, my intent was to create another global brand.

We would ultimately need a flagship store but, initially, our strategy was to launch online until we had re-established ourselves. We were back to being a brand in its infancy and, as Gary pointed out, we hadn't opened Walton Street until the product had done the legwork and momentum had built. Besides, in an increasingly interconnected world, we figured that an online presence was as good as going global, being open 24–7 in a virtual sense.

The early feedback from our sneak previews to journalists was encouraging. There is no knowing how a fragrance will be received but one acid test is putting it before those writers who feature and review new products. Charlotte had been spreading the word among the beauty and fashion editors, offering samples as teasers, and she kept returning to the office with good news. 'They're smelling Pomelo and saying, "That's a Jo fragrance" or

"You can tell that's Jo" – they knew the signature straightaway.'

I'd be lying if I said that I didn't punch the air a few times when I heard such comments because that had been a concern of mine – whether people would know it was me. I think that was when I truly felt I'd got my voice back after being muted for so long.

My gut had told me that Pomelo was going to be something special, and I would be proved right. The repeat purchases would be phenomenal and it would rightly earn its own cult status. I often say it's my 'best friend', simply because it was the first to break down the creative barrier and show me that I could still create fragrance like no one else in the world. That timeless scent will be working its magic thirty years from now. That's how much I believe in its power – I've heard, read and seen the lasting impressions. But I don't think any favourable reaction could top the time when, in the late spring of 2011, Pomelo opened the doors for us into Selfridges.

An early visitor to our new offices was Jayne Demuro, who had overseen the department store's famous beauty hall for the previous decade. Every luxury brand has to first pass through Jayne before having a chance of claiming counter space on that hallowed stage, and our announcement had clearly piqued her interest.

When we met in the 'think room', I didn't necessarily expect anything to come of this meeting – many curious executives and agents dropped by to take a sniff around, so to speak – but it felt good to be showcasing product again. Outside, the rain was tipping down, blown almost horizontal by a gusty wind. Jayne arrived with a raincoat that was wet through.

'Here, let me take that from you – I'll hang it up to dry,' I said.

Jayne detected the fragrance I was wearing. 'You smell *a-mazing*! What is that?'

Pomelo – once again doing all the talking for me.

I ran through the collection one by one, giving the story behind each, and Jayne seemed quietly impressed. We discussed my hopes and plans for the brand, the launch in November, and the eventual goal to put down roots with a flagship store. As she stood to leave and put her coat back on, I instinctively spritzed her coat. Spritzed is actually an understatement. I virtually spray-painted it in Pomelo.

The next morning, shortly after 10 a.m., she was on the phone. 'I got in the lift at work and someone asked me what fragrance I was wearing. I've never smelled anything like it, Jo – and it's still as present as it was yesterday,' she said.

By the end of that call, and thanks in no small part to the power of Pomelo, Jayne invited us to open a pop-up counter at Selfridges and use that as our launch pad, offering an in-store presence right through until Christmas.

Gary wasn't so sure. 'We're not ready to do this,' he said. 'Too big, too soon.'

'Please! We need to get product out there, and this is a fantastic opportunity,' I said, thinking he was overthinking it.

'It's a mistake. We haven't seeded properly. The brand hasn't gained momentum. We haven't even found our audience yet,' he said. 'We're running before we can walk, but if you want me to start the negotiations, I'm behind you.'

I heard him but, on this rare occasion, I thought I knew better. I also did something I had never done before: I crossed over into his lane – business and strategy – and made a decision with my heart. He had made all the right calls in the past but I was deaf to this one. My need to make a splash, to make my comeback known, and to do it with Christmas bells and whistles attached, proved louder than his wisdom. With my golden handcuffs removed, I was already galloping to the west end of Oxford Street. 'I can't think of a better time or better place to announce ourselves to the world – this is how we put ourselves back on the map!' I said.

The pride before the fall . . .

TWENTY-NINE

Selfridges was the only department store I visited as a little girl – a wonderland where Mum used to take me as a treat when she worked for Madame Lubatti. On rare Saturdays, after closing the salon, we'd walk down Baker Street and pass through Portman Square en route to the emporium that, to my young eyes, was as magnificent as any royal palace with its 'Queen of Time' statue and the Ionic columns of its famous frontage.

I'd shuffle through those revolving doors, tucked in tight behind Mum, and watch her browse the beauty hall, dabbing different scents on the inside of her wrist. I'd stand there, at eye level with the product-filled glass cabinets, peering up at the purse-lipped sales ladies with perfectly coiffed hair, who were so glamorous they might as well have wandered off a film set. Mum purchased many of her fragrances there. She also bought me my first Mary Quant grape-crush lipstick and a pair of new school shoes – the shiniest black shoes that I treated like glass slippers because they felt so posh. But *the best bit* was going to the Brass Rail cafeteria where, on a dark-wood mezzanine outside the food hall, we'd have the most amazing salt beef sandwiches with coleslaw and gherkins, and a hot chocolate. Now *that* was a real treat. I don't think I had ever seen so much meat stuffed into a hearty sandwich before! Everything about that store, from its sandwiches and its Easter chocolate to its shiny school shoes, was from a different world, as far as I was concerned.

Even today, I never fail to feel the extraordinary sense of adventure that founder Harry Gordon Selfridge wanted shoppers to experience when he opened the store to much razzmatazz in 1909. His American vision brought a revolutionary creative flair to London and changed the face of retail forever, from the glamorous showcasing of merchandise and 'splendid' in-store promotions to the spectacle of crowd-pulling 'window shows'. You can still sense his theatrical spirit, even within the modernity of its decor and style. And one thing that never changes is the marketplace buzz of retail activity.

There was none of the usual hustle and bustle when we arrived on the eve of our launch on Monday 6 November 2011, the day after my forty-eighth birthday. That's because it had just gone midnight, and the store was deserted save for a scattered team of cleaners and the odd cleaning truck trundling along the aisles with its rotating brushes polishing the marble floors. Selfridges at witching hour is a surreal place to be. All the Christmas decorations were up – sparkling blue bows strung between Roman columns and magnificently decorated trees – but the festive music, like the air conditioning, had been turned off. Each floor was as still and silent as the mannequins in the windows. Every word Charlotte and I spoke, together with every footstep, seemed to echo within a library-like hush.

Having left Gary at home with Josh, I oversaw the team of shopfitters who would construct our unit through the small hours of Monday morning, ready for opening at 9 a.m. The pop-up had become its own phenomenon in my time away but it wasn't anything new – the concept of a temporary retail presence had been around for years in the form of trunk shows, which was how we first became a blip on the American radar in the 1990s. Only now, the stage was far bigger and the radar global, which was probably why I felt a rush of excitement as the workmen unwrapped our unit and crates of product. At that hour, it was like being caught in a dream watching our counter get built, piece by piece.

There were some apprehensions, too, mainly because pop-ups don't 'pop up' at all. When you're there, witnessing the construction, it's actually an agonisingly slow process. It would take them eight hours and I'd count every minute of that race against the clock, leaving us one hour to stock the shelves and be bright-eyed and bushy tailed for the first customers.

Another reason for my nervousness was down to our location – fifty feet away from Jo Malone London. It was a proximity I hadn't even considered, or looked for, until half an hour after arriving. I had been so wrapped up in getting everything ready that I hadn't paid attention to the sleeping brands around us. My view was partly obscured by other counters but the irony was stark – the old brand I had boxed away in my head would now be a near neighbour and, come morning, I'd be in direct competition with my own name.

I won't lie, part of me wanted to go over, touch the boxes, smell and breathe in the memory of Lime Basil & Mandarin, and almost put my arms around the counter while no one was looking, pretending for a second that it was still mine. Two things stopped me: a sense of respect for keeping the past where it belonged; and the fact that one of the country's leading beauty bloggers, Jane Cunningham, was shadowing me. At Charlotte's prompting, I had embraced the new world of media and invited Jane to share the experience, allowing her to 'live' blog what she referred to as a 'complete overnighter with Jo Malone'. So, you can see why it made PR sense to keep my sentimental temptations to myself.

But over the course of that night, I did catch myself looking over a few times, thinking, 'How on earth did it come to this?'

Looking at my established name fifty feet away and seeing Jo Loves slowly forming right in front of me was the strangest feeling. Mr Selfridge once famously said, 'To work is elevating. To accomplish is superb. To fill one's time with profitable enterprise is to leap forward in the world's race and to place beside one's name the credit mark of effort.' I now saw two credit marks under the same iconic roof, and I think that will probably be the closest I'll ever come to an out-of-body experience. It felt like I had been split down the middle: half of me over there, dressed in cream and black; and the other half with me, trying on red and black for size. And the new me felt like the underdog. An underdog against my own name. With no idea whether success or failure lay ahead.

Indeed, my new packaging provided another degree of trepidation, not just on this night but in the weeks beforehand. When I had first seen the designs for the pop-up, I'd had my doubts about how our red boxes would look in the classy environs of Selfridges. Those doubts didn't go away when I showed Isy Ettedgui, who had inspired our first brand's packaging. 'It's not you. It's too loud, too hard,' she said. But I chose to overlook that advice, the same way I pushed away Gary's caution, telling myself that it would look better in reality than on paper.

The pop-up was a complex design that relied on a lot of technology because it incorporated a 'Smell Pod' – a booth where customers could step inside and use touch screens to select each fragrance's story, or a quick spray of each scent. As a result of that elaborate facility, and due to other hitches along the way, progress was painfully slow.

Jane Cunningham summed up the atmosphere at 2.54 a.m. when she 'live' blogged and wrote: *'It's a bit like* Night at the Museum *... but no Ben Stiller. Jo can't keep still – it's clearly all so* *exciting for her – but, like all of us, she is looking tired now. We just want to start putting bottles of Pomelo on the shelves but the fitters are nowhere near ready for us, but they couldn't go any faster . . . there's really a lot at stake and there just isn't room for any error at all.'*

Without endless coffee and the sugar rush from a shared box of Quality Street, I don't know how we would have kept going. Not until 4 a.m. did the counter truly start to take shape – and that's when my earlier doubts were confirmed. Our brand image was all wrong. It *didn't* look better in reality than it did on paper.

I had gone downstairs to stretch my legs and was standing on the escalator, coming up from basement level to the first floor, when I first caught sight of our big, hard-edged, matt-finish, vivid red-and-black box, amplified by the luxury setting of brass, glass, copper and silver. Everything else sparkled; we were loud and brash – a galling realisation five hours from opening time.

Up ahead, I could see Charlotte chatting with our guest blogger, who was no doubt awaiting my gleeful reaction, when all I could think was, 'Oh my God. What have I done?'

Isy was right: it wasn't me. Gary was right: we hadn't been ready. I can't remember what I 'officially' said to Jane but her blog observed that I looked 'remarkably laid-back', so my poker face must have been effective. I might not have had straight aces in my hand but that's hardly something I was going to admit when the stakes were so high – that would have been PR suicide. No one would have a clue that Jo didn't love the clothes that Jo Loves wore; only Charlotte would know, along with Gary, who would arrive at nine. But what else could we do but take the hit, deal with it and move on?

Behind the brave face, I quietly kicked myself, but I soon put this tone-deaf error into context: yes, it didn't look great, and nor was it the dream start I had envisaged, but it wasn't fatal. I had every confidence that the main star of the show – the fragrance – would still shine through. My name would be back out there and each bottle of product would make itself known, backed by that morning's press launch. Don't get me wrong, I didn't *hate* the red and black – it grated more than anything else – and I accepted that we'd have to live with it for the immediate future. But I knew there and then that we'd rebrand, although not straightaway – that would have looked even worse, and the last thing I needed to do was make another hurried decision.

When you've messed up, even when you feel sick on the inside, business is about pushing through the mistake and learning from it – and the humbling lessons are the most valuable. If any part of me thought that my return was going to be straightforward and obstacle-free, then here was the abject reminder that building a brand doesn't work that way and doesn't respect past glories.

In my blinkered focus to get the fragrances right, and in my rush to get back in the game, I hadn't looked carefully enough at the packaging. Those colours were never me, but what is red if not an alert or an attention-seeking cry that yells, 'I'm here! I'm back!' It was all about being heard again, rather than an identity that represented who I am. I had been so hell-bent on putting daylight between the old and new – to appease the lawyers and tick all the contractual boxes – that I had gone to another extreme. And when Selfridges came knocking, all I could see was a repeat of our Bergdorf Goodman moment – the chance to accelerate and short-circuit a young brand's necessary growth. I stupidly believed that we could shoot to the top straight out of the starting gate. How ironic it seems to me now that I, this person so terrified of failure and humiliation and being imperfect, could make such a monumental misjudgement. Had I taken a breath, stepped back and waited another year, I'm sure the mistake would have made itself known and the red-black episode would never have happened.

But one imperfection aside, there remained lots to smile about, and not even the issue of the packaging could ruin what remained a momentous day.

The counter was built by 8 a.m. and Vera, our sales manager, arrived to stack the shelves while I attended a breakfast launch for all the Selfridges employees, so that they were briefed on the latest in-store product. I then returned home, changed, and was back on the floor to meet the press later that morning. To be fair, the day couldn't have gone better as we created the kind of in-store hype that I had missed. Trade in the run-up to Christmas was swift, and the write-ups and reviews, in magazines and on blogs, raved about the new fragrances. And seeing our bags walk out into Oxford Street felt wonderful. I even managed to convince myself that red and black looked festive.

Come New Year, and having had the taste of being back on the department store floor, I knew that we'd have to find our brand a permanent home. But, as Gary said, we first needed more fragrances and ancillary products before we even started thinking about a shop. 'Product, product, product, PR, PR, PR!' he said. 'Let's give this six months and dedicate the time to getting our ducks in a row. Far rather get it right within the next five years than get it wrong within two.'

And this time, I listened.

In many respects, the following year was a period of re-evaluation. After our successful stint at Selfridges, more agents and buyers came to see us, exploring our readiness for entering into partnerships with other department stores, but my lesson had been learned – we needed to regroup and establish the true identity of the brand first, before taking it out elsewhere.

I actually enjoyed the freedom and used it to create more fragrances – Pink Vetiver proved an addictive addition, as did the artistic Mango shot collection. I started to think of ways to present fragrance differently, and toyed with rebranding ideas, trying to figure out what we could look like if red and black didn't fit and we couldn't be cream and black.

It's important for any entrepreneur to realise that going back and putting things right is not admitting failure but guaranteeing success further down the line. I endlessly asked myself, 'How can I put this right?' 'What do I need to do to make this a global brand?' And there were times when I asked myself, 'Do you *really* want this? Are you hungry enough for the second climb?' The answer each and every time was a resounding yes — I hadn't come this far to quit now.

There are five heartbeats to a successful business: first, you need passion for, and pride in, your product — that's *inspiration*; second, in daring to be different, you think of ways to stay separate from the herd and strive for originality — that's *innovation*; third, you stamp your identity on everything you do as creators, without compromising who you are — that's *integrity*; fourth, you put the foundations in place and create hunger for the brand, building momentum for the moment of lift-off — that's *ignition*; and, lastly, you seize the moment by learning to tune in to and trust your gut, way more than you do the mind because the mind wasn't designed to make decisions, the gut was — and that's *instinct*.

Five heartbeats: Inspiration, Innovation, Integrity, Ignition, Instinct.

In my haste in 2011, I hadn't applied three of those principles. I ignored my instinct, compromised my integrity, and turned the key when the ignition was inadequate. But, by the summer of 2012, we had started to see the hunger build as sales maintained an upward trend. I had also developed the ancillary products of body crèmes, bath colognes, cleansers and body lotions. And now, seven months on from the Christmas at Selfridges, my instinct was flaring about our need for a shop; or at least to start the search.

We could pull on the reins as much as we liked, and continue with our online presence, but if people didn't know where I was, and couldn't smell the fragrances, we were operating with one hand tied behind our backs. In beauty and cosmetics, when the sense of smell or touch determines sales, online platforms are only effective if the offline groundwork is done in tandem. The biggest mistake for any business is to become detached from the consumer, and, for me, that detachment could not have been more keenly felt than when operating via the ether of the internet.

I remember standing in the 'think room', looking at our product-filled shelves, and it felt more like a perfume house reception than a shop. It felt like the fragrance equivalent of inviting someone to dinner without having a home to host them. And so Gary brought out his reliable clicker once again and started the search, both for new office headquarters and a prime retail location.

Finding the bigger office was no problem – we moved around the corner to a building off King's Road in Chelsea – but the perfect shop wasn't so easy to locate, either because the clicker count wasn't impressive or the leases were too prohibitive. After Walton Street and Sloane Street – premises that felt magical the moment we stepped inside – it was hard to imagine that we could be so lucky again, especially as the weeks dragged on. But Gary kept on being his optimistic self. 'We keep looking. There's a shop out there with your name on it and we're going to find it.'

As we looked ahead with the business, I would also face the saddest task of saying goodbye to my mum, dad and sister, who would all pass away within the space of eighteen months. At this time, the fact we had been estranged didn't seem to matter; the sense of loss still felt profound, and it pained me to remember the bridges we hadn't rebuilt.

I remember sitting by Tracey's hospital bed while she was in intensive care at the end of a long period of sickness and, as I held her hand, all I thought about was how much I wished things could have been different. I stood at Mum and Dad's funerals and felt the same way, hoping that they knew, deep down, beyond everything that had happened, how much I loved them. And it was love – and forgiveness – that I chose to focus on in my grief, allowing the memories of our early years, however imperfect they may have been, to sustain me. I couldn't change the past. But I could change how to frame it, without hurt, resentment or bitterness.

I asked for one sentimental item of my parents, something that I could remember them by. I received Mum's ornate letter rack with decorative leaves and a heart-shaped handle. It's not worth anything but it used to sit on her desk and that's where she kept all her notes and telephone messages; today, I use it to hold all my fragrance strips. And the one keepsake from Dad was a series of six watercolour paintings that he had done for me, placed into an envelope with my name on. I never knew he had done those paintings, and each one depicts colourful, antique perfume bottles. His way of capturing the art of fragrance.

The fruitless search for the ideal shop continued and I thought we were never going to find anywhere until, that was, I had a catch-up with Ruth Kennedy. A cup of coffee and a conversation with a good friend can often change our destiny or lead to a light-bulb moment, and that's what happened when we met at her offices in Ebury Street, Belgravia.

Over the years, we had shared many chapters of our lives, including our very different retail journeys. On this particular morning, I was moaning – and boring myself in the process – about the struggle to find a shop when she stopped me. 'You know there's a lease coming up in Elizabeth Street?'

'No – where?'

Five minutes later, after she had called the tenant, we were walking to the nearby street where I had first earned gainful employment as a teenager. We passed the cake shop, and then the flower shop where I was fired for throwing a bucket of water over the manageress. I shared that funny story as we kept strolling along, and then, up ahead – 'No, it can't be,' I thought.

'Here we are – it's this one,' said Ruth.

'You've got to be kidding me.'

'Why? What's wrong?'

'This is where I worked when it was a deli!'

We were staring in the window of No.42 Elizabeth Street – Justin de Blank's mini-food hall that was now a fashion designer's, selling kaftans, fabrics and textiles. I was standing in the spot where I had first started out. I don't think Ruth could believe it either.

As soon as we stepped inside, I got goosebumps. It felt like I had arrived home. The configuration was different – there was a downward staircase on the right and dark paisley-print wallpaper that made the space feel tighter – but my mind's eye still saw everything as it used to be: Justin standing at the counter; Tom unpacking the fruit and veg; Roy the butcher having banter with a customer. At the back, where two girls typed away in an office, I could visualise the kitchen where I'd cut overgenerous slices of salmon. 'I have to have this place,' I told Ruth, pulling out my phone to call Gary. At that moment, I set my heart on No.42 Elizabeth Street.

Gary started negotiating the lease but, as ever with commercial property, we had to wait for what felt like an inordinate amount of time. All I seemed to ask him, day in, day out, was, 'Are we close to signing yet?' I don't know which one of us wanted to finalise terms quicker: me, so that we could get cracking; or him, so that I would get off his back. I was like the annoying kid in the back of the car, repeatedly asking, 'Are we there yet? Are we there yet?'

From memory, there were several sticking points, not least of which concerned the building regulations in respect to the interior alterations we wanted to make. Throw in Gary's haggling for favourable terms and it's not hard to see why the process dragged on, but I started to believe that it wasn't ever going to happen. 'I'll stop asking,' I said, somewhat forlornly. 'Just tell me if and when we get it.'

On the morning of 5 November – my forty-ninth birthday – we maintained the tradition of gathering in the living room before Josh, now almost twelve, got ready for school. I lit candles. Gary made tea. We sat around in our dressing gowns as I opened my cards and presents. Later that afternoon, Gary joined me at the office. My head was down and I was concentrating on something when he walked in and placed a small white box on my desk. 'An extra birthday present,' he said.

All around the office, the team stood, paying closer attention than they ordinarily would.

Earrings, I thought. He's got me earrings and everyone's in on the surprise.

I pulled the lid off the box. A single silver key rested on a bed of scrunched-up white tissue paper. My first thought was that he had bought me a car. But why would he buy me a car when he knows I can barely drive?

And then the penny dropped: it was the best birthday present ever.

'We signed? THE LEASE IS SIGNED?!'

Gary's grin was almost as wide as mine. 'Time to go and be a shopkeeper again.'

THIRTY

As I turned the key in the lock, life turned full circle – the completion of a thirty-three-year journey that had brought me back to where everything had effectively started. Stepping inside those premises was like stepping into my past and future at the same time, walking Gary through the memory while simultaneously visualising what we were going to do with this empty space.

There is something amazing about going back to a place where you first set out as an innocent teenager, only to return with a wealth of experience. I remember admiring Justin de Blank's passion and pride in his shop, wanting to make it a special place for the customer; he unwittingly showed me the way long before I had glimpsed the possibilities of a career in retail. Now, there I was, standing in the shoes of the man who had taught me by example, with the opportunity of doing something special myself.

Having had so much time to think, my vision for No.42 Elizabeth Street was clear: to showcase fragrance in an original way and do more than rely on tester bottles and blotter strips; to create an environment that looked different and felt different, where people could indulge the senses and linger in a creative space, not only browse and shop but savour an *experience*.

I wanted to create a fragrance brasserie, complete with its own bar.

When I had first mentioned the idea to Gary, his face was a picture. 'A *brasserie!* We're not selling food, darlin'!'

'Not a bar where you come to eat but one where you come to smell,' I said. 'Think fragrance served in cocktail shakers, Martini glasses, velouté guns and big red bottles!'

Gary says there was a reason I was born on Bonfire Night, 'because when you start thinking about ideas, you're like one of those unpredictable fireworks, and there's no knowing which direction you'll shoot off'.

This experiential concept had its origins in both London and New York. One of my favourite things to do on a Friday afternoon was to take myself to the Harrods food hall and sit at the semi-circular tapas bar, enjoying a glass of wine and tapas. I've always been happy in my own company, sitting with my thoughts while I do a spot of people-watching, and I constantly observed how uniting the whole set-up was – lots of men and women on their own, savouring the tapas, engaging in conversation. All I could think about was how to recreate this little scene within the world of fragrance. 'How could I use product in a tapas format?'

Then came an evening in Manhattan, at the Four Seasons Hotel, when I watched a bartender turn cocktail-making into an art, creating elaborate drinks with a flourish. I noticed how people sitting at the bar never took their eyes off him as he grabbed vodka and added a shot of something, or poured the contents of a cocktail shaker into a Martini glass, drizzling the froth on top. He managed to make the presentation of alcohol and spirits entertaining.

Over time, this combined theme of tapas and cocktails would inspire me in many ways, as well as influence different products, but the central idea it inspired was the brasserie – something that I knew would be an industry first. It's not enough these days to have a bricks-and-mortar store and rely solely on product. Shopping has to become more of an experience, and that's what I set out to create. Friends tell me that I like to think outside the box, and maybe that's true, but on this occasion, I didn't want to think outside or inside the box. I didn't even want the box to be there. I wanted to open up a whole new arena.

As Gary and I stood in the side doorway of the shop, in the same spot where Tom and I used to grab lunch, looking out into the alleyway, I outlined my idea in detail to the architect Martin Steele, who had joined us on this site visit.

We were going to dispense with a standard retail counter and install a brasserie bar, offering a tapas-style menu to amuse the nose and scent the skin; instead of an *amuse-bouche*, an *amuse-nez*. Each customer would get to sample product by selecting three courses. The first course: a shot of bath cologne poured into a mini-tagine and served in hot water that releases a scented steam, to enjoy the fragrance as you would when taking a bath. For the second course, how about two shots of shower gel mixed in a cocktail shaker before being served on the rocks in a Martini glass with the resulting foam poured on top, creating the same froth as a shower? And for the third 'dish', the customer receives a shot of body crème from a velouté gun, whipped and sprayed on to a porcelain spoon before being painted on to the skin with brushes in an updated, and artistic, version of the hand and arm massage.

There's a quote from Maya Angelou that says, 'People will forget what you said, people will forget what you did, but people will never forget how you made them feel.' Nothing makes us *feel* and *remember* more than the sense of smell, so it was important that our flagship shop provide an immersive, unforgettable experience. Everyone remembers their first kiss, and I wanted to conjure that 'first kiss' moment with the brand, because falling in love with fragrance is rooted in first impressions, first feelings, first connections.

The more Gary heard, the more onboard he was, but he had concerns about the bar fitting the floor space. When Martin took out his tape measure and we used a felt-tip pen to map out a rough shape on the floor, it's fair to say that things didn't look encouraging. But instinct sent me over to the left side of the shop and I tapped the wall, recalling the precise layout thirty-three years on.

'This wall goes back a bit. Pass me that,' I said, pointing to a screwdriver on the ground. I dug into the plasterboard and, sure enough, there was a gap that must have been three feet wide. 'Take this wall back and we *can* have a brasserie.'

I always did like to push the boundaries.

I stepped into the middle of the floor and faced the rear of the premises. 'And those offices can be a creative studio.'

'What's going to be in the creative studio?' asked Gary.

'Something amazing,' I said, throwing him a wink. 'You'll see.'

'More money then?' he said, raising his eyebrows knowingly.

'Yup. And we're going to start the rebranding process, too.'

'Wonderful – *even more* money. Do you even know what that rebranding looks like?'

'I have a few ideas,' I said, smiling. 'I'm still working on them.'

'*Of course* you are,' he said.

Due to the usual red tape and not inconsiderable design snags, it would take another nine months before we opened, but at least that provided ample time to ensure everything was perfectly executed. One morning, in the spring of 2013, while Gary and I were having yet another site meeting, one of the builders handed me a folded piece of paper. 'A lady came by and left you this note – she asked that you call her when you get a chance,' he said.

I didn't recognise the number or the name 'Michelle' but I called her that evening – it was Justin de Blank's wife. When we talked, it transpired that she had no idea that I had previously worked for Justin. The reason for her note was that he had passed away, at the age of eighty-five, a few months earlier in the December. 'Would it be okay to come and have a look at the shop?' she asked.

'Of course, any time,' I said.

I understood that the place held many memories for her, too.

A few days later, we shared some of those memories over a cup of coffee, which seemed fitting in the weeks leading up to opening. Justin had been a part of my journey, and, in a small way, through Michelle, through reminiscing, I was able to express the 'thank you' I hadn't been able to say to him personally.

Dreaming up the concept for the brasserie was the easy part; the design would prove to be a little more challenging because I was essentially looking outside of the industry for my inspiration, and it mattered to me that it felt authentic, not gimmicky.

Fortuitously, when Gary and I attended a black-tie charity dinner at the Roundhouse, I found myself sitting next to Jeremy King, one-half of Corbin and King, the partnership behind restaurants such as The Wolseley, The Delaunay, Café Colbert, and Brasserie Zédel. Step into any one of those establishments and you'll see why these two visionaries know everything there is to know about brasseries.

When you find yourself sitting next to someone like Jeremy and you have no idea where to start with a bar's design, there's only one thing to do – you ask for help. I've never been backwards in coming forwards, and there's no harm in admitting you don't know how to do something. People can only say 'No', and entrepreneurs can ill afford to be afraid of that two-letter word. There are bigger risks to be taken in business than asking someone for a favour.

When Jeremy heard my concept, he was happy to help. The next day, he stopped by for a coffee in 'the think room', and that's where he took out his pen and sketched a rough design on a piece of paper. 'You need something like this, something that curves and looks classical.'

He didn't miss a detail, even drawing the foot-rail and the handbag hooks beneath the bar top. He then put me in touch with interior designer Shayne Brady, who would turn that exact sketch into the reality that customers enjoy today: a zinc-topped bar with a curved, ruby glass body which, when seen from above, is the letter 'J'. It is the centrepiece of a shop that remains aesthetically me: a minimalist, all-white decor that mirrors my own home.

Drop in and you'll find the bar with its high-top stools on the left; the recessed shelving filled with product on the right; and straight ahead, at the back, behind a double set of white doors, the purpose-built creative studio. We still had to grin and bear the red-and-black packaging for a while longer – rebranding would take another eighteen months. But even those original colours looked softer and less pronounced when better framed by the white frontage and our first window display – a giant bloom of red and white paper flowers erupting from a Jo Loves gift bag.

We opened our doors on 11 October 2013, and I commemorated the occasion, and my history with the address, by launching a new fragrance: a floral-scented collection called 'No.42 The Flower Shop', themed around my two jobs as a sixteen-year-old, evoking memories of a florist's filled with lilies, sweet peas, and roses, and a floor scattered with crushed green stems.

The whole day was hugely nostalgic, not only due to the Justin de Blank era but because Elizabeth Street felt like Walton Street all over again, no more so than the way the community of shopkeepers embraced us. Mauro the restaurant owner sent over pizza. Peggy Porschen brought round her cupcakes. And the boys from Jeroboams wine shop dropped off a bottle of champagne. With those kind of shopkeepers, the team I had around me, and the loyal customers we would attract, I would once again be surrounded by a wonderful retail family. I was back where I belonged, with a shop, in a local street, surrounded by my fragrances. Standing tall again.

I almost didn't want that first day to end, and yet I looked forward to many more like it. So determined was I to capture the details of our opening that I bought a red leather visitors' book so that every customer could leave their name and a message. It's still in the shop today. Second time around, I didn't want to forget a thing and, as those pages collected names, I soaked up the atmosphere, the laughter, and the nonstop activity. I watched people's reaction to the brasserie bar and the 'tapas', loving how both men and women engaged with the experience, not only leaving with heaps of product but with a better understanding of fragrance; its art, its beauty, its alchemy, its power to stir creativity.

That evening, back at home, I shared a glass of wine with Gary, toasting our first day's trade. And then I did something that we couldn't do after opening in 1994. I tweeted. I took out my mobile, logged on as @JoMaloneMBE, and tapped out a quick message that summed up how I felt: *'Once a shopkeeper, always a shopkeeper.'*

When it came to rebranding, we hired the expertise of Pearlfisher, a company I had worked with on *High Street Dreams*, led by the creative eye of Jonathan Ford. When we met at a local Italian trattoria, he asked what 'look' I had in mind. My answer amused him. 'I know everything I don't like and I'll know what I like when I see it,' I said. 'The gap in the middle is where you find me right now and I need help.'

I'm sure he's had more detailed briefs over the years, but it's not easy branding yourself for a third time, and I wanted to get it right and explore every option regarding textures, papers, colours, and fonts. We needed the equivalent of the Nike swoosh or Apple's bitten apple. 'I want to look at the packaging and say, "That's me. That's my signature."'

'We've certainly got a lot to work with,' said Jonathan, with a wry smile.

While that work began in earnest, I received a call from Downing Street, inviting me to be one of the creative ambassadors for Britain's GREAT campaign – an international promotion of the UK, building on the national pride generated by the Diamond Jubilee and 2012 London Olympics. I soon found myself at a dinner at No.10 hosted by Prime Minister David Cameron, sitting alongside the likes of David Bailey, Stella McCartney, Katherine Jenkins, Kelly Hoppen, Barbara Broccoli, and Ken Hom – a team of fellow ambassadors selected from the arts, fashion, design, and business.

The GREAT campaign would take us to Istanbul and Shanghai, and, as someone who is proud to be a British creator, I couldn't have been more honoured to be involved. I'll champion our nation's culture and enterprise as loud as anyone because I believe our small island has a continent's worth of creative and innovative talent.

Istanbul saw the first Festival of Creativity in May 2014, where the other ambassadors and I presented our wares and stories. Shanghai followed in March 2015, with HRH Prince William leading proceedings – the first time in thirty years that a member of the Royal Family had visited mainland China. Our prince was a trouper. Not once did it feel like he was a far-removed royal; it felt like he was one of us, an enthusiastic part of team GB, standing together as one voice, telling the story of great British business.

The one thing I expected to do in Shanghai was demonstrate

creativity by introducing my fragrance brasserie. What I *didn't* expect was to provide a lesson in how entrepreneurs have to think on their feet when plans go wrong.

Twenty-four hours before I was due to give a speech and 'set up shop' at a building on The Bund – a famous waterfront area on the banks of the Huangpu River – I was sitting with a client from Singapore, listening to a merchant's speech in the main hall of a conference centre, when Charlotte whipped in from nowhere and sat beside me, looking rattled.

'*I'll talk to you after this*,' I mouthed.

But she shook her head firmly. 'I need to speak to you *right now*.'

It transpired that we had a slight problem. A month earlier, we had shipped our tapas inventory to China in preparation for the big event. The shipment had reached land – it just hadn't reached Shanghai. The props we relied on – the tagines, cocktail shakers, glasses, paintbrushes, velouté guns, boxes and gift bags – didn't have a hope of arriving in time. All we had with us were three bags of product and some branded boarding that the campaign had organised. At the very festival where our future king was present, Jo Loves was in danger of being the only British brand that was closed for business even before opening.

One of the organisers looked as flummoxed as we felt. 'As I see it,' he said, 'you have two choices: fix it or cancel.'

I looked at Charlotte; she smiled because she already knew my response.

'We'll fix it,' I said. 'We'll make it work.'

How I said that with a straight face, I've no idea. But when encountering a brick wall in business, you have to find a way over, around, under, or through, even when the answer doesn't appear so readily apparent. Fortunately, in Charlotte I had someone who, like me, doesn't dwell on a problem; it's find a solution or go home. Which is why we found ourselves tearing around Shanghai that afternoon in a mad panic, trying to source makeshift materials. That search was starting to look hopeless when, at the eleventh hour, I spotted a building in the distance and could have sworn it was a mirage – an IKEA store; a little corner of Brent Cross in Shanghai. I could have wept with joy, especially when we ran inside and realised that it stocked almost everything we needed and more. We ended up adding red chopsticks, rice bowls, and soup spoons to my tapas routine. As for the cocktail shakers, I called a friend at The Langham and he kindly let me borrow a pair. I think that might count as my best ever recovery in retail!

The next morning, to please the local crowd, I came up with an idea for serving a fragrant version of dim sum – cotton-wool balls left to soak in a rice bowl filled with bath cologne before being picked up with chopsticks in order to breathe in the scent. We served this 'dish', along with the rest of the 'tapas', four times an hour. Within the first fifteen minutes, ten people had gathered around our bar. Within the hour, as word spread, and as four local TV crews took an interest, we had more than a hundred people queuing up, including three generations of different families. Dim sum proved a big hit, but it wasn't the only addition to my repertoire that month.

As part of the GREAT campaign I had been asked, along with four other perfumeries, to interpret our country through a fragrance. Without even thinking about it, I knew my theme had to be the Union Jack, and the hook had to be the Norma Jeane white rose. White roses were in my garden, my grandmother's garden, and the Queen's garden; they formed my wedding bouquet; and they are the flower that Gary or Josh buy me every Friday evening. And the white rose note, which I braided with the fresh, clean, citrus of lemon leaves, feels quintessentially British and classic. That's why White Rose & Lemon Leaves will always be my 'flying the flag' fragrance – a reminder of the trip when we needed a good dose of never-give-in British resilience, with a bit of help from our Swedish friends at IKEA.

Back in the autumn of 2010, in the months before announcing our new brand, I was walking through Times Square in New York City when I noticed a ridiculously long queue outside Pop-Tarts World – a pop-up café from the makers of the biscuit-like pastry that was seemingly a staple snack of most American childhoods.

Curious about the product that led to such foot traffic, I wandered over to find people lined up at a machine called The Varietizer, which custom-made Pop-Tarts. I watched as women and men, and boys and girls, used a touch screen to select six different flavours before a robotic arm compressed their flattened pastries. I thought it was pure genius – customers could have a hand in making their own favourite snack. And this is the direction that retail is headed – the millennial consumer has a taste for interaction with brands, whether it's sharing a creative experience or being part-involved in the creation of a product. Consumer and creator can become one in so many ways, and the Pop-Tart World example got me wondering if I could do the same with a candle.

In May 2015, after four years in development, we finally unveiled the fruits of that wondering: the Candle Shot Studio, based in the back room at Elizabeth Street – the creative space I had always intended to use as a way of involving and engaging the customer. Here, they can co-create their own bespoke Shot Candle, choosing one base scent and a 'shot' of another. The base is already set within the glass, hollowed out so that the 'shot' slots into its centre. A Tahitian gardenia base could be shot with mango, or Mint Mojito with petitgrain. Each pairing is melded together with a quick blast of a blowtorch. What I love about this is watching people choose their fragrances, leading to a combined scent that they have played a part in building.

This is what I want to keep doing as Jo Loves continues to grow: pursue more innovative products, experiential concepts, and memorable fragrances. The journey of this brand has taken me across the spectrum of emotions, and it has challenged every part of who I am. It's been tougher than I could possibly have imagined and yet the power of a retail adventure, combined with my passion for fragrance and the prospect of seeing us go global once more, continues to motivate me on a daily basis. And as we build and expand, we do so with colours and packaging that now resonate and represent who I am, because that final element – the rebranding – finally fell into place in 2015.

In the weeks before leaving for China, I had been at my desk in the office, staring at an uninspiring sheet of product labels – all white, bearing only the black font of our name. I remember noting the void of emotion in those labels, wondering if we needed a silver colour, or a gold, or a striking symbol to inject some energy.

In previous weeks, each proposed design for our new look that I had been shown hadn't resonated, although the team at Pearlfisher had already locked in two ideas: the use of a Union Jack and a mass of white space, representing patriotism and undiluted creativity.

As I continued idly to toss ideas around my head, I started to play with a bottle of Shanghai Red nail varnish that a friend had sent ahead of my trip. I was just fiddling around when – and don't ask why – I dipped the end of a pencil into the varnish and let one drop fall on to a label; it landed as a neat red globule just beneath the words Jo Loves.

Behind me, our new product development manager, Naomi Harford, whose desk was out of sight and around the corner, shouted out, 'Have you red-dotted that candle for approval, Jo?' By now, I had bought reams of adhesive red dots from Ryman's to continue our product-approval system.

I was about to answer Naomi, and reach for another sticky red dot, when the light bulb above my head switched on. I looked down at the label where the drop of varnish was beginning to dry – a red dot. That's it! My signature, my seal of approval, the mark that said a product was mine.

I jumped up and hurried over to Naomi, taking the label with me.

'That's me – that's our logo,' I said.

Charlotte came over, and we stuck that one label on a bottle of Pomelo, and we all had the same wow-moment. My name, above a slightly raised dot, suspended in lots of white space: vivid, emphatic, yet simple.

And that was the final piece of the jigsaw that the Pearlfisher team needed to go away and bring everything together for the subtle but sophisticated design that is our branding today: the dominant white with red lining and bows for the boxes and gift bags, and a colourless, embossed Union Jack wrapped around each box. Four years on from that humbling moment in Selfridges, we now had the impactful first impression we needed.

Look out for that red dot – it's a stamp I intend to leave all over the world.

In many ways, 2015 represented a turning point – the first time since launching that I felt we were swimming with the tide. But never one to rest on my laurels, I decided to take Naomi to Grasse, the place where I first fell in love with fragrance. I hadn't returned to the town since my maiden trip in the 1990s, so it seemed the most obvious place to be reinspired and seek new ideas.

Naomi joined Gary, Josh and me on a weekend visit and, as we touched down at Nice airport, I couldn't wait to roam the market and sit in the square in that same spot outside the brasserie.

After checking in at our hotel, we headed into the old town but, as we rounded the corner and the square came into view, my expectations received a rude awakening. Everything had changed. The abundance of flower stalls had been replaced by merchants selling second-hand clothes, bric-a-brac, and touristy souvenirs. The brasserie was closed. Even the fragrant air of jasmine and rose seemed to have lost some of its regality. The charm and magic – everything I had once fallen in love with – was missing. Only the cobbled streets and the picturesque backdrop were unchanged; the beautiful frame was there but the oil painting was missing. I had stepped into nostalgia only to find that nostalgia was all that remained, and the sense of disappointment was crushing.

Once back at the hotel, I voiced my sadness to the concierge at the front desk, but I could tell from his easy sympathy that I wasn't the first devotee to complain about change. 'Have you been to Mougins?' he asked.

'No.'

He picked out a pen from his breast pocket and wrote down the route on the tourism leaflet he handed me. 'Go there tomorrow – you will feel better,' he said, as if he was a doctor writing out a soul prescription.

Mougins is six miles to the east of Grasse and, as we approached this old medieval citadel, my heart beat a little faster, sensing something around the corner. I wasn't to be disappointed this time. The tourism bureau described it as 'a place that time forgot' and it certainly felt ancient in character.

As we explored the old town, the history that seized me was that of Pablo Picasso, who withdrew from public gaze to spend his final years at a farmhouse on the village outskirts. Mougins, with its hilly location and beautiful landscape, had been his artistic refuge, and it was not hard to see why – I could almost smell the creativity in the air as much as the scent of pine and French rural life. I assume that's why Christian Dior and Yves St Laurent also bought homes locally. Instead of perfume houses and the celebration of fragrance, this was a place that embraced artistry and innovation, and the geniuses who had been residents.

As we walked the narrow streets in between tall, compact townhouses, my nose wasn't filled with notes but my head was filled with inspiration. Every signpost I saw – from the bronze sculptures in the street to the painters sitting in the sun with their easels and paintbrushes – pointed me towards deepening and expanding my creativity.

For a long time, I think part of me had wanted time to stand still, and for things not to have changed. I probably looked over my shoulder more times than I should have done, trying to maintain an attachment to the past, looking to reconnect with an old feeling that could never be the same. Maybe part of me had returned to Grasse for that same reason – to go back to a familiar setting and re-enact the same magic. But not every memory can remain intact, and not every circle can be completed.

Instead, I found myself in a different place that resonated for different reasons and, as I stood outside a building where Picasso used to paint – a studio, I think it was – I started to understand the shift. The brasserie. The tapas. The Candle Shot Studio. The red dot. The new look. The new me. I came to realise that Grasse represented who I once was – the past, the beginner, the search for myself in fragrances. Mougins represented who I am now – the future, the designer, and the pursuit of artistry within my creativity *not just* fragrance. Happiness in a different landscape.

Josh, who was honing his own creativity with a camera, took a photo of me in one of Mougins' streets. It shows me looking up from a set of stone steps; behind me, there is a dark archway, the other side of which is the light from a sunlit courtyard. Every time I look at that image, I'm transported back to Mougins, and reminded of the fact that, as much as the environment might alter around us, the entrepreneur's journey is as uncertain as it is exhilarating, and all we can do is keep moving forward, keep building, and keep our eyes on the horizon, remaining true to who we are.

Dubai, April 2016: I'm sitting on the front row of an auditorium packed to the gills, feeling more nervous than I've felt in a long time, and with good reason.

Behind me, among the one-thousand-strong audience, are the great and the good of retail, plus representatives from international governments and the media. In front of me is the vast stage where I'm soon going to deliver one of the most important speeches of my life. For this is the annual World Retail Congress, and the day I'm being inaugurated into its Hall of Fame, one of the most prestigious awards a retailer can receive.

I got the call a few weeks after returning from Mougins and, at first, I thought there had been a mistake – the organisers must not have realised that I only have one shop now, not an empire. In my head, why would they want to honour a one-location shopkeeper? 'It's not about your old brand or your new brand,' Charlotte had said. 'It's about you, the entre-preneur, in recognition of your contribution and vision, Jo.'

I'm sure I'm not the only one in the industry who has spent so long focused on brand recognition that personal recognition still feels strange. But what makes this feel extra special is the fact that it's a tip of the hat from my peers. Now I'll join the ranks of previous inductees, such as the Nordstrom family, Sir Paul Smith, Martha Stewart, Miuccia Prada, Laura Ashley and Anita Roddick. And today, alongside me, Tommy Hilfiger and Solomon Lew will be added to the list as well. Regardless of the success I've achieved, there will always be a part of me that sits in such eminent company and wonders if I've walked into the wrong room.

It's only now that I am sitting here in the arena, with its cinema-sized screen and stage set that appears to dwarf the lectern where I'll stand, that the enormity of the occasion truly hits me.

It seems apt that we're in Dubai for this moment because it was here, in 2012, that Jo Loves had her first public overseas outing. I can see them now: thirty glass bottles on a table at an Easter Sunday lunch hosted by our dear friends Mark and Elizabeth Horne at their home on Arabian Ranches. This couple, and their son Archie, have been with us through thick and thin, and they wanted to do everything they could to do their bit for our new brand at a time when we had no idea what the future held. And none of us had seen this day coming.

I look around the audience and see all the different nationalities, from Europe to the Far East, from America to the Middle East; CEOs of international companies and heads of industry. When I think back, there was a time as I was starting out when I would have given my right arm to have just ten minutes with any one of them. And now I'm going to address them all about brand-building, in a speech entitled 'Scents of Success'.

The hall quietens as BBC presenter Naga Munchetty walks on stage to introduce me. As she does, my name and picture flash up on the screen above her.

I lean forward and look along the front row and see Charlotte, and I think of all the adventures we've shared and the territories and stores we've opened. In her, I don't see a member of staff, I see a best friend. Sitting to her right is our new general manager Jessica Clark, who has taken hold of the reins to steer the business. Her influence has been immediate, because what no one knows — until I announce it during my speech — is that we have just signed a deal with Net-a-Porter, the online luxury 'department store', to curate a Jo Loves collection. Five years after launching, we will have global distribution in place.

I glance to my left and see Josh listening intently to Naga's glowing introduction for his mum, and it feels like only yesterday that he was the infant strapped to my hip as I signed bottles of fragrances during personal appearances in New York. And to my right is my soulmate, Gary. No one knows more than him what it has taken to get here. I don't know where I'd be without him but I know this much: I wouldn't be in Dubai on this unforgettable day receiving such an honour.

He's been telling everyone since we arrived how proud he is of me, but what no one will truly appreciate is his role and what I see: him telling me to get out of bed and make a decision after parting ways with Mum; standing by my side in our tiny kitchen in Chelsea, working until gone midnight to help me make bath oils; the man who negotiated the first deals that put foundations under our feet; and the constant laughter through the hard times.

What none of my team know is that in the speech I'm about to give – and I've given countless speeches to schools, women's organisations and business conferences before this – I'm going to start by acknowledging the two people who are not here to share this moment: my mum and dad. They were the ones who unwittingly shaped me into the entrepreneur I have become. Mum, from her Revlon days to Madame Lubatti; Dad, the magician and market trader.

Naga Munchetty is wrapping up her introduction. I'm about to be called on stage. I look down at the red, A4-sized notebook in my lap. Engraved into its leather cover is the Oscar Wilde quote: 'Be yourself. Everyone else is taken.' Resting on top of that are two cream cards that I'll use as my prompts: one full of dates that mark the story of my journey; the other has three words written on it that say—

'So please do give a very warm welcome to Jo Malone,' I hear Naga announce.

Applause breaks out as I walk up the steps to a stage where, the moment I reach the lectern, my nerves melt away and I feel instantly calm. Or is it content? Or proud? I place my notebook and cards down. I look out beneath the haze of the bright lights and I take a breath before beginning.

I suppose I haven't done that badly for the girl who was once told by a teacher that she wouldn't make anything of her life. I'll mention that, too, telling this audience that I might not have any qualifications but I do have the vital ingredients that every entrepreneur needs to succeed, and they are the three words written on the card in front of me: PASSION. RESILIENCE. CREATIVITY.

ACKNOWLEDGEMENTS

Until sitting down to write this book, I don't think I knew what it would entail, or the memories I would unpack. I have been reminded of the amazing people who have travelled this journey across the years with me, and I have emerged with a new-found appreciation for what it takes to put one's life story on the shelf. I would therefore like to thank the following:

First and foremost Gary and Josh, you are the loves of my life. Thank you for putting up with all the highs and lows. Aunty Dot, for helping with certain details and jogging my memory.

Kerri Sharp, my commissioning editor at Simon & Schuster, who saw this book before I did; her belief in me, and passion for my story, have been a constant source of encouragement. Jonathan Lloyd and Jacquie Drewe, thank you for your guidance. Thank you to the ghostwriter, Steve Dennis, for his collaboration in bringing my story to life. Jo Roberts-Miller, the copy-editor, for your polish and expert eye; Iain MacGregor, the non-fiction publishing director, for pursuing the artistry for scenting this book; Julia Marshall and Jo Edgecombe in production, and executive editor Trish Todd in New York.

My stellar team at Jo Loves, who provide invaluable support and

help me fulfil the vision. Special mention goes to my executive
assistant Ruthie Burgess, who keeps me organised and makes
everything run like clockwork. Thanks for all that you do.

All our suppliers and creators for helping me create a great
brand. And not forgetting the first twelve face clients who spread
the word all those years ago. Josh Wood, Gary Glossman, Shaun
Johnson, Beverley Pond-Jones and Liz McAulay, who never fail
to make me look glamorous at every occasion.

Jeremy Pennant and his team at D. Young & Co. Alan Marshall,
Gary Hampton and Paul Ingram. Plus, Jeremy Courtenay-Stamp,
Amanda Pattison and all at Macfarlanes; and Peter Hansen and
everyone at Sapient. Ron Dennis for his friendship. Thank you
all for your wisdom and guidance.

Dearest Larry Norton, Joseph Disa, Alexandra Heerdt and
Mary Massie – thank you for helping me fight the biggest battle
of my life and win; also every nurse and doctor at Sloan Kettering,
who not only saved my life but save thousands of others every
year. Thank you for your love and kindness.

Lucy Perdomo-Ruehlemann, Cathy O'Brien, Pamela Baxter,
Terry Darland and everyone else at Lauder, especially John Larkin
and the late Evelyn Lauder. The GREAT campaign and everyone involved with flying the flag around the world. Sarah Sands,
Jim Armitage and Alex Lawson at the *Evening Standard* – the best
editorial team I have worked with. Those members of the press
(and now blogosphere) for every story and piece you have written
about both my businesses over the years. I would never be where
I am today without your continued support. A big thank you to
Jeremy King for designing the Brasserie Bar in Elizabeth Street
and Shayne Brady for bringing it to life.

Dr Guy O'Keeffe, Anna Albright and Dr Michael Pelly, I
am indebted to all three of you and what you have done. Rich
and Emily Powers, Linda Adeson, and Martin and Christine

Falkner – my wonderful Thanksgiving family. Nicky and Pippa Gumball, for all your prayers. The Hornes, Haddocks, Cadburys, Vigors and Farrs for the memories, celebrations and best holidays in the world. Also, 'The Girls Rose Club' of Jane Moore, Ruth Kennedy, Caroline Gallagher and Dame Betty. Magoo Giles, David Goodhew, Catriona Sutherland-Hawes and Tamás Kovács, thank you for inspiring the next generation. And Flo – you are a treasured friend to our family.

To all my amazing friends – you know who you are – thank you for every Friday night dinner, Sunday lunch, celebration, and special occasion. Every time you were there to laugh and dry our tears. You are without doubt my Solomon's riches.

And lastly, I'd like to express my gratitude to every person across this world who, over the last thirty years, has bought a product I've created, be it a fragrance, a bath oil, candle or face cream – thank you for helping make a shopkeeper's dream come true.

Jo, summer 2016

RECIPE FOR A
YOGHURT FACE MASK

I wanted to end this book by leaving you with a recipe for the face mask that I've made throughout my life, from my years with Madame Lubatti to this very day. It's perfect for when you need to rehydrate your skin, and I use it every time I travel.

Ingredients

1 small pot of natural yoghurt
freshly squeezed juice of 1 lemon
1 teaspoon warm liquid honey
2 drops jojoba oil
2 drops avocado oil

Method

Add all of the ingredients to the yoghurt, stir together and store overnight in the fridge. Remove from the fridge and apply to thoroughly cleansed skin using your fingertips or a brush. Leave on for approximately twenty minutes until the mask starts to dry and go hard. Next, gently massage the skin using a little extra avocado oil, which will help to remove the mask and any dead skin cells. Finally, completely remove the mask with a warm face cloth and spritz the skin with cold water. You now have a completely clean canvas on which to apply your moisturiser.

INDEX

JM in an index entry refers to Jo Malone